MEETING GOD

Face to Face

MEETING GOD

Face to Face

BILL JOHNSON

CHARISMA
HOUSE

Most CHARISMA HOUSE BOOK GROUP products are available at special quantity discounts for bulk purchase for sales promotions, premiums, fund-raising, and educational needs. For details, write Charisma House Book Group, 600 Rinehart Road, Lake Mary, Florida 32746, or telephone (407) 333-0600.

MEETING GOD FACE TO FACE DEVOTIONAL by Bill Johnson

Published by Charisma House
Charisma Media/Charisma House Book Group
600 Rinehart Road
Lake Mary, Florida 32746
www.charismahouse.com

of Christian Education of the National Council of the Churches of Christ in the USA. Used by permission.

Scripture quotations marked TPT are taken from The Passion Translation. Copyright © 2017 by BroadStreet Publishing® Group, LLC. Used by permission. All rights reserved.

Visit the author's website at www.ibethel.org.

Library of Congress Cataloging-in-Publication Data:
An application to register this book for cataloging has been submitted to the Library of Congress.
International Standard Book Number: 978-1-62999-581-6
E-book ISBN: 978-1-62999-582-3

Portions of this book were previously published by Charisma House as *Face to Face With God*, ISBN 978-1-62998-186-4, copyright © 2007, 2015.

19 20 21 22 23 — 987654321
Printed in the United States of America

Introduction

A LIFE DEVOTED TO HOSTING THE PRESENCE OF GOD

GOD HAS GIVEN Himself to His children as an inheritance. Nothing stretches the imagination more than this truth. The God of the universe not only makes Himself—every aspect of His being—available to us, but He also actively pursues our hearts. My life's great honor is to guard and cultivate my relationship with Him. However much I long to see cancer eradicated, blind eyes opened, or the oppressed set free, these quests come second to my desire simply to be in His presence.

The pursuit of His presence is foundational for every other aspect of our lives. Matthew 6:33 says, "But seek first His kingdom and His righteousness, and all these things will be added to you." God is the great rewarder. Awareness that He rewards is so important for our understanding of Him as a good Father. However, if we become focused on the "all things added," our walk with God will always be measured by external conditions. It is a relational journey. Period.

My prayer is that this devotional would stir up a hunger within you, drawing you closer to God's presence and deeper into His truth. As you read these pages, may you have the kind of real encounters with His power and grace that leave you transformed forever. I challenge you to step toward Him boldly and let His face shine upon you so that you can be light to the world.

BILL JOHNSON

Day 1
THE JOURNEY BEGINS

Seek first His kingdom and His righteousness,
and all these things will be added to you.
—MATTHEW 6:33

THE AIR IS pregnant with possibility—can you feel it? Heaven itself is longing to invade the natural realm. Darkness may cover the earth, but God's glory upon His people is becoming more and more realized, bringing hope to the most hopeless situations. And what is this day that God is unveiling? It is a day of divine encounters, at least for those who will *pursue* what this revelation is making available. Are you ready to pursue Him?

POINT TO PONDER

Today is the first day in my quest for more of God's presence in my life.

PERSONAL REFLECTION

_____

_____

_____

_____

_____

_____

_____

_____

_____

_____

_____

_____

Day 2
WISDOM AND REVELATION

*That the God of our Lord Jesus Christ, the Father
of glory, may give to you a spirit of wisdom and
of revelation in the knowledge of Him.*
—Ephesians 1:17

In your quest for God it's important to understand that the spirit of wisdom and revelation is not given to make you smarter but to make you more aware of unseen realities. The purpose of the spirit or anointing is to give you wisdom and revelation *in the knowledge of Him*. It works not merely to increase your understanding of kingdom principles but also to reveal the King Himself. Presence always wins out over principles. When you encounter His divine presence, transformation occurs that goes beyond the reach of merely good ideas; it is transformation that first takes place *within you* that you might cause transformation around you. Do you believe that encountering His presence takes priority over understanding kingdom principles?

Point to Ponder

*I put everything I know about God aside in order to pursue Him
to the fullest and allow Him to transform my life for His glory.*

Personal Reflection

_____

_____

_____

_____

_____

_____

Day 3

GOD'S TREASURE HOUSE OF TRUTH

*If you seek [wisdom] as silver and search for her as
for hidden treasures; then you will discern the fear of
the Lord and discover the knowledge of God.*
—**Proverbs 2:4–5**

GOD IS OPENING up His treasure house of truth and releasing it all over mankind in remarkable ways. Like birth pangs signaling the time of delivery, things are being released in revelation knowledge that have been preserved through the ages for this particular hour. In other words, this exponential increase in wisdom and revelation is being precipitated by the day that God is releasing in our time in history. I'm not talking about new books of the Bible or other holy writings. I'm talking about the Holy Spirit unlocking the very Scriptures you hold in your hands. How do you respond to what God reveals to you in the pages of Scripture? Do you believe these treasures are available to you?

POINT TO PONDER

*I receive the spirit of wisdom and revelation so that I can understand
every facet of what God is saying to me today through His Word.*

PERSONAL REFLECTION

Day 4
TASTE AND SEE

*Taste and see that the L*ORD *is good.*
*—*PSALM 34:8

THE HEART TO seek God is birthed in us by God Himself. Like all desires, it is not something that can be legislated or forced, but rather it grows within us as we become exposed to God's nature. He creates an appetite in us for Himself by lavishing us with the reality of His goodness—His irresistible glory. God's love for people is beyond comprehension and imagination. He is for us, not against us. God is good 100 percent of the time. These realities burn deeply into the hearts of all who simply take the time to behold Him. When was the last time you experienced the reality of His goodness in such a way that your desire to seek God intensified? How did you respond to this desire?

POINT TO PONDER

I need more of the revelation of God's goodness to draw me to Him.

PERSONAL REFLECTION

_____

_____

_____

_____

_____

_____

_____

_____

_____

Day 5

TRANSFORMED TO HIS IMAGE

*But we all, seeing the glory of the Lord with unveiled
faces, as in a mirror, are being transformed into the same
image from glory to glory by the Spirit of the Lord.*
—2 CORINTHIANS 3:18, MEV

PAUL DESCRIBES THE place of beholding God as the absolute center of the new covenant we have been brought into. The impulse that drives the life of the believer isn't the need to perform for God but to commune with Him. Only when we perceive the face of the One in whose image we were made do we come to know who we are and the One for whom we were made. And because of who He is, to behold Him and remain unchanged is impossible. As He infects us with His presence, we are drawn into an ongoing mission by the One who longs for us. This mission is simply the mission to become more and more fit to see Him in His fullness. Does the need to perform for God drive your thinking and behavior at all? Would you say you find your identity in the face of Christ or in what you do?

POINT TO PONDER

*To truly see God is to be changed by Him
and to become more like Him.*

PERSONAL REFLECTION

_____

_____

_____

_____

_____

Day 6
THE MANIFESTATION OF CHRIST

*He who loves Me will be loved by My Father, and
I will love him and manifest Myself to him.*
—JOHN 14:21, NKJV

THE DEGREE TO which you perceive the face of God corresponds directly to the degree to which you have yielded to the Holy Spirit's work of transforming you into the image of Christ. The question is whether you will be satisfied with only a partial transformation or whether you will be so captivated by who He is that you will allow Him to kill everything in you that would inhibit you from becoming a mature manifestation of Christ. What are the markers of a mature manifestation of Christ, and why are they attractive? Do you believe these are promised to you as you yield to the Spirit's work in you?

POINT TO PONDER

*I yield myself completely to the Holy Spirit's work
of transforming me into the image of Christ.*

PERSONAL REFLECTION

_____

_____

_____

_____

_____

_____

_____

_____

_____

Day 1
THE BEST DEAL EVER

For to me, to live is Christ.
—Philippians 1:21

This quest for His face is the ultimate quest. But to embrace the quest for the face of God, you must be ready to die. Thus, this quest is not a journey for the faint of heart. It is far too costly to pursue from mere curiosity. You might be asking, What is the cost of fully seeking His face? I must warn you—it costs everything. In reality what you get in return makes the price you pay embarrassingly small by comparison. The bottom line is that you give all of yourself to obtain all of Him. There's never been a better deal. When you go through with the exchange, you find that what used to matter doesn't anymore. Life without passion gives way to a life of reckless abandon. Not only does everything in your life that is inconsistent with the kingdom of God start to die the moment you encounter Him, but the superior, supernatural reality of His kingdom starts to come alive in you. It is not possible to encounter One so overwhelming and maintain the status quo. Are you ready to leave it all and run after Him with reckless abandon?

Point to Ponder

I am willing to let everything about me die so that I might know Him more fully and experience the power of His Spirit within me.

Personal Reflection

_____

_____

_____

_____

Day 8
DON'T MISS OUT

O God, You are my God; I shall seek You earnestly;
my soul thirsts for You, my flesh yearns for You, in
a dry and weary land where there is no water.
—Psalm 63:1

THIS JOURNEY IS so sacred, so all-consuming, that very few respond to its call. While the seeds of this quest are found in the heart of every man, woman, and child, most seem to be numb to its existence. Many things work to stifle your desire to seek the face of the One in whose image you were created. Whether you are overwhelmed by the prevailing winds of secular reasoning or the pain of religious disappointment, such forces cause you to abandon the ultimate quest and give in to the other impulse that has infected man since the fall—the impulse to hide from God. Have you allowed distractions and deception to stifle your desire for God or lead you to hide from Him?

POINT TO PONDER

I receive God's wisdom and grace to recognize
things that keep me from pursuing Him.

PERSONAL REFLECTION

_____
_____
_____
_____
_____
_____
_____

Day 9

DON'T SETTLE FOR LESS

Blessed are those who hunger and thirst for
righteousness, for they shall be satisfied.
—MATTHEW 5:6

THE ULTIMATE QUEST of seeking His face is quite doable and within reach. It is so all-inclusive that the smallest child may come. Every other journey and every other ambition pale in comparison. One might say this one challenge adds meaning and definition to all of life's other pursuits. Those who respond to the invitation find little else to live for. Those who say no spend their lives looking for an adequate replacement. And there is none to be found, anywhere. Have you been satisfied with a status quo life or a partial transformation into Christ's image? Are you hungry for more? It's time to let your heart be captivated by who He is!

POINT TO PONDER

I know I'm pursuing the very purpose I was made for, and
I refuse to settle for substitutions or replacements.

PERSONAL REFLECTION

_____

_____

_____

_____

_____

_____

_____

_____

Day 10
ANSWER THE CALL

"But the Levitical priests…shall come near to Me to
minister to Me; and they shall stand before Me to offer
Me the fat and the blood," declares the Lord GOD.
—EZEKIEL 44:15

IN MY LIFE the quest for deep encounters with God started the moment I said yes to His call on my life. Not a call to ministry. A call to God Himself. It happened in 1971 when my dad, who was also my pastor, taught a message from Ezekiel 44 about our ministry to the Lord in thanksgiving, praise, and worship. He taught that there is a difference between ministry to God and ministry to people. Ministry to God is the most important responsibility of all, and it is available to every believer. This call to worship is not about music, instruments, or worship teams. As far as music is concerned, not even the great songs written *about* Him are appropriate; you need songs you can sing *to* Him. It is all about ministering directly to the Lord in His actual presence. Have you felt Him calling you to this ministry? How will you answer?

POINT TO PONDER

I answer the call to minister to the Lord in true worship.

PERSONAL REFLECTION

_____

_____

_____

_____

_____

Day 11

THIS IS YOUR MOMENT

While they were ministering to the Lord and
fasting, the Holy Spirit said, "Set [them] apart
for…the work to which I have called them."
—Acts 13:2

As you've read the first few days of this journey to seek God's face, I pray that you have been stirred beyond anything you ever felt before. While it isn't typical to give an altar call in a devotional book, I want to challenge you to respond right now in this moment. Right where you are as you read this, pray, "Heavenly Father, I give You the rest of my life to teach me this one thing."

This was the prayer I prayed back in 1971. It was my moment. I had already given my life to Christ in a way that I held nothing back. But I was now saying that in my surrender to Christ I had one specific agenda that outweighed every other—my ministry to the Lord Himself. Did you pray this prayer, or one like it? If you did, I can promise you that your life will never be the same.

Point to Ponder

I will spend the rest of my life in pursuit of
one thing—my ministry unto God.

Personal Reflection

_____

_____

_____

_____

_____

_____

Day 12

GET READY FOR MORE

For He has satisfied the thirsty soul, and the
hungry soul He has filled with what is good.
—Psalm 107:9

I BELIEVE THE LORD has already started to respond quickly to your lifestyle of abandonment to His presence by confirming, through unfolding revelation, that this is indeed the purpose for which He has made and redeemed you. Scripture is saturated with the theme that we were made for a relationship that allows us to know by experience the supernatural God who created us, and it will soon become evident to you that the encounters God had with people in the Bible were not reserved only for those of that era. Encounters of that magnitude will actually start to look possible, even probable, again. Perhaps you've never thought you qualified for anything extraordinary. I feel the same way about myself. It's actually perfect because it's all about Him anyway. All you need to know is that He loves you, and, in turn, you will find yourself increasingly hungry for Him. Do you believe God desires to make His presence evident in and through your life?

Point to Ponder

God gives me revelations of what is available to me through
divine encounters in the Scriptures, in history, and around me.

Personal Reflection

_____

_____

_____

_____

Day 13
FOLLOW AFTER GOD

My soul follows close behind You.
—Psalm 63:8, nkjv

I HAVE TRAVELED TO many cities where God was visiting in unusual and notable ways in my personal quest for increased power and anointing in my life. Some people belittle such pursuits, saying, "Signs and wonders are supposed to follow you, not you follow them." My perspective is a bit different: *if they're not following you, follow them until they follow you.* God has used my experiences in such places to set me up for life-changing encounters at home. After one such trip in 1995 I cried out to God for months, "God, I want more of You at any cost! I will pay any price!" Then one night God came in answer to my prayer. I encourage you to read about my powerful encounter with God in my book *Face to Face With God.* It was the most overwhelming experience of my life. It was raw power. It was God. He had come in response to the prayer I had been praying. What about you? Do you believe that God will respond to you if you seek His face?

Point to Ponder

I will follow after God's signs and wonders until they follow me.

Personal Reflection

_____

_____

_____

_____

_____

_____

13

Day 14
HUNGRY FOR MORE

*As the deer pants for the water brooks, so
my soul pants for You, O God.*
—Psalm 42:1

HAVE YOU ASKED God to reveal more of Himself to you no matter the cost? There's no right or wrong way to do this. Simply confess your hunger and thirst for Him. Back in 1995 I wasn't sure of the correct way to pray, nor did I understand the theology behind my request because I knew He already dwelt in me as a result of my conversion. All I knew was I was hungry for God. There were times I even woke in the night because I was asking for more in my sleep. My powerful encounter with God in the mid-'90s didn't come in the way I expected—although I couldn't have told you what I expected. It was a glorious experience, because it was Him. But it was not gratifying in any natural sense. Are you ready to receive Him, even if it's not what you expected?

Point to Ponder

I am hungry for more of God's presence in my life.

Personal Reflection

_____

_____

_____

_____

_____

_____

_____

_____

Day 15
SAY GOODBYE TO RESPECTABILITY

*It happened when the ark of the covenant of the LORD
came to the city of David, that Michal the daughter of Saul
looked out of the window and saw King David leaping
and celebrating; and she despised him in her heart.*
—1 CHRONICLES 15:29

PERHAPS BY NOW you've realized your request for more of God carries a price. In 1995 as I cried out for more of God, I was gripped by the realization that God wanted to make an exchange—an increased manifestation of His presence in exchange for my dignity. After all, I *had* prayed, "at any cost." One night, in the midst of tears, I cried, "More, God. More! If I lose respectability and get You in the exchange, I'll gladly make that trade. Just give me more of You!" Is the sacrifice of your respectability one you are willing to make in order to have more of God and become like Him?

POINT TO PONDER

*Respectability cannot fulfill my heart's desire; only
greater measures of God's presence will satisfy me.*

PERSONAL REFLECTION

_____

_____

_____

_____

_____

_____

_____

_____

THE PURPOSE OF DIVINE ENCOUNTERS

Whenever Moses entered the tent, the pillar of cloud would descend and stand at the entrance of the tent; and the LORD would speak with Moses.
—EXODUS 33:9

SOME PEOPLE MIGHT wonder what a divine encounter accomplishes in one's life. It's difficult to explain exactly how one knows the purpose for divine encounters. All I can say is you *just know.* You know His purpose so clearly that every other reality fades into the shadows as God puts His finger on the one thing that matters to Him. Some of the most important things that happen to us during these times are the most difficult to explain to others, yet they are undeniably from God. The person having the encounter knows, and that's what matters most. Are you willing to embrace an encounter with God, even if you can only know its purpose in your heart and not in your head?

POINT TO PONDER

I'm not going to overthink what God is doing; I'm going to embrace His work in my life and let it accomplish His purpose.

PERSONAL REFLECTION

_____

_____

_____

_____

_____

_____

Day 11
DIVINE ENCOUNTERS CHANGE US

Whenever Moses went in before the LORD to speak with
Him, he would take off the veil until he came out; and
whenever he came out...the skin of Moses' face shone.
—Exodus 34:34–35

THINK ABOUT JACOB and the encounter where he wrestled with an angel throughout the night. He limped for the rest of his life after his meeting with God. And then there was Mary, the mother of Jesus. She had an experience with God that not even her fiancé believed was true. It took a visit from an angel to help change his mind. As a result, she bore the Christ child—although she bore a stigma for the remainder of her days as the mother of an illegitimate child. As you consider these stories, something should become clear: from Earth's perspective the favor of God sometimes looks different than from heaven's perspective. How does looking at your circumstances from a heavenly perspective change what you perceive?

POINT TO PONDER

I will focus on heaven's perspective and let
my quest for God change my life.

PERSONAL REFLECTION

_____

_____

_____

_____

_____

Day 18

ONE SIZE DOESN'T FIT ALL

God sees not as man sees; for man looks at the outward
appearance, but the LORD looks at the heart.
—1 SAMUEL 16:7

BECAUSE YOU'RE READING this book, I assume you are seeking to experience a face-to-face encounter with God. If you study such encounters in the Scriptures and in the testimonies of saints, you'll find that face-to-face encounters with God often look very different from each other. He reveals Himself to us according to His purposes, and sometimes He fashions the way He does it according to what He sees in people's hearts. Moses encountered Him in a burning bush. Paul was knocked off his horse by a blinding light. Regardless of the form they come in, such experiences have one thing in common—they make it nearly impossible for people to live as they did before they had them. Has your quest for the face of God changed you yet? In what ways?

POINT TO PONDER

I know that God knows me better than I know myself, and He
will reveal Himself to me in the way I need Him the most.

PERSONAL REFLECTION

_____

_____

_____

_____

_____

_____

_____

Day 19

GETTING GOD IN EXCHANGE

*But whatever things were gain to me, those things
I have counted as loss for the sake of Christ.*
—**Philippians 3:7**

TRADING ANYTHING FOR more of God really is the greatest deal ever offered to mankind. What could I possibly have that would equal His value? I know that many say revival is costly. And it is. But when I get Him in the exchange, I find it difficult to feel noble for what I've paid. Many pray for and study about revival, but then they miss it when it comes. They aren't willing to pay the price. But revival only costs in the here and now; the absence of revival will cost throughout eternity. Has your desire for revival cost you anything yet? If so, how?

POINT TO PONDER

*I willingly surrender all I have to God as He
prepares me to be a catalyst for revival.*

PERSONAL REFLECTION

_____

_____

_____

_____

_____

_____

_____

_____

_____

_____

Day 20

NOT EVERYONE WILL UNDERSTAND

*You've been given the intimate experience of insight
into the hidden truths and mysteries of the realm of
heaven's kingdom, but they have not. For everyone who
listens with an open heart will receive progressively
more revelation until he has more than enough.*
—MATTHEW 13:11–12, TPT

IN 1996 I became the pastor of Bethel Church in Redding, California, and within a month an outpouring of God's Spirit began. Lives were changed, bodies were healed, and divine encounters increased in amazing proportions, along with the unusual manifestations that seem to accompany revival. When this happened, approximately one thousand people left the church. This wasn't the kind of revival they wanted. Understandably, it was difficult for people with that opinion to coexist happily with the perspective I held, which was that we should take whatever He gives us until He gives us something else. Let's apply this experience to your life. Have you considered that some people will distance themselves if they don't embrace what God is doing in and through you?

POINT TO PONDER

*I have decided that what God thinks is more
important than what people think.*

PERSONAL REFLECTION

_____

_____

_____

_____

Day 21

LIVING ON SUPERNATURAL GRACE

*We know that God causes all things to work
together for good to those who love God, to those
who are called according to His purpose.*
—Romans 8:28

FEW THINGS ARE more devastating to pastors than when people leave the church. It often feels like rejection. Yet in the strange season of exodus in our early days at Bethel, my wife and I were immune to the devastation. Usually that is only possible if your heart is calloused to the point where no one can affect you either negatively or positively, or you are in denial about the impact such a loss is causing in your heart. Thankfully, there is one other possibility, and that is that God has actually given you a supernatural grace to live opposite to your circumstances. Have you experienced this type of grace from God that allows you to live in the peace of knowing you are obeying Him, even when those around you don't understand?

POINT TO PONDER

*My mind is at ease because I know God is causing
all things to work together for His good.*

PERSONAL REFLECTION

_____

_____

_____

_____

_____

_____

Day 22
GOD IS PREPARING YOU

He who prepared us for this very purpose is
God, who gave to us the Spirit as a pledge.
—2 Corinthians 5:5

In those early days at Bethel, because of the grace given to us, not one day was spent in discouragement or questioning God. Our food really was doing His will. It provided all the nourishment and strength we needed. Plus, His presence was the reward. The public criticisms and slander, the humiliation of decreased numbers, the daily calls of complaint to our denomination for close to a year—none of it had teeth to its bite. The need for respectability had all but disappeared on the night of my first visitation. God knew what had been lying underneath it all when He asked for my respectability in exchange for the increased manifestation of His presence. It was the kindness of God that made it all possible. Have you experienced this type of divine preparation in your life?

POINT TO PONDER

I trust that what God is doing in me now will divinely
prepare me for where He's taking me next.

PERSONAL REFLECTION

_____

_____

_____

_____

_____

_____

Day 23

TIMES OF LOSS CAN BE PRECIOUS

Those who know Your name will put their trust in You,
for You, O Lord, have not forsaken those who seek You.
—Psalm 9:10

THAT FIRST YEAR at Bethel, along with the increased manifestation of His presence, God simply made His will too obvious to miss. God often spoke to my team or me in dreams or visions. Sometimes He brought forth a prophetic word that confirmed or added understanding to a direction we were to take. There was never a question. The fruit of this move of God was undeniable. It included an increased measure of His presence along with the bounty of transformed lives. That was all we needed to make us smile in the face of such apparent loss. To this day we consider that time of our greatest loss as one of the most precious and delightful seasons of our lives. Are there times of loss in your life when God became more real to you than ever before?

POINT TO PONDER

I know I can count on God to be faithful no matter what season I'm in.

PERSONAL REFLECTION

_____

_____

_____

_____

_____

_____

_____

_____

Day 24

THE SIGNS OF HIS FAVOR

For it is You who blesses the righteous man, O Lord,
You surround him with favor as with a shield.
—PSALM 5:12

WHEN GOD INVADES your life, things change. Not only that, but the impact of your life on the world also changes. The measure of God's glory that rests upon your life following these unusual divine encounters affects every person you touch. The supernatural becomes natural as God takes center stage in the places where you have influence. When His glory is present, the things that you used to work hard for, such as miracles of healing and transformation in people's personal lives and families, come with little or no effort. Have you seen Him start to move in your life to make the supernatural become natural?

POINT TO PONDER

I am expecting God's favor and glory to
work in amazing ways in my life.

PERSONAL REFLECTION

_____

_____

_____

_____

_____

_____

_____

_____

_____

Day 25
GOD'S FACE SHINES UPON YOU

Arise, shine; for your light has come, and the
glory of the LORD *has risen upon you.*
—ISAIAH 60:1

PROVERBS 16:15 SAYS, "In the light of a king's face is life, and his favor is like a cloud with the spring rain." Scripture describes those individuals whose lives are marked by the power and blessing of the living God as those upon whom *God's face shines.* God's countenance is toward His people, and the result is that their lives are marked by His favor. Now is the season when all who confess Christ must give attention to the role of the favor of God in our lives. Have you ever asked God for favor? Are you sure you know what it means?

POINT TO PONDER

As I seek God's face, His light shines upon me, revealing His glory.

PERSONAL REFLECTION

_____

_____

_____

_____

_____

_____

_____

_____

_____

_____

Day 26

THE FAVOR OF HIS FACE

For now we see in a mirror, dimly, but then face to face.
—1 Corinthians 13:12, nkjv

THE HEART TO seek God is birthed in you by God Himself. Like all desires, it is not something that can be legislated or forced, but it grows within you as you "taste and see that the Lord is good" (Psalm 34:8). For while you have been given the capacity to perceive God's goodness through the new birth in the Spirit, that capacity is something that must develop in you throughout your life. The quest for the face of God has two central dimensions—the quest for His presence and the quest for His favor. For the next several days we will explore the quest for His presence, and then we'll take several days to look at the quest for His favor. Are you ready to see Him face to face?

POINT TO PONDER

*I am continuing to grow in my understanding
of God's goodness as I seek His face.*

PERSONAL REFLECTION

_____

_____

_____

_____

_____

_____

_____

_____

Day 27

GREATER MEASURES
OF HIS PRESENCE

For He gives the Spirit without measure.
—John 3:34

SEEKING THE PRESENCE of God is not about trying to get Him to do something. He's already given you His Holy Spirit without measure. All measurements are set up on your end of the equation, determined by the degree to which your life is in agreement with God and His kingdom. Scripture gives you some specific clues about how you can bring your life into greater agreement with God and "host" greater measures of His presence. Significantly, all these measures correspond with deeper truths about who God is. If you are going to bring your life more fully into agreement with God and His kingdom, the primary thing you need is a burning conviction that *God is good*. What things are you doing to bring your life into complete agreement with God?

POINT TO PONDER

I will bring my life into complete agreement with God and receive as much of His as I can.

PERSONAL REFLECTION

_____

_____

_____

_____

_____

_____

_____

Day 28

GOD'S PRESENCE IN CREATION

In Him all things consist.
—COLOSSIANS 1:17, NKJV

ANOTHER FOUNDATIONAL REVELATION about the presence of God is that God actually holds all things together. Take a look at Colossians 1:17 above. *Consist* means "to hold together." The pantheist worships all things, believing all things to be God. While it is crazy to worship a tree as God, it is correct to realize that God holds every cell of that tree in place. He is everywhere. And since I can't imagine a place where He isn't, I might as well imagine Him with me. This truth about God brings me into a measure of awareness of His presence. Have you ever thought about this level of awareness of God's presence before?

POINT TO PONDER

Any place I go on this earth, God is already there.

PERSONAL REFLECTION

_____

_____

_____

_____

_____

_____

_____

_____

_____

_____

Day 29

GOD'S PRESENCE IN HIS CHILDREN

*Your body is a temple of the Holy Spirit who
is in you, whom you have from God.*
—1 Corinthians 6:19

A MORE PROFOUND TRUTH about God's presence is that God has come to live in each person who receives Jesus Christ through His work on the cross as the necessary payment for sin. In one sense He was already in me as the One who actually holds my cells in place. But when I receive Him, He comes to make my body His temple—the eternal dwelling place of God. He has come in an increased measure of His presence. How are you surrendering your body to God's will? What do you think of the idea that all of your body belongs to God?

Point to Ponder

*My body is not my own; it is His dwelling
place, and I surrender it to His will.*

Personal Reflection

_____

_____

_____

_____

_____

_____

_____

_____

_____

_____

Day 30

GOD'S PRESENCE IN OUR MIDST

*For where two or three have gathered together
in My name, I am there in their midst.*
—MATTHEW 18:20

WE PROGRESS TO an even deeper truth when we learn that whenever there are two or three people gathered in God's name, He is in their midst. He is already in you as a part of His creation, and He is in you as His temple, but that measure of His presence increases still more when you come together with other believers in His name. "In Jesus' name" means more than an ending to a prayer. It is, in fact, the attempt to do and be what He would do and be in that given situation. To gather in His name means that your gathering should look as it did when Jesus met with people two thousand years ago. If that is a correct definition, then how many of your gatherings are actually *in His name?*

POINT TO PONDER

*When my life is lived in Jesus' name, I become
a reflection of His life and presence.*

PERSONAL REFLECTION

_____

_____

_____

_____

_____

_____

_____

Day 31
GOD'S PRESENCE UPON HIS THRONE

You…are enthroned upon the praises of Israel.
—Psalm 22:3

In Psalm 22:3 David discovered a wonderful and even deeper truth that adds to this revelation of increasing degrees of God's presence. His throne is an even greater measure of His presence. He holds your being together with His presence, and then He moves inside to reign as God over your life. He increases your encounter with Him by having you gather with others in Jesus' name. Ultimately, His glory begins to fall on you as you learn the honor of serving Him through thanksgiving, praise, and worship. Do you make it a habit to "enter His gates with thanksgiving and His courts with praise," as instructed in Psalm 100:4?

Point to Ponder

My ministry to God takes me into His throne room where I experience the greatest degree of His presence.

Personal Reflection

_____

_____

_____

_____

_____

_____

_____

_____

_____

Day 32
THERE'S ALWAYS MORE

I saw the Lord...with the train of His robe filling the temple.
—Isaiah 6:1

THE LAST FEW days of reflection have provided the foundational concept in your quest for God Himself: the presence of the Lord can and will increase for those who embark on this quest. Isaiah seemed to tap into this understanding when he wrote the words of Isaiah 6:1 above. The word *filling* implies that God came into His temple, but He also *kept coming*. That explains why those who seem to have the greatest measure of God's presence on their lives tend to be the hungriest for more. There's always more to hunger for! This shouldn't be a hard concept to embrace, since we believe that He Himself fills the universe with His presence. King David declared that the universe is actually the work of His fingers. Isn't it exciting to know that there will always be more of God to seek and find?

POINT TO PONDER

I serve a really big God who has a lot more to give than I can imagine.

PERSONAL REFLECTION

_____

_____

_____

_____

_____

_____

_____

Day 33

AN INVITATION TO HIS INCREASING PRESENCE

Lo, I am with you always, even to the end of the age.
—MATTHEW 28:20

YOU AND I cannot live in mediocrity, content with merely knowing that there is more of God to experience and explore—and then do nothing about it. Truths that are not experienced are, in effect, more like theories than truths. Whenever God reveals truth to you, He is inviting you into a divine encounter. His promise to be with you always has to be more than a verse you quote in difficult times. His presence with you is the one factor that could make your impossible assignment to disciple nations a doable command. The promise must become an invitation to discover this increasing manifestation of His presence in your life so that you might fully enter into your purpose on the earth. Do you feel unqualified for what you've been called to do? How does knowing He is with you change that?

POINT TO PONDER

I am ready to experience more truths about God as I encounter more and more of Him.

PERSONAL REFLECTION

_____

_____

_____

_____

_____

Day 34

KNOWING FROM EXPERIENCE

*I will ask the Father, and He will give you another
Helper, that He may be with you forever.*
—JOHN 14:16

WE WILL BE Spirit-filled forever! Jesus didn't set limits on what we can have in this lifetime, but He did set a pace to be followed and not just admired religiously from a distance. God is to be known through encounters. Many people are content to live with the *concept* of the presence of God in their lives, but they fail to enter the intended *experience*. When I married my wife, I wasn't interested in the concept or the theory of marriage. I wanted to experience marriage in all its privileges and responsibilities. Can you say of your relationship with God that you know Him from experience, or do you only know *about* Him? It's time to experience Him today!

POINT TO PONDER

*I won't rest until I have personally encountered God
and experienced His presence in my life.*

PERSONAL REFLECTION

_____

_____

_____

_____

_____

_____

_____

_____

Day 35

STEWARDING THE PRESENCE

*Examine everything carefully; hold fast to that
which is good; abstain from every form of evil.*
—1 Thessalonians 5:21–22

We steward the presence of God by learning to obey the commands "Do not grieve the Holy Spirit" (Ephesians 4:30) and "Do not quench the Spirit" (1 Thessalonians 5:19). We grieve Him when we do something wrong; we quench Him when we fail to do what is right, stopping the flow of His love and power that comes from the Father. Have you ever thought about the difference between grieving Him and quenching Him before? Can you think of times in your life when you have stopped the flow of what the Spirit wants to do?

Point to Ponder

*I will not hinder the Spirit's flow in my life,
staying totally yielded to His work.*

Personal Reflection

_____

_____

_____

_____

_____

_____

_____

_____

_____

Day 36
A LIFE TO REST UPON

*I saw the Spirit descending from heaven like
a dove, and He remained upon Him.*
—JOHN 1:32, NKJV

JESUS MODELED WHAT life could be like when a person neither
grieves nor quenches the Holy Spirit. It is for this reason that
we see such a great measure of the presence of God in the person
of Jesus. Certainly, John 1:32 is not talking about the indwelling
presence of the Holy Spirit that was already in Jesus' life. The
Holy Spirit came to rest on Jesus as evidence of His faithfulness
to be perfectly trustworthy with the presence of God. The same
principle is true for us. The Holy Spirit lives in every believer, but
He rests upon very few. Why? It's not because He's fragile; it's
because He is holy! Few people give Him a life to rest upon. The
one whose life is not in agreement with God—which is what He
calls "entering His rest"—has not given Him a place to rest. Can
He trust you to be a resting place for His Spirit?

POINT TO PONDER

*I want to be trustworthy with the presence of God. I seek to live
in agreement with Him so His Spirit can remain upon me.*

PERSONAL REFLECTION

_____

_____

_____

_____

_____

Day 37

GROWING IN FAVOR WITH GOD

Jesus increased in wisdom and in stature
and in favor with God and men.
—LUKE 2:52, MEV

JESUS IS ALSO our model when it comes to pursuing and increasing in measures of God's favor, as we read in Luke 2:52. This is really a remarkable statement. Jesus Christ was perfect in every way, yet even He needed to grow in favor with God and man. It's easier to understand that He needed to grow in favor with man. No doubt favor opened many doors for life and ministry that would have otherwise been closed to Him. But how is it that the Son of God, who was perfect in character and sinless, needed to obtain more favor from God? While I can't answer that question to my own satisfaction, I do know that the implication is quite clear: if Jesus Christ needed to increase in favor with God, you and I need it much more. Are you ready to increase in wisdom and favor with God?

POINT TO PONDER

I thank God for my growth and progress in pursuit of His face. I haven't arrived yet, but I'm not where I used to be either.

PERSONAL REFLECTION

_____

_____

_____

_____

_____

_____

Day 38
FOLLOWING JESUS' FOOTSTEPS

If anyone wishes to come after Me, he must deny himself,
and take up his cross daily and follow Me.
—LUKE 9:23

IT'S POSSIBLE THAT Jesus embraced a life that required Him to grow in favor with God only because of *our* need to learn how to do the same thing. I'm convinced of one thing: Jesus definitively modeled the Christian life for every believer. He was fully God, yet He set aside the privileges of His divinity. Everything He did in His life and ministry He did to model the kind of life He would make available to each of us through His death, resurrection, and ascension. For our sakes He showed us how to grow in favor with God. Are you ready to follow Jesus' example and live the same kind of life He lived?

POINT TO PONDER

I'm thankful for Jesus' example of the kind of life I am called to live.

PERSONAL REFLECTION

_____

_____

_____

_____

_____

_____

_____

_____

_____

Day 39

WHAT IS FAVOR?

For of His fullness we have all received, and grace upon grace.
—John 1:16

IN ORDER TO grow in favor, you must first have favor. So what exactly is favor? I think we are most familiar with the idea that favor is preferential treatment shown to somebody. It denotes acceptance, approval, and pleasure. While the Greek and Hebrew words translated as *favor* in Scripture include these definitions, there is a deeper dimension to the Greek word for favor: *charis*. Almost everywhere in the New Testament this word is translated as *grace*. Grace (and favor) is essentially a *gift*. It's exciting to think that God's favor comes to us as a gift given by His grace. What are some of the ways in which you have received God's gift of favor in your life?

POINT TO PONDER

I thank God for His favor given to me as grace upon grace.

PERSONAL REFLECTION

_____

_____

_____

_____

_____

_____

_____

_____

_____

_____

Day 40

FAVOR IS ACCESS TO GOD

*Being justified as a gift by His grace through
the redemption which is in Christ Jesus.*
—ROMANS 3:24

IF YOU GAIN favor with people or, as you might say, get into their "good graces," you have special access to them and you receive something from them. The same thing is true about gaining favor with God, although the *charis* you receive from God is obviously different from the favor you receive from men. At your conversion you learned that God's grace is His *unmerited favor* toward men through the blood of His Son, but it also means that you have access to the very presence of God in the same way that Jesus did. Does the knowledge that you have the same access to the Father as Jesus affect your thinking and behavior?

POINT TO PONDER

*God's unmerited favor means that I have access to the presence
of God in the same way that Jesus has access to Him.*

PERSONAL REFLECTION

_____

_____

_____

_____

_____

_____

_____

_____

_____

Day 41

FAVOR IS POWER

My grace is sufficient for you, for power is perfected in weakness.
—2 CORINTHIANS 12:9

EVERY BELIEVER RECEIVES favor from God, but we don't all recognize the additional dimensions to the *charis* we receive. God's grace is also His operational power, the force of His nature. He gives you this grace to empower you to become like Christ. These two aspects of God's grace—access and power—set you up to understand what it means to grow in favor with God. At the heart of growing in favor are two aspects: (1) the pursuit of God, the practice of coming before God through the "new and living way" (Hebrews 10:20) that Christ has made available to you, and (2) receiving, in God's presence, measures of His own nature that empower you to be conformed to the image of the Son He loves. If growing in favor is primarily a matter of receiving God's grace to imitate and demonstrate His nature and character, then what are some signs of a life of divine favor?

POINT TO PONDER

I desire to pursue God more fully and to receive measures of His own nature to empower me to be conformed to the image of His Son.

PERSONAL REFLECTION

_____

_____

_____

_____

_____

_____

STEWARDING THE FAVOR OF GOD

*Now therefore, I pray You, if I have found favor
in Your sight, let me know Your ways that I may
know You, so that I may find favor in Your sight.*
—EXODUS 33:13

IF IT TAKES favor to get more favor and we have all been given a measure of favor with God through our conversion, that means the issue of growing in favor is a matter of stewardship. I believe that the failure to understand stewarding the favor of God has led many people to die in the unnecessary tragedy of never having their God-given dreams and desires fulfilled. Often those same individuals blame others around them for not supporting them in the pursuit of their dreams. The sober reality is that most dreams go unfulfilled because of the lack of favor with God and man. Where favor is increasing, we witness the power of exponential increase that comes through agreement. That is the by-product of favor. So the real question is, What have you done with the favor God has given to you?

POINT TO PONDER

I want to be an excellent steward of the favor of God.

PERSONAL REFLECTION

Day 43

GOD-GIVEN DREAMS REQUIRE FAVOR

*I sought Your favor with all my heart; be
gracious to me according to Your word.*
—PSALM 119:58

OUR AUTHENTIC DREAMS from God cannot be accomplished on
our own. If you can accomplish your dream on your own, that
is a sure sign that your dream is too small. We must dream so big
that without the support that comes through favor with God and
man, we could never accomplish what is in our hearts. While God
loves everyone the same, not everyone has the same measure of
favor. Yet everyone is positioned to increase in favor *if* each one of
us effectively stewards what we have. In other words, when we seek
His face from the favor we have, we increase in favor itself. What
authentic dreams from God are in your heart? What does it look
like for you to seek His face from the favor you currently have?

POINT TO PONDER

*I'm ready to dream big with God—to seek His face
from the place of favor He has already given me.*

PERSONAL REFLECTION

_____

_____

_____

_____

_____

_____

_____

_____

Day 44
THE SUPREME ISSUE

*From everyone who has been given much, much
will be required; and to whom they entrusted
much, of him they will ask all the more.*
—LUKE 12:48

GOD'S FAVOR IS given to all of us freely, with no strings attached, and it also comes with a purpose. Not everyone necessarily chooses to use it for its intended purpose, or to use it at all. But God's favor most definitely is something that we're supposed to use. Jesus taught on the subject when He told a parable about talents in Matthew 25. We'll unpack this story over the next several days, but before we begin, you need to understand that the word *talent* does not mean a natural ability to do something well. A talent was a sum of money in the ancient world. Because it can be measured, it represents the subject of favor very well, because favor also is a measurable commodity. How sweet is it to realize that God's favor comes to us freely—no strings attached. How much favor has God given you and for what purpose do you think He gave it?

POINT TO PONDER

*I will be purposeful to use God's favor on my life for His
intended purpose, rejoicing in this gift so freely given to me.*

PERSONAL REFLECTION

_____

_____

_____

_____

Day 45

GOD'S IDEA OF FAIR

For it is just like a man about to go on a journey, who called his own slaves and entrusted his possessions to them. To one he gave five talents, to another, two, and to another, one, each according to his own ability; and he went on his journey.
—MATTHEW 25:14–15

JUST AS THESE servants were each given different amounts of money, not everyone starts out with the same amount of favor. We can't allow ourselves to trip over this—where there is a debate between our idea of what is fair and God's, we'd be wise to stick with God's. God is sovereign (supreme authority, self-governing, not ruled by another), and He decides who starts with what.

"All men are created equal" is not a verse in the Bible. The statement is true as it pertains to God's love, for He loves everyone the same. But not everyone is given the same measure of favor. To consider God unjust because of this is foolish. He is God. And God is love, which means He does everything out of His goodness. The servants were given various amounts "each according to his own ability." They were given something because they had the capability to use it. What kind of balance do you see between your capability and the measure of favor God has put on your life?

POINT TO PONDER

God is sovereign. I accept His idea of fair, and am thankful for the measure of favor He gives me.

PERSONAL REFLECTION

_____

_____

_____

THE NATURE AND PURPOSE OF GOD'S FAVOR

Immediately the one who had received the five talents went and traded with them, and gained five more talents. In the same manner the one who had received the two talents gained two more. But he who received the one talent went away, and dug a hole in the ground and hid his master's money.
—Matthew 25:16–18

CLEARLY, PROPER STEWARDSHIP is *using* what we've been given in order to gain increase. Similarly, the word *traded* here is a word that simply means "to work with." The faithful servants put the money to work, just as we must put the favor we've received from God to work in our lives in order to bring increase. Now clearly someone who understands how money works will be able to work with money more successfully than someone who doesn't; in the same way we must seek to understand the nature and purpose of God's favor if we are going to put it to work successfully. How well do you understand the nature and purpose of God's favor to you?

Point to Ponder

I will put the favor I have received from God to work in my life in order to honor Him and bring increase.

Personal Reflection

_____

_____

_____

_____

_____

Day 41

THE ISSUE IS FAITHFULNESS

The one who had received the five talents came up and brought five more talents, saying, "Master, you entrusted five talents to me. See, I have gained five more talents." His master said to him, "Well done, good and faithful slave. You were faithful with a few things, I will put you in charge of many things; enter into the joy of your master."
—MATTHEW 25:20–21

GOD IN HIS wisdom gives us only what we can handle by His grace as we engage in this learning process. He doesn't expect us to solve calculus equations before we've learned addition and subtraction. That's not to say that God doesn't want full maturity in each of us. But He knows that the key to growth at every stage, whether we're in charge of much or little, is the same. The primary issue is always faithfulness. God, who is perfectly faithful, is looking for this trait in those who say they love Him. Each one of us is given the opportunity for increase by faithful use of what we've been given. In the kingdom of God faithfulness is the supreme value and is always rewarded. What is faithfulness to God, and how is it different from moral purity or religious observance?

POINT TO PONDER

God, who is perfectly faithful, is looking for me to be perfectly faithful to Him.

PERSONAL REFLECTION

_____

_____

_____

_____

Day 48

STAYING ON TRACK

And the one also who had received the one talent came up and said, "Master, I knew you to be a hard man, reaping where you did not sow and gathering where you scattered no seed. And I was afraid, and went away and hid your talent in the ground. See, you have what is yours."
—MATTHEW 25:24–25

ON THE OTHER hand, consider God's verdict on unfaithfulness: "But his master answered and said to him, 'You wicked, lazy slave, you knew that I reap where I did not sow and gather where I scattered no seed. Then you ought to have put my money in the bank, and on my arrival I would have received my money back with interest. Therefore take away the talent from him, and give it to the one who has the ten talents'" (Matthew 25:26–28). Is there an area of your life in which you have stopped trying to fulfill God's commands because obeying Him seemed too difficult or even impossible? What will it take for you to get back on track?

POINT TO PONDER

I will examine my life for areas of unfaithfulness so that I may be made ready to steward well what God has so graciously given me.

PERSONAL REFLECTION

_____

_____

_____

_____

_____

Day 49

DEMONSTRATING FAITHFULNESS

*For to everyone who has, more shall be
given, and he will have an abundance.*
—MATTHEW 25:29

IN THIS STORY the one who started with the most is the one who was found the most faithful. His responsibility was greater, and he was duly rewarded. But the opposite can also be true. I have observed that some of those who seem to have the greatest opportunities in life end up being the ones who squander them the most and therefore fall into the greater judgment. They are held accountable; they must give an answer for their unfaithfulness. Scripture is clear on this point: "From everyone who has been given much, much will be required" (Luke 12:48). The landowner honors the slave who started with the most and who earned the most by giving him the unused talent of the unfaithful slave. The first slave had the greater responsibility, *and* he proved to be the most faithful. Faithfulness is what God is looking for. How can you best demonstrate your faithfulness?

POINT TO PONDER

*I will be always mindful of the truth that God's
favor comes with responsibility.*

PERSONAL REFLECTION

_____

_____

_____

_____

_____

Day 50

HOLY FEAR OF GOD

*But from the one who does not have, even what
he does have shall be taken away. Throw out the
worthless slave into the outer darkness; in that place
there will be weeping and gnashing of teeth.*
—MATTHEW 25:29–30

IN THE SAME measure that faithfulness is rewarded, unfaithfulness is judged. God judges everything that opposes love. How did the lazy servant oppose love? Consider the master's rebuke to him. Interestingly he didn't correct the servant's view of him as a hard man, but he rebuked him for his wrong response to that view. Instead of being inspired by a holy fear of the master, which would have given him a correct sense of the weight of the trust that had been laid on him, he looked at the task and said, "Too hard." In ignoring his responsibility, he was dishonoring his master by essentially telling him that his expectations were too high. Are you living with a holy fear of God? Do you know what that means?

POINT TO PONDER

*I will fully embrace the responsibility God sets before
me so that He can receive the honor He is due.*

PERSONAL REFLECTION

_____

_____

_____

_____

_____

Day 51

REPRESENTING GOD WELL

*He who is faithful in a very little thing is faithful
also in much; and he who is unrighteous in a very
little thing is unrighteous also in much.*
—Luke 16:10

THE FAITHFUL SERVANTS didn't make excuses. They took what they were given and simply used it. They may also have known their master to be a hard man, but apparently they also thought him trustworthy and desired to please him. In fact, in going out and getting more talents with the ones they were given, they were acting like their master. They were aware that they represented the master in his absence and endeavored to rise to his level of doing business. Their love for him was demonstrated in actions that revealed their deep honor and respect for his authority and their sense that it was a privilege to represent him. What a great privilege we have been given to represent God well in the world. In what ways are you currently a representative for your heavenly Father?

POINT TO PONDER

*I want to live with a holy awe and reverence of God
that comes from my love of His divine nature and
inspires me to aim for perfect obedience.*

PERSONAL REFLECTION

_____

_____

_____

_____

Day 52

FULFILLING OUR COMMISSION

And as you go, preach, saying, "The kingdom of heaven is at hand." Heal the sick, raise the dead, cleanse the lepers, cast out demons. Freely you received, freely give.
—MATTHEW 10:7–8

I HAVE BEEN DISTURBED to see the attitude of the lazy servant operating in so much of the church when it comes to fulfilling our commission to imitate Christ in destroying the works of the devil and performing signs and wonders. The favor that we've been given to be like Christ has this commission included in its purpose. It uniquely positions us as representatives of His kingdom to carry out exploits that bring Him honor and to bring people into their God-given destiny. It can be intimidating to think that you are commissioned to destroy the works of the devil and perform signs and wonders like Jesus did, yet God is with you. How has God uniquely positioned you to represent His kingdom, and in what ways are you fulfilling Christ's Great Commission from this unique position?

POINT TO PONDER

I receive the favor I have been given to be like Jesus, and step into the position that is available to me to imitate Him in the work of the Great Commission.

PERSONAL REFLECTION

_____

_____

_____

_____

Day 53
THE GREATEST PRIVILEGE

Faithful is He who calls you, and He also will bring it to pass.
—1 Thessalonians 5:24

Faithful servants don't get hung up over *how* they're going to fulfill the Master's command before they've even tried or even after they've tried a few times and been unsuccessful. They trust the Master. If He said it, then apparently He thinks they're up to the task—if they use the talents He's given them. They see that being given the opportunity to represent Him in all His power and glory is the greatest privilege they could ever receive. Walking out God's call on your life means that you have to trust Him to be faithful to help you fulfill that call. Do you often feel as if all the responsibility for success falls on you, or do you live daily relying on Him to meet you at every point of need?

Point to Ponder

I will begin today to fully trust God to meet all my needs in the power of His Holy Spirit as I go into the world in His name.

Personal Reflection

_____

_____

_____

_____

_____

_____

_____

LIVE TO HONOR GOD

For, behold, those who are far from You will perish; You have destroyed all those who are unfaithful to You.
—Psalm 73:27

UNFAITHFUL SERVANTS LOOK at the commands to do the impossible and question the goodness and wisdom of the Master. Instead of pursuing Him to find a way to fulfill His commands, they put them out of sight and go about their business. Ignoring God while pretending to serve Him is a serious violation of relationship and cuts us off from being able to do the very thing we were put on the planet for—to live our lives to honor the One to whom we will give account. Oftentimes we put the commands of God out of sight because they seem too difficult for us to handle. If that is you, how can you retrieve those commands and begin to fulfill them in ways that honor God?

POINT TO PONDER

I commit to retrieve the commands of God that I have put out of sight and to go about fulfilling them to the glory of His name.

PERSONAL REFLECTION

_____

_____

_____

_____

_____

_____

_____

Day 55

HIS SELFLESS KINGDOM

For the word of the LORD is upright, and
all His work is done in faithfulness.
—PSALM 33:4

JESUS MODELED PERFECT faithfulness for us by taking on the form of a servant and perfectly fulfilling His Father's will. He showed us that the best service comes from those who aren't actually hired servants, but by intimate friends who take on a servant role as an expression of love. We have been given favor because it empowers us to serve more effectively. Favor is not to be used to draw attention or people to ourselves. His is a selfless kingdom. When people use the favor of God for personal gain and not for kingdom purposes, they have chosen where they will level off in their development and experience. Have you ever been tempted to use the favor of God for your own purposes? What turned you back to God?

POINT TO PONDER

I want the selflessness of Christ to be reflected in my life.

PERSONAL REFLECTION

_____

_____

_____

_____

_____

_____

_____

Day 56

AS IT WAS IN THE BEGINNING

The Scripture was fulfilled which says, "And Abraham
believed God, and it was reckoned to him as
righteousness," and he was called the friend of God.
—JAMES 2:23

AS JESUS SHOWED us, the way to becoming a faithful servant of God is by learning to be His friend. In fact, friendship is the purpose of our creation. Everything in creation was made for His delight and pleasure, but human beings alone were made with the capacity to draw close to God in intimacy. No other part of creation has been given the opportunity of becoming a friend of God, even becoming one with Him through His indwelling Spirit. You were actually created for friendship with God. How amazing! What are some of the ways in which you have learned to be His friend?

POINT TO PONDER

I am one with God through His Holy Spirit who
dwells in me. I delight in His friendship.

PERSONAL REFLECTION

_____

_____

_____

_____

_____

_____

_____

_____

GOD'S DELEGATED AUTHORITIES

Be fruitful and multiply, and fill the earth, and subdue it.
—GENESIS 1:28

IN THE BEGINNING God walked with Adam in the cool of the garden. His desire to spend time with those who love Him by choice set the stage for all the conquests that were to come. While Adam and Eve were placed in a garden of perfect peace, the garden itself was placed in the midst of turmoil. It was in this original setting that Adam and Eve were given the assignment to subdue the earth. As they increased in number, they would be able to establish and extend the rule of God over the planet by representing Him as His delegated authorities. What does it mean to be a delegated authority of God and how do you see yourself in that role?

POINT TO PONDER

The establishment and extension of the rule of God on the earth is an outgrowth of His intimate relationship with all who call Him Lord.

PERSONAL REFLECTION

_____

_____

_____

_____

_____

_____

_____

_____

_____

_____

Day 58

CO-LABORING WITH GOD

So He drove the man out; and at the east of the garden of Eden He stationed the cherubim and the flaming sword which turned every direction to guard the way to the tree of life.
—GENESIS 3:24

THE REASON THAT the territory beyond the garden was in turmoil was that Satan, one of the three archangels, had set up his rule there after being cast out of heaven for his rebellion and his desire to be worshipped like God. God in His sovereignty allowed the devil to set up his rule on earth because His intention was to bring eternal judgment to the devil through mankind, in particular, through the fruitfulness of intimate co-laboring between God and man. It is both profound and a bit scary to think that your relationship with God upsets the devil. In what ways are you intimately co-laboring with God in this regard?

POINT TO PONDER

God intends to bring eternal judgment to the devil through mankind—me.

PERSONAL REFLECTION

_____

_____

_____

_____

_____

_____

_____

Day 59
DIVINE JUSTICE

How you have fallen from heaven, O star of the
morning, son of the dawn! You have been cut down to
the earth, you who have weakened the nations!
—Isaiah 14:12

WE MUST ALWAYS remember that Satan has never been a threat to God. Instead, God chose to give those who were made in His image the privilege of executing the judgment of God on all the fallen hosts. God determined that it would be fitting for the devil's defeat to come at the hands of those made in the image of God, who worship Him by choice, because it would mean that the devil would be overcome by those who succeeded where he had failed. This divine justice strikes at the very heart of how and why Satan was removed from heaven in the first place. Why was Satan removed from heaven, and what do you think of God's divine justice regarding his fall?

POINT TO PONDER

I believe that it is a privilege for the people of God to execute
the judgment of God on Satan and the fallen hosts.

PERSONAL REFLECTION

_____
_____
_____
_____
_____
_____
_____

Day 60
DIVINE ROMANCE

You prepare a table before me in the presence of my enemies.
—PSALM 23:5, NIV, EMPHASIS ADDED

WE SEE GOD'S divine plan expressed by David in the psalm above. It's as though God said, "Satan! My people love Me, and I love them, and you're going to watch!" Such romance strikes terror in the heart of the devil and his hosts. At this table of fellowship our relationship with God deepens and overflows into a life of victory in conflict with the powers of darkness. Have you ever thought of the table of fellowship with God as a place of victory? How has God prepared a table before you in the presence of your enemies? How do His actions reflect His love for you?

POINT TO PONDER

The powers of darkness are no match for the love that comes from an intimate relationship with God.

PERSONAL REFLECTION

_____

_____

_____

_____

_____

_____

_____

_____

_____

_____

Day 61

BEING AVAILABLE FOR GOD

The heavens are the heavens of the LORD, but
the earth He has given to the sons of men.
—PSALM 115:16

GOD IS LOOKING for partnership, a partnership in which He empowers His people to become all that He intended them to be. He is the One who said that He made the heavens for Himself, but the earth He made for man. Through this partnership, He portrays the intended similarity between His world (heaven) and ours (earth). His people are to demonstrate His rule to a dying world. He has chosen us for this purpose, not because we're better, but because we're the ones who signed up. He enlists everyone who is *available*. Being available for God isn't always easy. How available do you make yourself to God? What happens when you do?

POINT TO PONDER

I want to partner with God to demonstrate His rule to a dying world.

PERSONAL REFLECTION

_____

_____

_____

_____

_____

_____

_____

_____

_____

_____

THE PERSON OF WISDOM

Christ Jesus... became for us wisdom from God.
—1 CORINTHIANS 1:30, NKJV

To WANT TO grow in favor with God is the most natural desire in the world. Wisdom knows how. Wisdom gives us the keys to understand and use the favor that we've been given in accordance with God's purposes in giving it to us. Increase in wisdom and increase in favor go hand in hand for us because they are interdependent. Jesus, once again, modeled this for us, as we see in Luke 2:52. He "increased in wisdom and in stature and in favor with God and men" (MEV). In fact, Jesus is the person of wisdom as we see in the above scripture from 1 Corinthians. This should convince us that studying the life of Christ and deepening our relationship with Him are central to stewarding our favor with God. Seeking God's wisdom and studying the life of Jesus are essential disciplines for every believer. How do these two disciplines help you steward well the favor He has put on your life?

POINT TO PONDER

I want God to set up a holy hunger in me to dig deep into His Word so that I might know Him more, love Him more, and look more like Him every day.

PERSONAL REFLECTION

_____

_____

_____

_____

_____

Day 63

THE WISDOM OF THE
WORD BRINGS FAVOR

*Do not let kindness and truth leave you....So you will
find favor and good repute in the sight of God and man.*
—**PROVERBS 3:3–4**

WE SHOULD ALSO study Proverbs, the book of the Bible that
best expresses wisdom. As such, this book gives us some of the
greatest instruction for growing in favor. The above verses from
Proverbs give practical instruction for how to pursue an increase
of favor. They describe those who embrace the instruction of the
Lord with diligence, committed to obey and not to lose sight of
His Word. By doing so, they position themselves for an increase
of divine favor. Placing high value in the voice and Word of the
Lord plays a big role in obtaining more favor from God. Is the
Book of Proverbs a "go to" place for you? If not, do you think it
should be? Reading your Bible daily is one of the best ways to get
to know God and understand His wisdom. How can you increase
your time in the Word?

POINT TO PONDER

*I want the Word of God to be a light to my path and
a lamp to my feet in all things and at all times.*

PERSONAL REFLECTION

_____

_____

_____

_____

_____

Day 64

WISDOM—THE CREATIVE
EXPRESSION OF GOD

For he who finds me finds life and obtains favor from the Lord.
—**Proverbs 8:35**

THE ENTIRE EIGHTH chapter of Proverbs reveals the person called Wisdom, which, of course, is Jesus Christ. The chapter primarily focuses on the role of Wisdom in the story of creation, and in doing so unveils the true nature of wisdom—it is the creative expression of God. This verse promises that finding the wisdom of God as it pertains to His creative expression in our fields of influence is a sure way to increase in God's favor. How would you explain to someone the true nature of wisdom as a creative expression of God? What does that mean to you? Perhaps a good place to start is to think of ways that you creatively express God in your sphere of influence.

POINT TO PONDER

I desire the wisdom of God as His creative expression in my fields of influence.

PERSONAL REFLECTION

_____

_____

_____

_____

_____

_____

_____

Day 65

UNIQUELY EXPRESSING AN
ASPECT OF GOD'S NATURE

So we, who are many, are one body in Christ, and
individually members one of another.
—ROMANS 12:5

ONE HELPFUL WAY to see how this promise works is to look at it within the picture we're given in the New Testament, where we are told that we are the body of Christ. Like the members of a human body, every part of the body of Christ is unique, yet each finds its significance and function only in relationship to the rest of the body, particularly the brain. Finding wisdom is the process of discovering and correctly aligning our lives in relationship with the head, Christ, and with our unique destiny to express an aspect of His nature in a way that no one else can. God's favor rests upon us when we are being and doing that which He created us in His wisdom to be and to do. Do you feel that your life is currently aligned in relationship with Jesus and His unique destiny for you? If not, how can you get into alignment to become your unique expression of God's nature?

POINT TO PONDER

I am committed to seek and find God's wisdom so that I may
live as an aspect of His nature in a way that no one else can.

PERSONAL REFLECTION

_____

_____

_____

_____

Day 66

DILIGENTLY SEEK HIM

But thanks be to God, who always leads us triumphantly
as captives in Christ and through us spreads everywhere
the fragrance of the knowledge of Him. For we are
to God the sweet aroma of Christ among those who
are being saved and those who are perishing.
—2 Corinthians 2:14–15, bsb

Proverbs 11:27 says, "He who diligently seeks good seeks favor." The word *good* in this passage means "things that are of benefit" or "pleasing." Those who put extra effort in pursuing the things that please the Lord and bring benefit to the King and His people cannot help but increase in favor with God and man. God loves to find people after His own heart. In what ways do you diligently pursue things that please God and bring benefit to Him and His kingdom?

Point to Ponder

I want my life to be a pleasing aroma to God.

Personal Reflection

_____

_____

_____

_____

_____

_____

_____

_____

_____

Day 67
CELEBRATE LIFE WITH GOD

A good man will obtain favor from the LORD, but
He will condemn a man who devises evil.
—PROVERBS 12:2

THE WORD GOOD here carries several other characteristics that I did not mention in the previous devotion. "Pleasant," "cheerful," "gracious," "generous," and "festive" are a few of the definitions that apply to this verse. The world wants to paint "good" people as boring, legalistic, and somber. But God's goodness can always be recognized in those who seem to overflow with joy, encouragement, forgiveness, peace, and generosity. Their goodness is the fruit of a life lived in celebration of their life with God, and because they are like Him, He is drawn to them. Good people are easy to promote. They automatically align themselves for the lifestyle of increased favor. How do you see yourself aligned for a lifestyle of increased favor? Do you think it begins with celebrating life with God?

POINT TO PONDER

I will live with gladness and singleness of heart,
loving the One who is worthy of it all.

PERSONAL REFLECTION

_____

_____

_____

_____

_____

_____

Day 68

SEEK GODLY UNDERSTANDING

*Good understanding produces favor, but
the way of the treacherous is hard.*
—PROVERBS 13:15

ONE OF THE primary commands in the Book of Proverbs is to seek understanding. Many Christians, recognizing that God is opposed to a purely intellectual gospel that is devoid of the Spirit of God and that consists of form without power, have fallen into the error of believing that God values mindless Christianity. But the truth is that none of us will reach maturity if we think we have to dumb down or cut off part of ourselves in order to serve God. If we are going to be successful in fulfilling the assignments that God has for us, we will need all our faculties and energies to be focused and engaged in what we're doing and what God is doing. A life lived steeped in God's Word in the power of His Spirit requires our full engagement. How fully engaged are you?

POINT TO PONDER

*I commit all my faculties and energies to be focused and engaged
in what God is doing and what He has for me to do with Him.*

PERSONAL REFLECTION

_____

_____

_____

_____

_____

_____

Day 69
LIVE LIKE JESUS

The king's favor is toward a servant who acts wisely,
but his anger is toward him who acts shamefully.
—**PROVERBS 14:35**

To "ACT WISELY" is to live as Jesus would live, with a deep-seated awareness of the King's thoughts and values. Such a lifestyle attracts the King's scepter of favor. After all, we're called to be *disciples*, that is, learners. Jesus certainly sought to bring His disciples into a deeper understanding of kingdom reality. Those who pursue understanding life from God's perspective please Him greatly. Practicing the principles of the kingdom positions a person for an increase in the favor of God. In order to practice kingdom principles, we need to have intimate knowledge of them, which comes from the Word. Think about some principles of God's kingdom that you are practicing. How are your actions positioning you for an increase in the favor of God?

POINT TO PONDER

Let every day be a day that I live like Jesus.

PERSONAL REFLECTION

_____

_____

_____

_____

_____

_____

_____

_____

Day 70

BECOMING ONE

He who finds a wife finds a good thing and
obtains favor from the LORD.
—PROVERBS 18:22

THE IMPLICATIONS OF this promise go far beyond simply getting married. Many have done that without any increase of God's favor. This promise is given to those who correctly steward the blessing of marriage. If you want to catch the attention of the king, treat his daughter well. By nature, it implies unity—becoming one—which illustrates the relationship of God with His people. The groom is to love his bride as Jesus loves the church and died for her (Ephesians 5:25). The bride is to honor and respect the groom as the church respects God. Stewarding marriage by maintaining honor and love in the relationship is to position oneself for increase of favor with God and man. It is when this relationship is held in proper esteem that the message of God's love is most clearly seen in this world. Marriage is often used in the Bible as a metaphor for Christ's relationship with us, His church. To what degree have you become one with the Father by loving His Son well?

POINT TO PONDER

I will receive the glory that has been given to me so
that I may be one with Jesus and the Father.

PERSONAL REFLECTION

_____

_____

_____

Day 11

MOTIVATED BY PASSION

Let him who boasts boast of this, that
he understands and knows Me.
—JEREMIAH 9:24

THOSE WHO GROW in favor are not those who are focused on jumping through hoops and crossing things off the list in order to get God's attention. That's the mentality of a hired servant, not a friend. A friend grows in favor by embracing a life of obedience, motivated by passion for Him and Him alone. This truth is important to remember when pursuing God's favor. Many people want more money, or open doors for their business or ministry, or even greater opportunities for their families. But God's favor is first and foremost about giving us the privilege of knowing Him, simply for the purpose of knowing Him. It could be said that divine favor comes to those who have chosen to keep the main thing the main thing—knowing and loving God. Would you say that knowing and loving God are the main thing in your life?

POINT TO PONDER

I want to be found on my knees today, fully embracing
the great privilege of knowing and loving God.

PERSONAL REFLECTION

_____

_____

_____

_____

_____

_____

Day 12
GOD'S FAVOR AFFIRMS
OUR IDENTITY

For when He received honor and glory from God the Father, such an utterance as this was made to Him by the Majestic Glory, "This is My beloved Son with whom I am well-pleased."
—2 PETER 1:17

As I MENTIONED earlier, we gain favor with God as we pursue His wisdom in order to discover and fulfill the destiny for which He created us. Vital to this process is one of the primary expressions of God's favor—declarations in which He recognizes our identity and asserts His approval and acceptance over our lives. Scripture is filled with these declarations, but there must be moments in the life of every believer in which we hear the voice of our Father speak them directly to us. That's when they become *ours*. *What declarations has God spoken directly to you, and how are you stewarding these declarations?*

POINT TO PONDER

Today I receive all the declarations that God has spoken over me.

PERSONAL REFLECTION

_____

_____

_____

_____

_____

_____

_____

_____

Day 73

TWO ARE BETTER THAN ONE

How could one chase a thousand, and two put ten thousand
to flight, unless...the LORD had given them up?
—DEUTERONOMY 32:30

IT SHOULDN'T SURPRISE us that we need God to show His favor toward us through declarations, because this kind of need for affirmation and approval is wired into our DNA. The pursuit of favor is a normal and deeply rooted human behavior. Everyone has a deep-seated awareness of incompleteness apart from outside recognition and affirmation. Even though the pursuit of man's approval has caused many to fall into an unhealthy fear of man, the basic desire for affirmation is authentic and necessary. When we receive this kind of favor, it increases the effect of who we are and what we've been given to do in life because it taps into the principle of *exponential increase through agreement*. It affirms the fact that *two are better than one* if they are united. With favor our potential increases as the strength of others is added to our own. If you are struggling in any area of your life with an unhealthy fear of man, how can you replace it with an authentic desire for God's affirmation?

POINT TO PONDER

I want the principle of exponential increase
through agreement operating in my life.

PERSONAL REFLECTION

_____

_____

_____

Day 14
CHILDREN OF GOD

Therefore, since we have so great a cloud of witnesses
surrounding us, let us also lay aside every encumbrance
and the sin which so easily entangles us, and let us
run with endurance the race that is set before us.
—HEBREWS 12:1

AT A VERY early age children can be seen pursuing recognition from someone important to them. "Daddy, watch me! Daddy, watch me!" was heard frequently in my home when my children were about to try something new or courageous. The attention they got from me and the subsequent cheers of support were essential building blocks of their self-esteem and confidence in life.

While I worked hard to give them my undivided attention in those moments, there was an even greater positive effect whenever I spoke highly of them to my friends in their presence. It seemed to communicate to them my *ultimate* sign of approval. That is something I still do even though they are adults now. God responds to hunger. How hungry are you for God's affirmation and approval?

POINT TO PONDER

I come like a child into God's presence—hungry and unafraid.

PERSONAL REFLECTION

_____

_____

_____

_____

_____

_____

Day 75

SEEKING GLORY FROM GOD

This is My beloved Son, in whom I am well-pleased.
—Matthew 3:17

IN THIS VERSE in Matthew the heavenly Father spoke of His Son, Jesus, in the hearing of bystanders. The mark of divine favor upon a life is always such a heavenly cry! The challenge for every one of us is to renew our minds and hearts so that our affections are anchored, keeping God's approval as our supreme goal and reward. If we fail to place our value for the favor of man in its appropriate subordinate position in our hearts, we will be vulnerable to tragedy. It's so easy to fall into the trap of fearing what others think of us. We so often just unconsciously want the favor of others and don't even think about God's favor. In what ways do you subordinate the favor of man to the favor of God in your life?

POINT TO PONDER

I will live in such a way as to continually renew my mind and my heart so that my affections are anchored to keep God's approval my supreme goal and reward.

PERSONAL REFLECTION

_____

_____

_____

_____

_____

_____

_____

_____

TAKING EVERY THOUGHT CAPTIVE

For God has not given us a spirit of timidity,
but of power and love and discipline.
—2 TIMOTHY 1:7

MOST OF US need to break our agreement with the spirit of the fear of man first in order to be free to develop the proper priorities when it comes to God's favor and man's favor. Many people don't recognize that their agreement with that spirit is still operating in their thinking, so they will not venture out in their passion for God without the approval of others. Seeking the recognition of man at the expense of approval from God is foolish at best and completely self-destructive at worst, but it is also the way of this world, and so we must be proactive in dismantling such thinking in ourselves and courageous in resisting the peer pressure to cooperate with it. This is where one of Jesus' warnings comes into play. He warned His disciples of the potential influence, like leaven, on their minds by the religious system (Pharisees) and the political system (Herod). Both have the fear of man as their common denominator. How are you proactive when it comes to dismantling thought patterns that lead you to the fear of man instead of passion for God?

POINT TO PONDER

I break all agreement with the spirit of the fear of man and
replace it with God's spirit of power, love, and discipline.

PERSONAL REFLECTION

_____

_____

_____

Day 11
THE ONE AND ONLY

How can you believe, when you receive glory from one another and you do not seek the glory that is from the one and only God?
—JOHN 5:44

JOHN 5:44 DOES not teach that honoring people is wrong. That would bring us into conflict with the rest of Scripture. What it does say is that faith cannot coexist with the fear of man, that is, being more concerned with what someone else will think of us for a particular decision than what God thinks of us. This is important for us to note because it is impossible to please God apart from faith. And the pursuit of favor has everything in the world to do with pleasing God. How willing are you to lay aside what others think of you in order to please God? Think of one situation in your life where you need to do this, and go over the outcome in your mind. Is pleasing God worth the price you have to pay?

POINT TO PONDER

Today I will do whatever it takes to love God with all my heart, with all my soul, with all my strength, and with all my mind.

PERSONAL REFLECTION

_____

_____

_____

_____

_____

_____

_____

Day 78

SEEKING HIS FACE

*Therefore let us draw near with confidence to the
throne of grace, so that we may receive mercy
and find grace to help in time of need.*
—Hebrews 4:16

NOTHING COMPARES WITH the satisfaction of pleasing the heart
of our heavenly Father. Embracing the ultimate quest for His
face means becoming a person whose every thought and action
is driven by the goal of hearing the declaration from heaven:
"Well done!" Thankfully, Scripture is filled with clues as to how
to become—and how not to become—such a person. We'll take
a look at how the history of Israel gives us rich revelation that
defines the kind of relationship God has called us into and the
choices we all have to make in walking out that relationship. What
kind of relationship do you hear God calling you into, and what
choices are you facing as a result?

Point to Ponder

*I will seek Scripture's rich revelation of what rela-
tionship with God looks like.*

Personal Reflection

_____

_____

_____

_____

_____

_____

_____

Day 19
HEADING TO THE PROMISED LAND

Jacob named the place Peniel, for he said, "I have seen
God face to face, yet my life has been preserved."
—GENESIS 32:30

JACOB IS THE first person mentioned in the Bible who had a revelation encounter with the face of God. We see it in Genesis 32:30 following his wrestling match with the angel of the Lord. Significantly, it was this encounter in which Jacob's name was changed to Israel. Hundreds of years later God designated a blessing to be spoken over the nation of Israel: "The LORD bless you and keep you; the LORD *make His face to shine upon you*, and be gracious unto you; the LORD *lift His countenance upon you*, and give you peace" (Numbers 6:22–27, MEV, emphasis added). God wanted the same mark that came upon Israel (Jacob) in his wrestling encounter to be upon Israel's descendants. The people of His name were to be recognized by the blessing of favor and peace in their lives—which comes from His face. How have you or how are you currently wrestling with God in an effort to receive His favor?

POINT TO PONDER

I see the promised land, and it makes me hungry to pay
the price for a revelation encounter with God's face.

PERSONAL REFLECTION

_____

_____

_____

_____

_____

FACE TO FACE WITH GOD

*The LORD spoke to Moses face to face, just
as a man speaks to his friend.*
—EXODUS 33:11, MEV

IT IS NO mistake that Moses was the one God spoke to about His face shining on His people, because Moses is the second, and certainly more significant, person associated with the revelation of the face of God. Exodus 33:11 tells us this, and in Exodus 34 we read that when Moses left these encounters, his own face was shining, reflecting the glory he had beheld. Until Jesus Christ Himself, no other person in Scripture is recorded as being one upon whom the real, physical glory of the Lord was visible in this way. Clearly Moses had a revelation of the face of God, and we need to turn our attention to what it means. The idea of coming face to face with God is found throughout Scripture, but what do you think the phrase really means? What is a "revelation of the face of God"?

POINT TO PONDER

I want to know God fully, just as I am fully known by Him.

PERSONAL REFLECTION

_____

_____

_____

_____

_____

_____

Day 81

FIXING OUR EYES ON THE HEAVENLY REWARD

By faith Moses... [considered] the reproach of Christ greater riches than the treasures of Egypt; for he was looking to the reward.
—HEBREWS 11:24, 26

IN ORDER TO understand the full significance of who Moses was and the revelation he carried, we need first to have a sense of where he stood in the narrative that God had been unfolding in the history of the earth. From the moment that Adam and Eve broke their fellowship with God through sin, God began to carry out His plan to bring mankind back into a relationship with Himself. But throughout the early history of mankind there was a wholesale rejection of God and His ways. So He chose a man, Abraham, from whom to build a nation, Israel, through which He could illustrate what He always had in mind for the whole of humanity. It was never intended that the people of Israel would enjoy God's love exclusively, but instead that they would become the example of what He offers to everyone. What God began through Moses, Jesus brought to perfection. Both experienced the reproach (disappointment) of man yet kept their eyes fixed on the heavenly reward that awaited them. Are you willing to surrender the praises of man for the rewards of heaven?

POINT TO PONDER

My eyes are focused on Jesus, the author and perfecter of my faith.

PERSONAL REFLECTION

_____

_____

_____

Day 82

THE ULTIMATE QUEST

Remember these things, O Jacob, and Israel.... You
will not be forgotten by Me. I have wiped out your
transgressions like a thick cloud and your sins like a
heavy mist. Return to Me, for I have redeemed you.
—Isaiah 44:21–22

THE BLESSING GOD assigned to Israel was the declaration of the favor of His face. Thus, it is through Israel that the rest of humanity has been invited into the ultimate quest. When we go deeper, we find that the history of Israel calls us to this quest by revealing the fact that God Himself is on a quest—the quest for our faces, as it were. He is on a quest to restore the face-to-face intimacy with His children that was lost through sin. Perceiving God's pursuit of us through Scripture is a vital ingredient in helping us come to the place where we can understand and become possessed by the impulse to pursue Him in the same way He has pursued us—with complete abandonment. Those who embrace the ultimate quest are simply those who have correctly perceived and responded to His invitation for restored relationship. Are you eager to restore your relationship with God? What are some of the ways in which you are responding to God's invitation for restored relationship?

POINT TO PONDER

My heart delights in knowing that God is
pursuing me with abandonment.

PERSONAL REFLECTION

_____

_____

_____

Day 83

MY REDEEMER LIVES

Shout for joy, O heavens, for the LORD has done it!...The LORD has redeemed Jacob and in Israel He shows forth His glory.
—ISAIAH 44:23

PERCEIVING GOD'S INVITATION to us through the Scriptures, particularly in the history of Israel, is not something that everyone does automatically. In fact, much of the history of Israel is the story of a people who fundamentally *didn't get* what God was inviting them into. Thus, we learn both positive and negative lessons from Israel's history—both how to respond to God and how *not* to respond to Him. As we'll see shortly, this is precisely where Moses stands out—he was one in a million who got it. Think of someone in your life who "gets it." What are their priorities in life? Now, examine your priorities in light of how you are responding to God.

POINT TO PONDER

I want to be found among the true worshippers who seek to worship the Father in spirit and in truth.

PERSONAL REFLECTION

_____

_____

_____

_____

_____

_____

_____

_____

Day 84

KNOWING GOD VERSUS
KNOWING ABOUT GOD

*For the sorrow that is according to the will of God
produces a repentance without regret, leading to
salvation, but the sorrow of the world produces death.*
—2 CORINTHIANS 7:10

THE REASON WE don't automatically get it is that we have to receive divine grace from God in order to see things from His perspective. This process of perceiving and coming into agreement with God's perspective is called *repentance*. Most of us usually associate this word with being sorry for our sin, and this is appropriate. Scripture tells us that godly sorrow leads to repentance. But being sorry is not repenting. We repent when our sorrow over sin leads us to the place where we receive power from God to change the *way* we think. We may all be able to change *what* we think about, but only God can give us a new perspective on reality. In particular, only God can build a paradigm in our thinking in which we live for and from a relationship with Him instead of going through religious motions and being content simply to know about Him. Think of one area of your life where you are content to know *about* God instead of knowing Him. What would it look like to flip that around?

POINT TO PONDER

*I will allow God to change the way I think
so that I can know Him better.*

PERSONAL REFLECTION

_____

_____

_____

Day 85

THE GIFT OF A RENEWED MIND

Repent, for the kingdom of heaven is at hand.
—MATTHEW 3:2

JESUS BEGAN HIS ministry with the above declaration. Christ came to earth as the culmination and explicit revelation of God's pursuit of mankind. But without receiving the gift of repentance, the very people He preached to, healed, and died for remained blind to this revelation. *Through His very declaration* He made the gift of repentance available to all who would listen. This is the nature of all God's commands. He spoke the universe into existence, and when He speaks to us, grace is released in the same way to enable us to accomplish what He has said. Our job is to appropriate that grace through trusting what He has said and stepping out in radical obedience to it. Trust is something that most of us really struggle with. How much are you willing to trust God?

POINT TO PONDER

I trust God whose grace is sufficient for me.

PERSONAL REFLECTION

_____

_____

_____

_____

_____

_____

_____

_____

Day 86

A HISTORY OF FAVOR

*By faith Abraham, when he was called, obeyed by going
out to a place which he was to receive for an inheritance;
and he went out, not knowing where he was going.*
—HEBREWS 11:8

APPROPRIATELY THE HISTORY of Israel begins, just as the Christian life does, with such an act of radical obedience—a man left the human boundaries that had hitherto defined his life and stepped into a journey of total dependence on God's perspective and commands. It was Abraham's response to God's invitation for relationship that qualified him to receive the tremendous favor by which God made a father of no one into the father of a nation. Let's spend some time looking at how the favor of God shaped the history of Israel into a story of redemption that prophesies the ultimate redemption that Christ would accomplish for us. How radically are you willing to respond to God's invitation for relationship, and what would that radical obedience look like for you?

POINT TO PONDER

I am willing for God to create a history of favor in my life.

PERSONAL REFLECTION

_____

_____

_____

_____

_____

Day 81

THE UPSIDE-DOWN KINGDOM

You are the LORD God, who chose Abram and
brought him out from Ur of the Chaldees, and gave
him the name Abraham. You found his heart faithful
before You, and made a covenant with him.
—NEHEMIAH 9:7–8

FIRST OF ALL, I want to clarify that while Abraham's faith enabled him to receive the favor God was offering to him, the story is clear that he was not receiving that offer because of some particular merit or strength he possessed. In fact, from Abraham right on through his descendants, the story tells us that it was God's choice alone that distinguished Israel as a people and that they were chosen because of their *insignificance*. How does the idea of being insignificant set with you? Are you willing to exchange your earthly power for God's grace to live life from heaven to earth instead of from earth to heaven?

POINT TO PONDER

God's strength is made perfect in my weakness.

PERSONAL REFLECTION

_____

_____

_____

_____

_____

_____

_____

Day 88

PERFECT STRENGTH

*Now as they observed the confidence of Peter and
John and understood that they were uneducated
and untrained men, they were amazed, and began
to recognize them as having been with Jesus.*
—ACTS 4:13

THE DIVINE STRATEGY of God, to take the lowly and despised
things and use them to display His glory, has been played out
over and over again throughout history. The reality is that people
are more likely to recognize the mercy of God and give Him glory
when He does this. Christ declared this to the apostle Paul when
He said, "My grace is sufficient for you, for My strength is made
perfect in weakness" (2 Corinthians 12:9, MEV). And Jesus' disciples experienced this in the religious leaders' response to their
preaching in Acts 4:13. This reality is one of the primary themes
in Israel's history, and it prefigures the life of every believer. Most
of us spend a lot of time trying to hide our weaknesses from others.
Is that you? What can you let go of to get into a place where you
can reveal your weaknesses to others?

POINT TO PONDER

*Like Peter and John, I want to be recognized
as one who has been with Jesus.*

PERSONAL REFLECTION

_____

_____

_____

_____

YIELDING TO GOD'S DIVINE GRACE

Now the LORD said to Abram, "Go forth from your country, and from your relatives and from your father's house, to the land which I will show you...." So Abram went forth as the LORD had spoken to him.
—GENESIS 12:1, 4

THE FAVOR GOD gave to Abraham had a place to land in Abraham's life because of his faith, which he demonstrated through radical obedience. Radical obedience always gives priority to what God has said over what He hasn't said. When God told Abraham to leave his country of origin, He didn't bother to tell him where he was going. He only made it clear that if he was going to be able to fulfill the assignment God was offering him, he couldn't stay in his old environment. When God only gives us the guidance we need for the moment, it tends to keep us closer to Him. This helps us to learn the all-important lesson of dependence on God—a lesson that every single person marked by the favor of God has to learn. Abraham's willingness to follow God on those terms was what was necessary for God to trust him with his amazing assignment. Is God's moment-by-moment guidance something you can accept in the middle of an assignment change? What does that look like for you?

POINT TO PONDER

My conduct and character are governed by God's divine precepts.

PERSONAL REFLECTION

_____

_____

_____

Day 90

FAVOR POINTS TO YOUR PURPOSE

*Know for certain that your descendants will live as
strangers in a land that is not theirs, and they will be
enslaved and mistreated for four hundred years.*
—GENESIS 15:13–14, MEV

GOD'S FAVOR WAS given to Abraham with a specific purpose in mind. Favor always goes with an assignment. In Abraham's case that assignment was to build a nation, which meant that the impact of the favor on Abraham's life and every one of his descendants had a momentum and purpose that extended beyond them for generations—in fact, to all the generations that would be a part of the revelation God intended to release on the earth through that nation. Thus, virtually all the encounters Abraham had with the Lord addressed the generations that God's favor was designed to shape.

In one of these encounters the Lord told Abraham his descendants would be enslaved for four hundred years. (See Genesis 15:13 above.) Though a prophesied captivity may not strike most of us as a sign of God's favor, once again this was simply God's divine setup for displaying His power and perfecting His strength in weakness. All of us experience difficulties. How do you see God's favor pointing to your purpose in your current difficulties?

POINT TO PONDER

*God's favor points to my purpose no matter
how difficult the circumstances.*

PERSONAL REFLECTION

_____

_____

_____

FAVOR CHANGES YOUR CIRCUMSTANCES

You meant evil against me, but God meant it for good in order to bring about this present result, to preserve many people alive.
—GENESIS 50:20

AFTER JOSEPH RECEIVED the revelation of God's favor on his life through two prophetic dreams, his journey immediately led him into circumstances that seemed to contradict that revelation completely. As he ended up thrown in a pit, sold into slavery, and tossed into prison, I'm sure he had no idea that the Lord's favor on his life was positioning him there to fulfill God's prophetic word over his family. But that, more than any plan of the enemy, was the ultimate truth of his circumstances. Divine favor causes you to rise to the top in your sphere of influence, and the reality is that favor can be recognized more easily if you start at the bottom. Thus, Joseph's darkest hour revealed the extraordinary measure of God's favor on his life. Favor enabled him to turn his adverse circumstances into the very training process he needed. What adverse circumstances are you experiencing and how are you feeling God's favor right now?

POINT TO PONDER

I will trust the Lord, even when my circumstances seem to contradict His promises.

PERSONAL REFLECTION

_____

_____

_____

_____

Day 92

FAVOR CAN BE VISIBLE

By faith Joseph, when he was dying, made mention of the exodus
of the sons of Israel, and gave orders concerning his bones.
—HEBREWS 11:22

AMAZINGLY THE FAVOR on Joseph's life was not merely to save his family but also to save the entire nation of Egypt. After all, if God's people were going to be coming out of this nation "with great possessions" in a few hundred years, it needed to be a prosperous nation, not one destroyed by famine. In this way the favor on Israel became very visible to the nation of Egypt. But after Joseph's death God allowed a pharaoh to rise up who perceived the blessed children of Israel with eyes of fear and jealousy, just as He had allowed the enemy, who hated and feared Adam and Eve because of their intimacy with God, to infiltrate the Garden of Eden. This pharaoh, in fact, is one of the clearest representations of the enemy in Scripture, and his reign of oppression over Israel is emblematic of the slavery of the human race to the enemy's kingdom of sin and death. Has God put favor on your life that extends beyond you? How are you stewarding that favor?

POINT TO PONDER

Today I lift my hands in worship regardless of my circumstances.

PERSONAL REFLECTION

FAVOR PROVOKES OTHERS

*Then Joseph had a dream, and when he told it
to his brothers, they hated him even more.*
—**GENESIS 37:5**

GOD'S FAVOR HAS a way of provoking those who don't have it. It's a reality that began in the garden and continued through Cain and Abel, Satan and Job, Jacob and Esau, David and Saul, up to Christ and the Pharisees and through every generation of church history. Each scenario simply reenacts the hatred of the enemy for the objects of God's affection. But you can't let this deter you from pursuing the place of favor that God has made available to you. As you've seen, when you pursue the glory and intimacy you were created for, God ends up with the perfect conditions in which to rise up and judge His enemies. How are you embracing the truth that you are an object of God's affection, created for glory and intimacy with Him?

POINT TO PONDER

*There is a place of favor that God has for me, and
I will pursue it with all my heart.*

PERSONAL REFLECTION

_____

_____

_____

_____

_____

_____

Day 94

GOD'S TRAINING GROUND

Faith prompted the parents of Moses at his birth to hide him for three months, because they realized their child was exceptional and they refused to be afraid of the king's edict.
—HEBREWS 11:23, TPT

THE FAVOR ON Moses' life was visible even when he was an infant. Like Christ, Moses was born into a hostile environment for baby boys. In Pharaoh's fear that a deliverer would rise up, he had ordered that all newborn male Israelites be killed. But Moses' mother saw that he was special and protected him as long as she could. Then he came under the protection of Pharaoh's daughter and, remarkably, ended up growing up in Pharaoh's household. When Moses learned that he was an Israelite, his passion grew to see his own people set free from the cruelty of slavery. He tried to accomplish his destiny under his own power and entered a season of exile that lasted forty years. But this, like Joseph's years in prison, became God's training ground for him, culminating in his stunning commission at the burning bush. Think about those things that brought you to your seasons of exile and what brought you out.

POINT TO PONDER

Only God can empower my destiny.

PERSONAL REFLECTION

FAVOR MATCHES THE ASSIGNMENT

*Holding faith's promise Moses abandoned Egypt and
had no fear of Pharaoh's rage because he persisted
in faith as if he had seen God who is unseen.*
—HEBREWS 11:27, TPT

THE FAVOR ON Moses' life was different from Abraham's or Joseph's because the assignment, to deliver the nation of Israel, required Moses to confront the spiritual principality oppressing Israel. Thus, the miracles He performed through Moses are on a completely different scale. It makes it easier to understand Moses' insecurity at the burning bush when we consider that nothing like what God was asking him to do had ever been done before. He was familiar with power. After growing up in Egypt, he probably knew exactly what he was up against when God told him to confront the demonic power behind Pharaoh's throne. But he hadn't yet seen the superior power of God on display. This was where Moses had to step out in radical obedience. In doing so, Moses received a revelation of the God who invades the impossible like no one before or around him. I believe this level of revelation explains why Moses had such a profound, unique relationship with God. How willing are you to step out in radical obedience to God even when you can't see what He's doing? Do you believe that God's favor matches the assignment He has for you?

POINT TO PONDER

God's fresh revelations come in my radical obedience.

PERSONAL REFLECTION

_____

_____

Day 96

THE BATTLE FOR WORSHIP

God...sent me to you with this message, "Release my
people so that they can worship me in the wilderness."
—Exodus 7:16, MSG

GOD INVOKED HIS rightful ownership of His people to Pharaoh by demanding that they be free to worship Him. This issue of worship is the defining issue of human history. We were made to worship the One in whose image we were created. Christ was crucified to restore our place of communion with God in worship. That is, the salvation He purchased for us is not only salvation *from* death but also, and even more importantly, salvation *unto* a life of communion with God. In that place of beholding the Lord in worship, we are transformed. Since we always become like whatever we worship, there is nothing greater that God could want for His people than for them to worship Him, for there is nothing greater than Himself. God doesn't long for our worship because He is an egotist in need of our affirmation. Instead He longs for our transformation that takes place in the glory of His presence, the glory that descends in times of extended worship. How integral is worship in your walk with the Lord?

POINT TO PONDER

The name of the Lord is majestic in all the earth!

PERSONAL REFLECTION

_____

_____

_____

_____

Day 97

WORSHIP BRINGS FREEDOM

*This is what the LORD says: By this you will know that I am
the LORD: With the staff that is in my hand I will strike
the water of the Nile, and it will be changed into blood.*
—EXODUS 7:17, NIV

WHEN ADAM AND Eve sinned, they didn't stop worshipping; they simply started directing their worship toward the wrong thing. The enemy's agenda has always been to rob our destinies by getting us to worship anything but God. We see this agenda demonstrated in the Exodus story through Pharaoh, who clearly understood the fact that Israel's worship of God was a threat to his kingdom. His responses to Moses, which we'll explore over the next several days, reveal the tactics the devil uses to keep people from entering into complete freedom, which is the true fruit of our lives when we live to worship the One worthy of our worship. And God's responses to Pharaoh reveal His passion to bring His people into nothing less than complete freedom. Total freedom is always on God's agenda. His love always works to make us free. The anger of God is always aimed at that which interferes with love. What are you wrestling with that is causing you to worship things other than God? How can you jettison those things from your life?

POINT TO PONDER

*I will throw all the idols in my life on the trash heap until there
is nothing left to hinder my love and devotion for God.*

PERSONAL REFLECTION

_____

_____

_____

Day 98

PHARAOH'S FIRST BARGAIN

Go, sacrifice to your God in the land.
—**EXODUS 8:25, MEV**

LET'S CONSIDER THE strategies behind Pharaoh's responses to Moses. When Moses first asked Pharaoh to release God's people to go and worship, Pharaoh gave the above response. The devil doesn't mind our worshipping God if it doesn't require change. True worship, and the freedom it brings, requires the dedication of our entire lives to God. Any offer that tries to convince us otherwise is a false one. If we try to keep worship "in the land" of the devil's domain, we give him legal access to influence and spoil our efforts. The fastest way to get out from under Satan's thumb is to give every area of your life over to God. What areas of your life do you need to surrender right now, and what will it take to do it?

POINT TO PONDER

I will not bargain with the devil.

PERSONAL REFLECTION

_____

_____

_____

_____

_____

_____

_____

_____

_____

_____

Day 99

PHAROAH'S SECOND BARGAIN

Only you shall not go very far away.
—Exodus 8:28

WHEN MOSES REJECTED Pharaoh's terms, Pharaoh offered to let Israel go but added the above stipulation. To allow for changes, but only partial ones, is still an effort to control God's people. This strategy usually works well with those who know it's right to worship God but who are still holding on to something. Such people can often be convinced that fully surrendering their lives to God in worship is too extreme. Consider what happened to the woman who prepared Jesus for His burial by pouring costly ointment over Him—ointment worth a whole year's income. Everyone but Jesus thought it to be excessive and extreme. But Jesus honored her by stating that the story of her extravagant worship would be told wherever His story was told. What others thought to be excessive and extreme, God considered reasonable. The only true worship is extreme worship, and only extreme worship brings extreme results—transformation. Extravagant and extreme worship impacts the heart of God. What would extravagant worship look like in your life? How do you think it might transform you?

POINT TO PONDER

I am ready for full transformation at the hand of God.

PERSONAL REFLECTION

_____

_____

_____

_____

PHARAOH'S THIRD BARGAIN

Go now, you that are men.
—Exodus 10:11, mev

Rejected again, Pharaoh enlarged his offer with the statement above. It becomes quite clear that the enemy fears entire families worshipping God together, united in purpose. There is a powerful spiritual agreement that is established when multiple generations join their efforts to honor the one true God, and it brings an exponential release of power and blessing that can't be obtained any other way. The devil knows it, too, and for this reason he seems to work overtime to destroy families. God Himself explains why He made the husband and wife into one—it was so He could have godly offspring. Unity breeds unity, especially when its purpose is to honor God. The family unit has always been a target of the enemy, and never more so than now. In what ways has the enemy worked to disrupt or destroy your family?

Point to Ponder

*I endeavor to stand with my family, united
in purpose that fully honors God.*

Personal Reflection

_____

_____

_____

_____

_____

_____

_____

PHARAOH'S FINAL BARGAIN

Go, serve the LORD; only let your flocks
and your herds be kept back.
—EXODUS 10:24, NKJV

PHARAOH'S FINAL EFFORT to bring Moses and Israel into compromise is found in his statement above. This statement reveals the ultimate test and potentially the ultimate place of blessing from God. It is to worship God with all our financial resources as well as with our families. A Christianity that costs little is worth little. Satan knows that if he can keep us attached to his fear-oriented economy, he can still influence our emotions and will and poison our thinking. The end result is that we become ineffective in reaching our divine purpose. Such a last-ditch effort on the part of Pharaoh reveals what Satan fears most—families who worship together with reckless abandon, using all their assets for the glory of God. This absolutely terrifies the devil, because nothing will be withheld from this kind of people. God wants us to trust Him with everything—our families, our resources, and our very lives. This may seem too costly until you consider that the return is priceless. Are you willing to make the greatest transaction, to give all you have to God for all that He has for you?

POINT TO PONDER

I choose God's economy for myself and my family, severing all
fear-oriented thinking that places me in Satan's economy.

PERSONAL REFLECTION

_____

_____

_____

Day 102

GOD'S COVENANTAL BLESSING

Speak to all the congregation of Israel, saying, "On the tenth of this month they are each one to take a lamb for themselves, according to their fathers' households, a lamb for each household."
—EXODUS 12:3

AND THIS WAS precisely the sort of group of people that God intended Israel to be. He didn't send Moses to make a bargain with Pharaoh. All his negotiations with Pharaoh were set up to earn Israel's trust by displaying God's superior power and to accomplish a deliverance that would prophesy the ultimate deliverance He would bring to the human race through the atonement. In order to fulfill the latter purpose, the confrontation by which Pharaoh finally capitulated to God's demands was a confrontation in which death came to all those who failed to sacrifice a Passover lamb and anoint their doorposts with its blood. (One of the wonderful truths of this story is that only one lamb was sacrificed per household. I believe that this signifies that there is a covenantal blessing made available to entire families when members of that family walk faithfully before God.) God has given you His Lamb, Jesus, for your household. When was the last time you reflected on this great gift in the context of your family?

POINT TO PONDER

I desire that my entire family walk faithfully before God and receive His covenantal blessing.

PERSONAL REFLECTION

Day 103

JESUS OUR STRONG DELIVERER

*Then he called for Moses and Aaron at night and
said, "Rise up, get out from among my people, both
you and the sons of Israel; and go, worship the Lord,
as you have said. Take both your flocks and your
herds, as you have said, and go, and bless me also."*
—Exodus 12:31–32

So, just as the Christian life begins by embracing the grace and
forgiveness Christ has provided for us by faith, Israel's deliverance began with embracing that which God had prescribed to
them for their protection. The Scripture is clear that if they had
failed to trust and obey His instructions, they would have been
no more immune to the angel of death than the Egyptians. Their
faith was an essential ingredient in their deliverance. When Pharaoh saw the power of Israel's God, he was through bargaining.
The people of God lived by faith, and God honored their faith. Do
you believe that you can live by that same kind of faith and see
God's deliverance for yourself and your family?

Point to Ponder

*I will walk by faith, not by sight, hanging on
to God's vision for my reward.*

Personal Reflection

_____

_____

_____

_____

_____

ALL THINGS ARE POSSIBLE

As Pharaoh drew near, the sons of Israel looked, and behold,
the Egyptians were marching after them, and they became
very frightened; so the sons of Israel cried out to the LORD.
—EXODUS 14:10

A LMOST IMMEDIATELY AFTER the Israelites took their first step
of faith, they found themselves between the Red Sea and the
Egyptian army. Most of us face this kind of test early in our faith. It
seems that God is leading us into a life of impossibly high standards,
and we are dogged by the pressure to go back to sin and the world.
In Israel's case, the presence of the Egyptian army and the prospect
of returning to slavery gave Israel the incentive to cross the sea that
had previously looked like an insurmountable obstacle. Had Pharaoh and his army not been on their backside, I doubt very much
that they would have had the courage to cross. God is so good that
He will even use the enemy to motivate us to get to where we need
to be. The devil is a pawn in the hands of the Master—his greatest
attempts to destroy are *always* reworked to bring glory to God and
strength to His people. Think of a time when God used the enemy
to motivate you to get somewhere that you needed to be. How did
you respond?

POINT TO PONDER

I choose to respond to the motivation of God in every
situation no matter how impossible things may seem.

PERSONAL REFLECTION

_____

_____

_____

Day 105

ENTERING HIS FULLNESS

By faith he lived as an alien in the land of promise, as in a for-
eign land, dwelling in tents...for he was looking for the city
which has foundations, whose architect and builder is God....
And indeed if they had been thinking of that country from which
they went out, they would have had opportunity to return. But
as it is, they desire a better country, that is, a heavenly one.
—HEBREWS 11:9–10, 15–16

OTHER THAN THE life, crucifixion, resurrection, and ascension
of Jesus, the exodus is probably the most astounding thing that
has ever happened. But from God's perspective the greater reality
for His people was not their deliverance but the *purpose* for their
deliverance. The same is true of the salvation Christ gives to us.
The significance and nature of this salvation is something we will
be learning about throughout our lifetimes. It never gets old to
meditate on the fact that we were once dead in our sins and have
been resurrected as a new creation with a living spirit, in which
the Spirit of God dwells. But the truth is, life in the kingdom is a
greater reality than our entrance into the kingdom. Among God's
purposes for the Israelites was to represent Him to the nations and
to be the lineage for Jesus. With that in mind, can you see yourself
representing Him from your position of godly inheritance?

POINT TO PONDER

It's time to discover and pursue the fullness
of God's purpose for my salvation.

PERSONAL REFLECTION

_____

_____

LIVING IN THE KING'S DOMAIN

The kingdom of God is not coming with signs to be observed; nor will they say, "Look, here it is!" or, "There it is!" For behold, the kingdom of God is in your midst."
—LUKE 17:20–21

WHEN THE ISRAELITES came out of Egypt, they passed through the Red Sea. This is a picture of water baptism, the prophetic act by which we declare faith in Christ and receive forgiveness for our sin. God didn't merely bring Israel *out* of slavery; He also brought them *into* the Promised Land. When He brought them into the Promised Land, they crossed through another body of water, the Jordan River. This speaks of the baptism of the Spirit. (Jesus referred to the Holy Spirit as a river, for example, in John 7:38–39.) The first baptism deals with getting us out of the red, so to speak—paying our debt of sin. The second baptism deals with getting us into the black—getting us filled with God so we can walk with Him and more effectively represent Him as His agents of power on the earth. The promised land for the believer is living life in the realm of the kingdom—the King's domain. This is the realm we were saved to live in. How are you doing on your journey through the Red Sea waters of baptism, to the Jordan River baptism of the Spirit, and into the promised land?

POINT TO PONDER

With my hand in the Father's, I'm going forward, into the promised land.

PERSONAL REFLECTION

_____

_____

Day 107

CROSS THE RIVER

*I seek you with all my heart; do not let
me stray from your commands.*
—Psalm 119:10, niv

In actuality two and a half tribes decided to live on one side of the river while nine and a half tribes crossed over into the Promised Land. God required them to work together to make sure that people on both sides of the river came into an inheritance. This "river" continues to be a point of division to this day, as a host of wonderful people have chosen to live on the other side of the river of God's intentions. They are not inferior, nor are they powerless. But they have settled for less. There is more across the river. Which side of the river are you living on? Have you seriously considered that you might be settling for less than what God has for you? If so, are you ready to cross the river?

POINT TO PONDER

*I am not content to settle for less than what God has for me. I
will keep going forward until I receive my full inheritance.*

PERSONAL REFLECTION

_____

_____

_____

_____

_____

_____

_____

_____

Day 108

INTO THE PROMISED LAND

Do not conform to the pattern of this world, but be transformed by the renewing of your mind. Then you will be able to test and approve what God's will is—his good, pleasing and perfect will.
—ROMANS 12:2, NIV

WHAT THE EXODUS story shows us is that it is possible for people to be brought out of slavery but stop short of entering into the land of promises. In fact, the entire generation that came out of Egypt failed to fulfill the destiny God had for them; they died in the small peninsula between Egypt and the Promised Land. The simple reason for these aborted destinies was a lack of repentance—a failure to allow God to retrain their thinking from the slavish mentality of Egypt to the mentality of those fit to walk in covenant with Him. Have you allowed God to renew your mind or are you still living as a slave instead of a beloved son or daughter?

POINT TO PONDER

I am a beloved child of God.

PERSONAL REFLECTION

_____

_____

_____

_____

_____

_____

_____

_____

_____

Day 109

ISSUES OF THE HEART

*Holding to a form of godliness, although
they have denied its power.*
—2 TIMOTHY 3:5

IN THE SAME way, many Christians repent enough to be forgiven but not enough to see the kingdom. As I stated earlier, Jesus' first instruction in His ministry was, "Repent, for the kingdom of heaven is at hand" (Matthew 3:2). But just as the Israelites did, such believers miss out on all that is available in the authentic Christian life, and they are in danger of settling for a life of religious form.

Religion is the antithesis of the kingdom of God. And the kingdom—the realm of the King's domain—is what every man, woman, and child longs for deep within their hearts. Religion creates appetites it cannot fulfill. By nature it carries a value for form without power, information without experience. It makes outward appearance a priority over the issues of the heart. For this reason religion does not provide an opportunity to actually know God, and it is therefore cruel, powerless, and boring. Is religion keeping you from the fullness of the kingdom of God?

POINT TO PONDER

I will seek God's wisdom and grace to discern those things that are keeping me from living an authentic Christian life.

PERSONAL REFLECTION

_____

_____

_____

Day 110
KNOWN BY GOD

But now that you have come to know God, or rather
to be known by God, how is it that you turn back
again to the weak and worthless elemental things, to
which you desire to be enslaved all over again?
—GALATIANS 4:9

WE MUST BE a people who are not willing to sacrifice the ideals of the kingdom for artificial substitutes. This present move of God is all about retraining us to lock into His manifest presence and live for nothing else.

The fundamental difference between authentic Christianity and religion is the issue of knowing and being known by God versus merely knowing *about* Him. In fact, the only thing more important than knowing God is to be known by Him. Jesus made that clear in Matthew's Gospel when He warned that the Father would say to some, "*I never knew you.* Depart from Me" (Matthew 7:23, MEV, emphasis added). Those who have no real affection for Jesus are not His sheep—not His beloved. Are you hungry to know God with all your heart and everything that is in you, and to be known by Him, or is it easier to just know *about* Him?

POINT TO PONDER

God is the One I care about the most, the One I want above all else.

PERSONAL REFLECTION

_____

_____

_____

_____

KNOWING GOD

*For the Father loves the Son, and shows Him all things
that He Himself is doing; and the Father will show Him
greater works than these, so that you will marvel.*
—JOHN 5:20

KNOWING ABOUT SOMEONE is not the same as knowing him or her. As a child, I was a great fan of Willie Mays, the Hall of Fame baseball player with the San Francisco Giants. I read everything I could read about him, collected his baseball cards, attended games, and listened to countless broadcasts of the Giants' games on the radio. I could tell you his birth date, give numerous statistics about his accomplishments on the field, and even show you my copy of his autograph. But I didn't know him, and he didn't know me. For that to happen we would have to spend time together, and then he would have to let me into his life, as I would also need to do the same for him. Only if that were to happen could I say, "I know Willie Mays." Jesus modeled what a relationship of intimacy with the Father looks like. Do you believe that God desires this kind of intimacy with you also?

POINT TO PONDER

*I will search the Scriptures in order to better
understand Jesus' model for intimacy with God.*

PERSONAL REFLECTION

_____

_____

_____

_____

Day 112

OPENING YOUR HEART TO GOD

*If we confess our sins, He is faithful and righteous to forgive
us our sins and to cleanse us from all unrighteousness.*
—1 John 1:9

WHILE GOD KNOWS everything about everybody, He does not
know everyone. He can give more facts about a person than
anyone could ever know of himself. But a relationship takes mutual
consent and cooperation. For Him to know me I must open up my
heart and give Him access to the secret things of my life. That is
why confessing our sins to God is so important. It is the beginning
of the relationship. He already knows all—the good, the bad, and
the ugly. But when I confess them to Him, I come into agreement
with Him about my sin being wrong. But a relationship must be
built on more than confession. That just removes the obstacles and
makes a relationship possible. By confessing sin, I open myself up
to Him to make personal relationship a possibility. Are you ready
to confess your sins to God or is something holding you back? If
so, what?

POINT TO PONDER

*I'm not going to hold back any longer; I'm going to confess all
my sins to God so that every obstacle between us is removed.*

PERSONAL REFLECTION

_____

_____

_____

_____

_____

Day 113
SURRENDERING ALL

Surrender your heart to God, turn to him in prayer, and
give up your sins—even those you do in secret. Then you
won't be ashamed; you will be confident and fearless.
—Job 11:13–15, CEV

RELATIONSHIPS ARE BUILT on trust, communication, common
interests, honesty, and time together. It is no different with
knowing God. And it is from that place of knowing God that we
find our greatest purpose in life. Yet being known *by* God is the
most important thing in life, and it won't happen without my surrender and response to Him. Many of us understand the call to
surrender all to God, but we hold on to things anyway because we
trust our wisdom more than God's. If that's you, what does surrendering all to God look like right now for you? Is your perspective in line with heaven's perspective?

POINT TO PONDER

I will focus on heaven's perspective and pursue
what it means to surrender all.

PERSONAL REFLECTION

_____

_____

_____

_____

_____

_____

_____

A KINGDOM OF PRIESTS

*But you are a chosen race, a royal priesthood, a holy
nation, a people for God's own possession, so that you
may proclaim the excellencies of Him who has called
you out of darkness into His marvelous light.*
—1 Peter 2:9

GOD INVITED ISRAEL to know Him on Mount Sinai when He declared in Exodus 19:6: "You shall be to Me a kingdom of priests and a holy nation." God intended the entire nation of Israel to be priests unto the Lord, giving each citizen unique access to His presence in order to fulfill the amazing honor of ministering to God Himself. This was the heart of God for His people—for everyone to have access to Him. He had brought them out of Egypt to practice this kind of worship. How exciting that we can proclaim the excellence of God. How are you taking advantage of your position as a royal priest to worship Him?

POINT TO PONDER

My heart is joyful because I have full access to minister to God.

PERSONAL REFLECTION

_____

_____

_____

_____

_____

_____

_____

_____

WALKING IN YOUR NEW IDENTITY

*All the people perceived the thunder and the lightning flashes
and the sound of the trumpet and the mountain smoking;
and when the people saw it, they trembled and stood at a
distance. Then they said to Moses, "Speak to us yourself and
we will listen; but let not God speak to us, or we will die."*
—EXODUS 20:18–19, EMPHASIS ADDED

THE GIVING OF the Law at Mount Sinai was intended to facilitate the process by which Israel would unlearn the thinking of Egypt and learn how to walk in their new identity as priests to the Lord. In describing what He required of them, God was unveiling His holy and righteous nature, which they would need to emulate in order to walk in relationship with Him. But Israel rejected God's invitation for relationship. We see this in the above quoted verses from Exodus chapter 20 during an amazing encounter between God, Moses, and Israel. Have you struggled with feeling so afraid of God that you wanted someone else to mediate?

POINT TO PONDER

*I will not fear an intimate relationship with God. He
loves me and wants me to draw close to Him.*

PERSONAL REFLECTION

_____

_____

_____

_____

_____

_____

AUTHENTIC RELATIONSHIP

Create in me a clean heart, O God, and
renew a steadfast spirit within me.
—PSALM 51:10

ONE OF THE most important features of being a minister unto the Lord is to have a heart for the voice of God. He speaks to make us clean—to qualify us to be able to draw near to Him. Rejecting His voice is rejecting His face, as it rejects the opportunity for an authentic relationship with Him. The Israelites were afraid they would die if they heard His voice, not realizing that the death they feared was in the absence of His voice. They not only rejected a relational encounter with God; they chose to have a mediator. There can be no authentic relationship with God for people who prefer a mediator over and above personal encounters. Has it ever occurred to you that some of the things you do may actually be a rejection of God?

POINT TO PONDER

I am thankful that God's loving-kindness and forgive-
ness are always there for me even when I reject Him.

PERSONAL REFLECTION

_____

_____

_____

_____

_____

_____

_____

GRACE UNDER GOD

As each has received a gift, use it to serve one
another, as good stewards of God's varied grace.
—1 Peter 4:10, esv

ISRAEL'S RESPONSE EXPRESSED their preference for the law instead of grace. The law consists of preset boundaries that don't require a personal relationship with God. Grace, on the other hand, is based on relationship. Perhaps an oversimplification would be to say that under the law everyone is given the same requirements. Under grace some things change according to God's unique plan for each individual. For example, God may say to one person that he or she cannot own a television, yet He allows another to have several of them in his or her home. Grace is that way. It is relationally based. This doesn't mean that there are no absolutes under grace—quite the contrary. It just means that under grace God enables us to obey what He commands. How does it make you feel to think that grace under God is different for each one of us because it is based on relationship?

POINT TO PONDER

I am continuing to grow in my understanding of God's grace.

PERSONAL REFLECTION

_____

_____

_____

_____

_____

_____

Day 118

INVITATION FOR RELATIONSHIP

Now the appearance of the glory of the LORD was like a devouring fire on the top of the mountain in the sight of the people of Israel. Moses entered the cloud and went up on the mountain. And Moses was on the mountain forty days and forty nights.
—Exodus 24:17–18, ESV

INTERESTINGLY, THROUGHOUT SCRIPTURE Moses is associated with the Law. We read, "The law was given through Moses; grace and truth came through Jesus Christ" (John 1:17, MEV). As a prophetic sign that life under the Law was not what God intended for us in the kingdom (the promised land), Moses, the mediator of that first covenant, died in the wilderness with the first generation of Israelites. Yet as an individual Moses was one of the few people in the Old Testament who understood and responded to God's invitation for relationship. We see this in the rest of the encounter in which Israel demanded a mediator. To what extremes will you go in order to respond to God's invitation for relationship?

POINT TO PONDER

I am willing to brave even the fire on the mountaintop if it means drawing closer to God.

PERSONAL REFLECTION

_____

_____

_____

_____

_____

Day 119

TRUE FEAR OF GOD

*"Do not fear, for God has come to test you, so that
the fear of Him may be before you so that you do
not sin." The people stood a distance away as Moses
drew near to the thick darkness where God was.*
—EXODUS 20:20–21, MEV

BECAUSE MOSES WAS more familiar with the Lord's voice and walked in a greater revelation of who God is, his perception of all the fireworks God set off on the mountain was completely different. The word *fear* occurs twice in Moses' statement above. Moses was pointing out that there was a wrong fear of God and a right fear. The wrong kind leads us to hide from God, while the right kind leads us to draw near to Him in purity and reverence. The fireworks on the mountain exposed the fact that Moses was the only one who understood and possessed the true fear of the Lord. Moses was not afraid because he knew the voice of the One who bid him to come. Do you know God's voice well enough to distinguish between wrong fear of God and right fear?

POINT TO PONDER

*I will learn to hear God's voice so well that nothing
can stop me from coming when He calls.*

PERSONAL REFLECTION

_____

_____

_____

_____

_____

INTIMACY WITH GOD

The fear of the LORD is the beginning of wisdom, and
the knowledge of the Holy One is understanding.
—PROVERBS 9:10

MOSES' UNIQUE INTIMACY with the Lord can be seen in a situation that arose later between him and his siblings. Aaron and Miriam had been very critical of Moses because of the wife he chose to marry. God asked them how they could be critical of one of His best friends.

> The LORD came down in a pillar of cloud and stood at the doorway of the tent, and He called Aaron and Miriam. When they had both come forward, He said, "Hear now My words: If there is a prophet among you, I, the LORD, shall make Myself known to him in a vision. I shall speak with him in a dream. Not so, with My servant Moses, he is faithful in all My household; *with him I speak mouth to mouth,* even openly, and not in dark sayings, and *he beholds the form of the* LORD. *Why then were you not afraid to speak against My servant,* against Moses?"
>
> **—NUMBERS 12:5–8, EMPHASIS ADDED**

Are you operating from a place of intimacy with God that brings wisdom into your relationships with others?

POINT TO PONDER

I want my fear of the Lord to be such that it brings
me wisdom to see clearly in every situation.

PERSONAL REFLECTION

_____

_____

_____

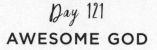

AWESOME GOD

Who is like the Lord our God, who is enthroned on high.
—Psalm 113:5

GOD HAD A certain way He would speak with His prophets. Not so with Moses. Moses was called to greatness as a child and given the favor that spared his life. But he misused that favor when he killed the Egyptian in his efforts to fulfill his assignment of becoming Israel's deliverer. The favor of God does not bless self-promotion. After forty years of tending sheep, he obtained favor when God came to him in a burning bush. When he turned aside from his agenda and stepped aside at the burning bush, God spoke. Has God ever had to remind you of who He is? Hopefully it didn't take forty years in the desert tending sheep for you to remember!

Point to Ponder

I stand in awe of God today, King of the whole earth.

Personal Reflection

_____

_____

_____

_____

_____

_____

_____

_____

_____

_____

Day 122

THE PLACE OF TRUST

Therefore, since we have such a hope, we are very bold. We are not like Moses, who would put a veil over his face to prevent the Israelites from seeing the end of what was passing away.
—2 CORINTHIANS 3:12–13, NIV

MOSES' STORY EXPANDS rapidly as God's relationship with him surpasses all the prophets'—God knew Moses face to face. The glory of God's face would actually rest upon Moses' face until the people finally asked Moses to put a veil over his head—the glory scared them. Moses is the ultimate example of using favor to increase favor. He had earned a place of trust that gave him access to the secret places with God, to see and experience what others could not have access to. He spoke openly to Moses, not in dark or mysterious sayings that needed an interpretation. Not only that, He also let Moses see His form, which was unheard of. How bold are you to let God's glory rest on you so that others may see it?

POINT TO PONDER

I am full of hope in Christ Jesus and that makes me bold for Him.

PERSONAL REFLECTION

_____

_____

_____

_____

_____

_____

_____

BEWARE THE SLANDERER

*Do not slander a slave to his master, or he will
curse you and you will be found guilty.*
—Proverbs 30:10

GOD TAKES IT personally when we dishonor those who carry His favor. Many self-appointed watchdogs in the body of Christ have some explaining to do before God. Their websites, books, and radio shows are filled with slander and criticisms of some of God's closest friends. Now these friends of God may not always have the best doctrine, and their mannerisms may offend many. They may even have areas of their lives that need serious adjustment and change. But they are recognized in heaven as those who will do whatever the Holy Spirit tells them to do. And the signs that are supposed to follow a believer actually follow them. When people have to disregard the signs that follow a person's life in order to feel justified in their criticisms of that person, they have ignorantly stepped into a place of judgment before God. "Do not slander a slave to his master, or he will curse you and you will be found guilty" (Proverbs 30:10). Are you willing to honor God's chosen ones even when they don't seem worthy of such honor? Can you let God be the judge?

POINT TO PONDER

*I will let God be the judge and not raise my voice
in slander or criticism of His friends.*

PERSONAL REFLECTION

_____

_____

_____

_____

Day 124

GIVE HONOR

*Love each other with genuine affection, and
take delight in honoring each other.*
—Romans 12:10, NLT

RECOGNIZING THE FAVOR of God on another believer plays a huge role in preparing us for the increase of God's favor in our own lives. If I see the favor of God on someone, I am responsible to give honor where it's due. And whoever honors the one that God honors is positioned for an increase of favor from God. Specifically, when we honor those who possess a deeper revelation of God and a deeper intimacy with Him, we position ourselves to receive the same revelation—to be guided deeper into a relationship with God ourselves as we walk in the footsteps of those who are ahead of us. If we are going to develop a heart to know God, we must learn to perceive the lives of His closest friends as examples of what God has made available for us and follow their lead directly to Him. How does honoring someone who has the favor of God on their life bring a heavenly perspective to the situation?

POINT TO PONDER

*I am ready to receive more of heaven's perspective
of what it means to honor others.*

PERSONAL REFLECTION

Day 125

COME STAND IN THE RIVER

And whosoever will, let him take the water of life freely.
—Revelation 22:17, KJV

CONSIDER MOSES' LIFE an invitation to a deeper revelation of God—and be even more encouraged, because he lived in a time in which sin had not yet been atoned for. Jesus, the Son of God, had not yet become a man, dying in our place, paying for our redemption. What that basically means is this—Moses experienced this amazing relationship of friendship with God under an inferior covenant. And it is improper to expect superior blessings from an inferior covenant. The invitation remains: "Whosoever will may come." If Moses was unafraid even though he was outside the saving grace of Christ, how unafraid are you under the new covenant to come before God and receive what He so freely gives?

POINT TO PONDER

As a new covenant believer, I will not be afraid to come before God's throne of grace and freely receive what He so freely offers.

PERSONAL REFLECTION

_____

_____

_____

_____

_____

_____

_____

_____

_____

Day 126

HOLY IS THE LORD!

The LORD reigns, let the peoples tremble; He is enthroned above the cherubim, let the earth shake! The LORD is great in Zion, and He is exalted above all the peoples. Let them praise Your great and awesome name; holy is He.
—PSALM 99:1–3

THE HUMAN RACE has been invited into the ultimate quest for the face of God through the story of Israel, those marked by the blessing of His face. Yet among those Israelites who came out of Egypt, only one embraced this quest. Something should provoke us to find out what possessed Moses to enter "the thick darkness where God was." After all, Moses knew better than the Israelites did that their fear of dying in the presence of God was far from unfounded. God explicitly told him, "You cannot see My face, for no man can see Me and live!" (Exodus 33:20). There is no question; to see the Lord in His fullness will kill anyone. We are not wired to be able to withstand that measure of glory, holiness, and power. Yet, apparently Moses felt that knowing more of this God was worth risking death. And later the same God who had said that any who saw His face would die declared that He spoke to Moses face to face. What are we to make of this? How willing are you to be a forerunner like Moses, to be so hungry for God's presence that knowing Him means more to you than life itself?

POINT TO PONDER

I will do whatever it takes to die to self if it means knowing God more.

PERSONAL REFLECTION

Day 127

UNION WITH CHRIST

*I have been crucified with Christ; and it is no
longer I who live, but Christ lives in me.*
—GALATIANS 2:20

SEVERAL PEOPLE IN Scripture saw God's face and were stunned
to find they were still alive. Gideon and John are two examples:

> So Gideon said, "Alas, O Lord GOD! I have seen the angel of the
> LORD *face to face*." Then the LORD said to him, "Peace be with you.
> Do not be afraid. *You will not die.*"
> **—JUDGES 6:22–23, MEV, EMPHASIS ADDED**

> I, John...was in the Spirit on the Lord's day, and I heard behind
> me a loud voice....And having turned *I saw...one like a son of
> man*....When I saw Him, I fell at His feet like a dead man.
> **—REVELATION 1:9–10, 12–13, 17, EMPHASIS ADDED**

John didn't die; he only fell "like a dead man." And yet, it was
not the same John who left that encounter. He, along with every
person who encountered the face of God in Scripture, "died" in
the sense that the person they were before the encounter and the
person they were after the encounter were two different people.
Have you been transformed into Christ's image, or are you still
embracing your old, sinful nature?

POINT TO PONDER

*I give God permission to crucify my old nature so that His
new nature can be re-formed in me by His Spirit.*

PERSONAL REFLECTION

Day 128

LOOKING LIKE JESUS

*So then, my beloved, just as you have always obeyed, not
as in my presence only, but now much more in my absence,
work out your salvation with fear and trembling.*
—PHILIPPIANS 2:12

SEEING GOD IS costly. Something in us always dies. But it's only the
part that is hindering us from becoming more like Jesus. It's like
the sculptor who was once asked what he was going to carve from
a particular piece of stone. His response was, "An elephant." Fasci-
nated with his abilities, the observer asked how it was that he could
actually carve an elephant out of stone. The artist responded, "Oh,
that's easy. I only chip off of the rock the parts that don't look like
an elephant." That is exactly what God does to us in our growing
experience with Him. He cuts off (brings death to) the parts that
don't look like Jesus. And there's no clearer way than through personal encounters with Him. Is the way in which you order your life
resisting or complementing the sanctifying work of the Spirit?

POINT TO PONDER

*In the power of God's Spirit, Lord, I will walk out Your process of
sanctification so that my life reflects the reality of Your work in me.*

PERSONAL REFLECTION

_____

_____

_____

_____

_____

BEYOND THE LAW

*The LORD looks down from heaven on all mankind to see
if there are any who understand, any who seek God.*
—PSALM 14:2, NIV

WHAT SEEMS CLEAR is that Moses and those who had personal encounters with God stepped into realms of truth that are simply not accessible to those who are content with the letter of the law and knowledge about God. The Bible can seem like a confusing, even contradictory book because it tells the stories of both kinds of people—those who choose relationship with God and those who choose religion, as well as God's different responses to them both. We see in these examples the stories of those who saw God and didn't die even though the Bible says they would. God intentionally includes these kinds of paradoxes in the Bible because they work to divide those who have a heart to know God from those who simply want to know about God. Jesus taught in parables for the same reason—so that only those who had a heart for Him would come to understand them. How much is your heart given over to seeking and knowing God?

POINT TO PONDER

*I surrender every area of my heart to God and invite
Him to come sit on the throne of my life.*

PERSONAL REFLECTION

_____

_____

_____

_____

Day 130
MYSTERY MADE MANIFEST

*If anyone supposes that he knows anything, he
has not yet known as he ought to know.*
—1 CORINTHIANS 8:2

THE ENTIRE BIBLE was written with the assumption that only those who have a personal relationship with God will truly be able to understand it. To those outside a relationship with God, the things that are only understood in the context of intimacy with God appear to be in conflict. Those who don't realize this live with an arrogant assumption that they have found weaknesses and inconsistencies in the Scriptures. Yet God has used His own willingness to appear weak to expose pride and independence in people. Those who see the pride of their ways have the opportunity to repent. Those who don't see and repent get harder in their hearts until a shaking brings a breaking.

He often chooses to lead us deeper into this knowledge by putting His favor on individuals that we would never have thought of as ideal candidates. It's our job to learn that this is one of His ways. We need to humble ourselves and learn to recognize the favor of God wherever it rests. How do you respond to what seem like contradictions in Scripture? Do you seek the Spirit who leads us in all truth or do you tend to rely on your own understanding?

POINT TO PONDER

*I will rely on the instruction of the Holy Spirit
when I encounter God's mysteries.*

PERSONAL REFLECTION

_____

_____

Day 131
STAND ON SCRIPTURE

All Scripture is inspired by God and profitable for teaching, for reproof, for correction, for training in righteousness; so that the man of God may be adequate, equipped for every good work.
—2 TIMOTHY 3:16–17

As a pastor I sometimes invite speakers who come in a rough package but carry a great anointing. I do this to train my congregation to recognize the anointing and to celebrate who people are, not who they aren't. People want to be doctrinally safe, not relationally safe. Often people expect me to publicly rebuke a previous speaker for teaching against what we believe. I will do that only if it's actual heresy. *Heresy* has become the term used to describe anyone who disagrees with a particular leader, but that is not so. We need to give more grace to those who differ from us. The essential doctrines of the church—the Virgin Birth, the divinity and humanity of Jesus, the atonement, and the like—qualify as issues we should fight for. That being said, I will purposely bring speakers into our church that I know I disagree with theologically *if* they are people of great anointing and integrity. It makes people nervous. But that's not necessarily a bad thing. Insecurity is *wrong security exposed. When someone disagrees with your theology, how do you respond?*

POINT TO PONDER

I surrender my insecurity when faced with those whose theology differs from mine, choosing instead to stand on Scripture.

PERSONAL REFLECTION

Day 132

TRUE FRIENDSHIP

Elijah said to Elisha, "Stay here please, for the LORD
has sent me as far as Bethel." But Elisha said, "As
the LORD lives and as you yourself live, I will not
leave you." So they went down to Bethel.
—2 KINGS 2:2

WE ARE COMING out of a season where people gathered around doctrinal agreement and formed organizations we call denominations. In recent years the Spirit of the Lord has been bringing about a shift. People are correctly changing their priorities by starting to gather around fathers. In the past the church has often sought for a safety in doctrine at the expense of the profound safety that is only found in godly relationships. Can you think of other examples of friendship in the Bible besides Elijah and Elisha, such as Daniel and Shadrach, Meshach, and Abednego? How do they serve as examples of the type of friendships you want in your life?

POINT TO PONDER

I will seek out godly relationships with spiritual mothers and fathers
and brothers and sisters in the joy of Christ-centered community.

PERSONAL REFLECTION

_____

_____

_____

_____

_____

_____

_____

Day 133

DEEPER REALMS OF HIS TRUTH

That you, being rooted and grounded in love, may
be able to comprehend with all the saints what is the
breadth and length and height and depth, and to know
the love of Christ which surpasses knowledge, that
you may be filled up to all the fullness of God.
—Ephesians 3:17–19

In order to gain a heart that longs to know God, we must sacrifice our need to be right, to understand or explain things. We have to trust Him enough to let Him shatter our boxes of understanding and lead us into deeper realms of His truth. He promises to take us line upon line, precept upon precept and "from glory to glory" (2 Corinthians 3:18). He didn't bring us out of Egypt to camp out in the wilderness, but to take us into the promised land of ever-expanding life in the knowledge of Him. Are you willing to throw the door of your heart wide open so that God can enter in ways that you never imagined?

Point to Ponder

I will lay aside my concerns and wade out into deep waters
with God in order to receive more of His divine revelation.

Personal Reflection

_____

_____

_____

_____

_____

_____

THE JOY OF HIS PRESENCE

*Surely you have granted him unending blessings and
made him glad with the joy of your presence.*
—PSALM 21:6, NIV

W E HAVE TO recognize that full repentance and transformation can only take place through real encounters with God—through actual experiences with His power and grace. Moses had a divine perspective because he had been exposed to the power of God more than anyone else in Israel. All throughout Scripture, God invites us to experience Him as we read the stories of His encounters with past saints. He invites us to "taste and see" that He is good (Psalm 34:8). In what ways have you experienced the joy of God's presence in your life? Are you able to taste and see that God is good?

POINT TO PONDER

I love to taste and see that God is good.

PERSONAL REFLECTION

_____

_____

_____

_____

_____

_____

_____

_____

_____

ON EARTH AS IT IS IN HEAVEN

Your kingdom come. Your will be done, on
earth as it is in heaven.
—MATTHEW 6:10

MANY FOLLOWERS OF Jesus Christ are satisfied with the simple promise of going to heaven instead of seeing that their destiny is to press in for encounters with the face of God and live in the corresponding increase of favor. They are satisfied with figurative promises, not their fulfillment. To some people this may seem like a strength, but it works against the very promises of God, which were given to us for our life on earth as much as our life in heaven. In fact, God gave us His promises so that as we appropriate them, heaven could come to earth. I'll say it again: we can only live in the kingdom, our promised land, if we are willing to embrace the adventure of experiencing God as He is. Are you living as if the promises of God can come to earth through you here and now?

POINT TO PONDER

I'm not going to be satisfied with figurative promises any
more. I will appropriate God's promises here and now and
watch His kingdom come on earth as it is in heaven.

PERSONAL REFLECTION

_____

_____

_____

_____

_____

_____

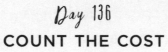

COUNT THE COST

In your seed all the nations of the earth shall be
blessed, because you have obeyed My voice.
—**Genesis 22:18**

ICHALLENGE YOU TO count the cost and, like Moses, to step boldly into the thick darkness where God is. There is nothing worth more on this earth than encountering His manifest presence and responding to the invitation to know and be known by Him. It is what we were made for, what we were saved for, and the only thing that will satisfy the deepest longings of our hearts. What will it take for you to truly count the cost, step out of your comfort zone, and boldly enter God's presence?

POINT TO PONDER

My heart longs to encounter God and His love, and
to respond to His invitation for relationship.

PERSONAL REFLECTION

_____
_____
_____
_____
_____
_____
_____
_____
_____
_____
_____

Day 137

HIS MANIFEST PRESENCE

And it will be that, afterwards, I will
pour out My Spirit on all flesh.
—JOEL 2:28, MEV

O NE OF THE greatest promises in Scripture is that the Holy Spirit would be poured out upon all mankind in the last days. This promise is most memorably stated in Joel 2:28. We can recognize this promise elsewhere in Scripture by paying attention to biblical prophetic imagery. The primary image associated with the Holy Spirit in the prophetic books of the Old Testament is *water*. We find this metaphor in such verses as Psalm 72:6: "He shall come down like rain upon the grass before mowing, like showers that water the earth" (NKJV). In a similar way, Hosea 6:3 says, "He will come to us like the rain; like the spring rains He will water the earth" (MEV). And the parallelism is perhaps most clearly seen in Isaiah 44:3: "For I will pour *water* on him who is thirsty, and floods on the dry ground; I will pour out My *Spirit* on your descendants, and My blessing on your offspring" (MEV, emphasis added). Have you experienced the water of God's presence—the promise of His Spirit poured out in your life?

POINT TO PONDER

When I am dry and thirsty, I will stand on God's
promises to pour out His Spirit on me.

PERSONAL REFLECTION

Day 138

AND IT SHALL COME TO PASS

*And in that day the mountains will drip with sweet wine,
and the hills will flow with milk, and all the brooks of
Judah will flow with water; and a spring will go out from
the house of the LORD to water the valley of Shittim.*
—JOEL 3:18

AT TIMES THE prophets refer to "rivers," "streams," "springs," or "pools," and at other times they use the terms *rain* or *outpouring*. But the most interesting part of studying the image of water in the prophetic books of the Bible is the fact that no matter the problem the people of God were having, water seemed to be the answer. In other words, whether they were facing a military conflict, a moral collapse, or even a natural drought, the answer was always the same—they needed the Holy Spirit. The outpouring of the Spirit really is the Bible's cure-all. It's not that there aren't things we are supposed to do in the natural; it's just that in the end we need more of Him than anything else. And He comes like rain—in heavenly downpours! Are you living in a dry and barren place in need of the spiritual prosperity of God? If so, there is a fountain in the house of God that flows from His throne to water every dry place in your life. Come receive it!

POINT TO PONDER

I will stand in the heavenly downpour of God.

PERSONAL REFLECTION

_____

_____

_____

_____

SPRING RAIN BRINGS THE HARVEST

*So rejoice, O sons of Zion, and be glad in the L*ORD
*your God; for He has given you the early rain for
your vindication. And He has poured down for you
the rain, the early and latter rain as before.*
—JOEL 2:23

O N THE DAY of Pentecost, Peter declared that the promise of Joel
2 was fulfilled. The remarkable events of that morning were all
part of an outpouring of the Holy Spirit. Yet, that day was only
the initial fulfillment of the promise—the Spirit was poured out
on that day, but there is a day coming in which He will truly be
poured out on *all flesh*. This is a fulfillment of the promise of the
Spirit being poured as the early and latter rain. The early rain was
the first century, and the latter is now. If the early rain referred
to in this passage from Joel is about the time of planting that has
already taken place—of sowing seeds for the kingdom—can you
see how the latter rain is the spring rain for the great harvest of
souls that is to come in revival?

POINT TO PONDER

*I trust what God is doing regarding the outpouring of
His Spirit because His timing is always perfect.*

PERSONAL REFLECTION

Day 140

THE BEST IS YET TO COME

*Every man serves the good wine first, and when the
people have drunk freely, then he serves the poorer
wine; but you have kept the good wine until now.*
—JOHN 2:10

THE ULTIMATE FULFILLMENT of Joel's prophecy will take place as the church enters her finest hour of impact in the world. Tragedy comes when the church skims over the great exploits in history and assumes that our finest hour is in the past. This misreading of history derives from a misunderstanding of God's nature. He always saves the best for last—so much so that Jesus even saved the best wine for the end of the wedding celebration. And when He restores things that are destroyed or broken, He restores them to a place greater than before. For example, Job lost everything in the devil's assault on his life. But when God restored him, he was given twice what he lost. It is God's way. To expect anything less of Him for the last days is at best pure ignorance or at worst unbelief. Do you find it interesting that the first recorded miracle of Jesus in the Bible is a revelation of God's nature? Perhaps Jesus was giving us a picture of the nature of God up front because He knew that relationship flows from understanding.

POINT TO PONDER

*I believe that God is good and that there is nothing
in His nature that contradicts His goodness.*

PERSONAL REFLECTION

_____

_____

_____

JESUS THE DESIRE OF ALL NATIONS

Do not quench the Spirit; do not despise prophetic utterances.
But examine everything carefully; hold fast to that which
is good; abstain from every form of evil. Now may the
God of peace Himself sanctify you entirely; and may your
spirit and soul and body be preserved complete, without
blame at the coming of our Lord Jesus Christ. Faithful
is He who calls you, and He also will bring it to pass.
—1 Thessalonians 5:19–24

THE CHURCH IS destined by God to fulfill a particular assignment in the last days, and the promised outpouring of the Spirit is directly connected with that assignment. We have been commissioned to do what Jesus did and teach what Jesus taught so that we might be able to fulfill the assignment to disciple nations. The outpouring of the Spirit comes to anoint the church with the same Christ anointing that rested upon Jesus in His ministry so that we might be imitators of Him. Only when Jesus Christ, who is called the Desire of the Nations, actually lives through His people can we be successful in His command to disciple nations. Do you see God as faithful to the end of time—when He restores the earth—even though what you see in the natural does not always look like the faithfulness of God?

Point to Ponder

Jesus, the Desire of the Nations, will be faithful to the end
even when circumstances seem to indicate otherwise.

Personal Reflection

_____

_____

_____

Day 142

PARTAKING OF HIS DIVINE NATURE

His divine power has granted to us all things that pertain to life and godliness, through the knowledge of him who called us to his own glory and excellence, by which he has granted to us his precious and very great promises, so that through them you may become partakers of the divine nature, having escaped from the corruption that is in the world because of sinful desire.
—2 PETER 1:3–4, ESV

IT IS IN the heart of God for His people to actually represent (or "re-present") the aspects of His nature that people hunger for. He must be expressed through us. God has set us up to be successful at representing Christ by giving us the promise of His Spirit who would come upon us in power. Peter expressed this wonderfully when he said that we "have been given…exceedingly great and precious promises, that through these [we] may be partakers of the divine nature" (2 Peter 1:4, NKJV). To what extent have you undergone the kind of radical spiritual transformation that enables you to be a partaker of His divine nature?

POINT TO PONDER

I am a child of God, a member of His family, transformed by the power of His Spirit to partake of His divine nature for both my salvation and so that I might represent Him well in the world.

PERSONAL REFLECTION

_____

_____

_____

_____

Day 143

HIS SPIRIT IN US AND UPON US

And Jesus came up and spoke to them, saying, "All authority has been given to Me in heaven and on earth. Go therefore and make disciples of all the nations, baptizing them in the name of the Father and the Son and the Holy Spirit, teaching them to observe all that I commanded you; and lo, I am with you always, even to the end of the age."
—MATTHEW 28:18–20

SCRIPTURE TEACHES US that every believer receives the Spirit as the down payment of our full inheritance, which is God Himself. We are heirs of God and have the wonderful privilege of being His dwelling place. The indwelling presence of the Spirit comes about at our conversion, when the Spirit of resurrection brings our spirits to life, just as He breathed into Adam's nostrils in the garden and he became a living being. In the lives of Christ's disciples we see this take place in John 20:22, when Jesus met with them, "breathed on them and said to them, 'Receive the Holy Spirit.'" But at His ascension, Jesus told these same people that the Holy Spirit was going to come upon them. The Holy Spirit was already in them, but He was going to come upon them with power in order to make them witnesses. Are you willing to let the Holy Spirit come upon you in power?

POINT TO PONDER

I will step into God's Great Commission as a faithful and capable witness in the power of His Spirit poured out upon me.

PERSONAL REFLECTION

THE SPIRIT POURED OUT

The kingdom of God is not eating and drinking, but
righteousness and peace and joy in the Holy Spirit.
—ROMANS 14:17

A S THE WORD *outpouring* suggests, the promise in Matthew 28 is fulfilled as the Spirit of God comes upon His people like rain. In such seasons God permeates all we are and do with deluges of Himself. This heavenly invasion of God into our lives is God's first answer to the prayer Jesus taught us to pray: "Your kingdom come. Your will be done, on earth as it is in heaven" (Matthew 6:10). The kingdom of God is in the Holy Spirit. When He is poured out on us, the King's domain becomes manifested in our lives. This kingdom first creates heaven on earth in the "earth" of our lives, which enables us to mature as co-laborers with heaven to bring transformation to the earth. Thus, the outpouring of the Spirit deals directly with God's destiny for humanity. Christ accomplished salvation for mankind to put us right with God so that He could rest upon us, creating a people who could co-labor with Him to bring heaven on earth. Are you ready for God's heavenly invasion to permeate all of you so that you walk hand in hand with Him to bring His transformation to the earth?

POINT TO PONDER

I'm ready for God's Spirit to come upon me like rain, for His heavenly
invasion to touch every part of me and transform me for my destiny.

PERSONAL REFLECTION

_____

_____

THE KEY FOR EVERY BELIEVER

And now, Lord, take note of their threats, and grant that
Your bond-servants may speak Your word with all confidence,
while You extend Your hand to heal, and signs and wonders
take place through the name of Your holy servant Jesus.
—ACTS 4:29–30

As we see in Acts 2, the outpouring of the Spirit is intrinsically linked to the baptism in the Holy Spirit. This experience has been the subject of debate for decades. But there was no debate when it was given to the church two thousand years ago. It was so essential to the believer's life that Jesus warned the disciples not to leave Jerusalem before they received it. Even more important, some time after that initial experience, we find the disciples getting another level of that same outpouring in Acts 4:30. If the baptism of the Spirit was promised for the last days and was the key to the disciples' success when they began to obey Christ's command to disciple nations, then it seems clear it is the key for every believer and every generation in the last days. We must continue with that assignment until it is fulfilled. What would it look like for you to speak boldly on behalf of God in a very public way, trusting that His Spirit will be given to you in a measure equal to the task?

POINT TO PONDER

I believe that the baptism of God's Spirit is a neces-
sity for me and for all believers.

PERSONAL REFLECTION

ON SOLID GROUND

And without faith it is impossible to please God, because
anyone who comes to him must believe that he exists
and that he rewards those who earnestly seek him.
—HEBREWS 11:6, NIV

THE BEST GROUND for us to stand on when considering the baptism of the Spirit is the Scriptures. Much of the confusion and debate that has arisen over this issue derives from people evaluating it on the basis of their experience, or lack of experience, rather than inviting the Holy Spirit to bring their level of experience into alignment with what He has already declared. Those who intentionally ignore elements of Scripture that are outside their experience betray a lack of trust in the God who wrote it. And because faith is essential to please God and know Him, those who resist such experiences and teach others to do the same rarely have the profound encounters with God and the corresponding miracles taking place in their lives.

All who are called to salvation are in line to receive the baptism in the Holy Spirit. What scriptures help you better understand the baptism of the Spirit? What do you find when you examine Scripture for evidence of the power of the Spirit operating in the lives of those who received the baptism of the Spirit? What do you find when you examine your own life?

POINT TO PONDER

I will continue to grow in my understanding of the baptism
of the Holy Spirit by reading and studying God's Word.

PERSONAL REFLECTION

_____

_____

Day 147

THE RENEWED NATURE

If we live by the Spirit, let us also walk by the Spirit.
—GALATIANS 5:25

I WAS RAISED WITH the teaching that speaking in tongues is the initial evidence of the baptism of the Holy Spirit. That's not a point I'm willing to go to war over, though I will go so far as to say that this gift of praying in tongues is available to every believer who receives this baptism. As the apostle Paul said, "Do not forbid to speak in tongues" (1 Corinthians 14:39). I personally feel that the baptism itself and its purpose are infinitely more important than the question of what is or is not the initial evidence of the experience. This profound encounter with God is given to us so that we might be filled with His power and be enabled to authentically demonstrate the life of Jesus before this world. In what ways is your renewed nature enabling you to demonstrate the life of Jesus to the world around you?

POINT TO PONDER

I will live and walk by the Spirit, filled with His power so that I reflect Jesus in every situation.

PERSONAL REFLECTION

Day 148

WAIT FOR IT!

*Do not leave Jerusalem, but wait for the gift my
Father promised, which you have heard me speak
about. For John baptized with water, but in a few
days you will be baptized with the Holy Spirit.*
—ACTS 1:4–5, NIV

UNFORTUNATELY, MANY CAN pray in tongues but have little power in their lives. Their example has hurt those who are looking for evidence that this is still a promise of the Lord that is for us today. Somewhere along the line they have bought into the lie that once they can pray in tongues they have all that was promised. Such a response is akin to Israel camping on the banks of the Jordan and never going in to take possession of the actual land that was promised. While the gift of tongues is one I take great delight in, there must be more to Spirit baptism than to be given a tool for personal edification, which is the purpose of tongues. All the other gifts are to be used so that I might be able to represent Jesus in power to the world and affect the course of world history. Therein lies the purpose for such a baptism— power! How often are you truly thankful for the great gift of the Holy Spirit given to empower you for God's glory?

POINT TO PONDER

*I will wait, for God's purpose in the baptism of His Spirit is to bring
me His power so that I may accomplish His will on the earth.*

PERSONAL REFLECTION

_____

_____

_____

Day 149

GOD'S INCOMPREHENSIBLE PROMISE

*Now to Him who is able to do far more abundantly beyond
all that we ask or think, according to the power that
works within us, to Him be the glory in the church and in
Christ Jesus to all generations forever and ever. Amen.*
—Ephesians 3:20–21

God's ultimate provision for the believer in the outpouring of
the Spirit is for us to become "filled with all the fullness of God"
(Ephesians 3:19, MEV). For the apostle Paul, it was so obvious that
we were to be filled with the Spirit that he actually commanded
it. It is one thing to get accustomed to the idea of God actually
wanting to live in us. But it's quite another to realize that God
intends to fill us with His fullness. I cannot comprehend such a
promise. But I know that His purpose in filling us is so that He
can overflow through us to the world around us. A glass of water is
not really full until it overflows. Similarly, the fullness of the Spirit
in our lives is measured by the overflow of the Spirit through us
in order to touch the world around us. How does it make you
feel to think that God intends that you become filled with *all* His
fullness?

Point to Ponder

I receive the fullness of God's Spirit working in me to bring Him glory.

Personal Reflection

_____

_____

_____

_____

Day 150
WHY POWER?

The Lord your God is with you, the Mighty Warrior who saves. He will take great delight in you; in his love he will no longer rebuke you, but will rejoice over you with singing.
—Zephaniah 3:17, niv

It would be incorrect for me to say that everything we experience is for the sake of others. That simply isn't true. Some think that God will heal them so that a relative or friend will get saved. Of course, it is a great side benefit of a miracle that others are touched by God's goodness. But it distorts the issue. God touches your life because He loves you. In fact, He delights over you. Many people find that hard to believe. How does that knowledge change how you think about yourself and about God?

Point to Ponder

I thank You, God, that You love me so much that You save me fully and for all time, from every spiritual enemy and every worldly enemy, and then put Your power on me so that I can stand in Your victory.

Personal Reflection

_____

_____

_____

_____

_____

_____

_____

_____

TO TELL OF GOD'S GREAT NAME

Then they called them in again and commanded them not
to speak or teach at all in the name of Jesus. But Peter
and John replied, "Judge for yourselves whether it is right
in God's sight to listen to you rather than God. For we
cannot stop speaking about what we have seen and heard."
—ACTS 4:18–20, BSB

GOD DELIGHTS IN us and showers us with blessings just because we belong to Him. He delights over us and gives us access to realms of God simply for our pleasure. Yet there is also an overriding principle in this kingdom: it is nearly impossible to experience more of God and keep it to ourselves. As stated by Peter and John: "For we *cannot stop* speaking about what we have seen and heard" (Acts 4:20, emphasis added). This is the nature of a life with God—giving is the most natural thing to do. As you experience more of God, what do you want to do as a result—hold the experience close, share it, or both?

POINT TO PONDER

Count me among those who cannot stop speaking
about what I have seen and heard from God.

PERSONAL REFLECTION

_____

_____

_____

_____

_____

_____

Day 152

THE MIGHTY NAME OF JESUS

*How much more, then, will the blood of Christ, who
through the eternal Spirit offered himself unblemished
to God, cleanse our consciences from acts that lead
to death, so that we may serve the living God!*
—HEBREWS 9:14, NIV

THE KINGDOM OF God must never be reduced to talk, ideas, and principles. The kingdom of God is power. Unlimited power has been granted to those who encounter Him over and over again. Each encounter works deeper in our hearts, bringing about the needed transformation so that we might be entrusted with more of Him. The more profound the work of the Spirit is within us, the more profound the manifestation of the Spirit flowing through us. That in essence is the purpose behind the promise found in Ephesians 3:20: "Now to Him who is able to do far more abundantly beyond all that we ask or think, *according to the power that works within us*" (emphasis added). When was the last time you allowed the blood of Jesus to cleanse your conscience?

POINT TO PONDER

*I want all the power of Jesus, Lord of heaven
and earth, operating in my life.*

PERSONAL REFLECTION

_____

_____

_____

_____

_____

THRIVING ON THE IMPOSSIBLE

At the name of Jesus every knee will bow, of those who
are in heaven and on earth and under the earth.
—PHILIPPIANS 2:10

NOTICE THAT WHAT goes on around us is *according* to what goes on inside us. That qualifier is all too often overlooked. This power enables us to present Jesus to others in a way that meets every human need. This lifestyle thrives on the impossible. Our delight is seeing the impossibilities of life bend their knee to the name of Jesus over and over again. Those who encounter Him on this level are much more prone to take risks so that miracles would happen. The absence of the supernatural is intolerable. When you consider the amazing provision of the Lord for those who surrender all, powerlessness becomes inexcusable. Are you seeing the impossibilities of life bend their knee to Jesus?

POINT TO PONDER

I will live a life that thrives on the impossible
because all things are possible with God.

PERSONAL REFLECTION

_____

_____

_____

_____

_____

_____

_____

Day 154

THE SWEET AROMA OF CHRIST

But thanks be to God, who always leads us triumphantly as captives in Christ and through us spreads everywhere the fragrance of the knowledge of Him. For we are to God the sweet aroma of Christ among those who are being saved and those who are perishing....And who is qualified for such a task?
—2 CORINTHIANS 2:14–16, BSB

GOD'S PURPOSE WAS announced by the psalmist: "God be gracious to us and bless us, and *cause His face to shine upon us*— that Your way may be known on the earth, Your *salvation among all nations*" (Psalm 67:1–2, emphasis added). Once again there is a profound connection that must not be ignored between the face of God shining upon His people and the salvation of souls among the nations. There is a connection between the two that must not be ignored. Many resist the blessing of the Lord because they don't want to be selfish. Yet it is His blessing upon His people that is supposed to turn the hearts of the unbelievers to the discovery of the goodness of God. Have you experienced God's face shining upon you? If so, what was the result? If not, how much do you desire this experience?

POINT TO PONDER

I will stop resisting God's blessings and become a sweet aroma for Him.

PERSONAL REFLECTION

_____

_____

_____

_____

Day 155
THE STUNNING PROMISE

This is what the LORD says—he who made you, who
formed you in the womb, and who will help you: Do not
be afraid, Jacob, my servant, Jeshurun, whom I have
chosen. For I will pour water on the thirsty land, and
streams on the dry ground; I will pour out my Spirit on
your offspring, and my blessing on your descendants.
—ISAIAH 44:2–3, NIV

GOD MADE A promise that combined two of the greatest experiences for the believer contained in the whole Bible—the outpouring of the Spirit and the encounter with His face. As we will see, they are in essence one and the same. He put it this way, "'I will not hide My face from them any longer, for I will have poured out My Spirit on the house of Israel,' declares the Lord GOD" (Ezekiel 39:29). In this declaration this extraordinary *promise* has been linked together with fulfillment of the ultimate *quest*.

God's face is revealed in the outpouring of the Holy Spirit! When the Holy Spirit comes in power to transform lives, churches, and cities, the face of God is within reach. His face expresses the heart of who He is and what He is like. How do you see God's ultimate promise linked with the ultimate quest in your life?

POINT TO PONDER

I receive God's ultimate promise as I pursue the ultimate quest of
my heart—to know Him fully so that He might be fully known.

PERSONAL REFLECTION

_____

_____

Day 156

REVELATIONS OF HIS FACE

But to each one is given the manifestation
of the Spirit for the common good.
—1 Corinthians 12:7

Not all can recognize God's face in the outpouring of His Spirit. When the rain of the Spirit comes, most people fixate on the effects of the storm and miss the One revealed in the cloud. The extreme joy, the weeping, the shaking and trembling, the visions and dreams, the healing, the deliverance, and the manifestation of the gifts of the Spirit, including tongues and prophecy, all are revelations of His face. Some people love these manifestations, and some people reject them. But the sobering thing to realize is that our response to the move of the Spirit is not a response to manifestations. Rather, it is a response to the face of God. To reject the move of the Spirit of God is to reject the face of God. Have you found yourself rejecting manifestations of God's Spirit? If so, what was the reason?

Point to Ponder

When God manifests Himself, I will respond
to His face and nothing else.

Personal Reflection

_____

_____

_____

_____

_____

Day 157

MOSES SAW WHAT
OTHERS COULDN'T

*He made known His ways to Moses, His acts to the sons
of Israel....But the lovingkindness of the LORD is from
everlasting to everlasting on those who fear Him, and His
righteousness to children's children, to those who keep
His covenant and remember His precepts to do them.*
—PSALM 103:7, 17–18

THE DEGREE TO which we perceive the face of God through the manifestations of His presence is largely determined by what is in our hearts. There is a great contrast in the way Moses experienced God and the way the people of Israel experienced Him. Moses' heart to know God gave him access to revelation that the people of Israel never perceived. Moses was allowed to see God's form, and Israel wasn't. Also, Psalm 103:7 states that Moses knew the ways of God, and Israel knew His acts. Are you stalled at a place where you know God's acts but not His ways? Do you desire more? Open your heart fully to Him today and receive Him fully!

POINT TO PONDER

*I refuse to settle for less than the fullness of
His countenance shining on me.*

PERSONAL REFLECTION

_____

_____

_____

_____

_____

Day 158

GOD THE PROVIDER

Ask a sign for yourself from the LORD your God;
make it deep as Sheol or high as heaven.
—ISAIAH 7:11

THE WAYS OF God are discovered through the acts of God, but they are only recognized by those who are hungry for Him. For example, whenever we see an instance of God's provision, that provision is a sign. A sign points to something greater than itself. In this case the sign of provision points to God, the provider. Taking time to recognize where a sign points to is not that complicated. However, our value system, which grows from the affections of our hearts, determines whether we will be motivated to take that time. If our value system places more importance on what God does than who He is—if we are religiously motivated rather than relationally motivated—we will not be drawn to recognize the greater revelation behind God's acts. The sad reality is that some are satisfied with what God can do and have little concern for who God is. Such a preference is costly in the long run. Many have missed out on the purpose for their creation by settling for the acts of God, thus failing to come under the influence of the face of God— the ultimate quest and our ultimate destiny. What is your value system, and how does it reflect the affections of your heart?

POINT TO PONDER

I will give my full affection to God, not based on
what He does for me, but on who He is.

PERSONAL REFLECTION

_____

_____

Day 159

STAYING IN GOD'S PRESENCE

Then he said to Him, "If Your presence does not go with us, do not lead us up from here. For how then can it be known that I have found favor in Your sight, I and Your people?...The LORD said to Moses, "I will also do this thing of which you have spoken; for you have found favor in My sight and I have known you by name."
—EXODUS 33:15–17

WE NEED TO pay a price to see more clearly. Moses' whole life groomed him to see God. His success as Israel's leader depended entirely on his ability, moment by moment, to perceive and follow the presence and voice of the Lord. But at one point, God gave him the opportunity to be successful as Israel's leader in a different way. He offered to assign an angel to take the people of Israel into the Promised Land. This angel would have made sure that every success came to Moses as God promised. But Moses was hungry for God alone, not merely for what God could do to make him successful. He insisted on following the presence of God Himself. What price are you willing to pay to see God more clearly? Moses gave up a great deal. What are you willing to give up?

POINT TO PONDER

I am so hungry for God that I will give up all earthly successes just to be close to Him.

PERSONAL REFLECTION

_____

_____

_____

Day 160
A NOBLE CHOICE

You shall do what is right and good in the sight of the LORD,
that it may be well with you and that you may go in and possess
the good land which the LORD swore to give your fathers.
—DEUTERONOMY 6:18

MOSES WAS THE great leader he was because he was not focused on personal success but on the God who could be known. Moses preferred the wilderness *with God* to the Promised Land *without God*, a noble choice for sure. Many in our ranks have failed that test. They have chosen the gratification of fulfilled dreams over the realms of God that seem so costly. They chose the inferior and lost out on the heavenly realities that were at hand, yet unseen. Heavenly realms are made available to us in this lifetime. They are not reserved just for eternity. What heavenly realities do you want God to make available to you in your lifetime?

POINT TO PONDER

I will only be satisfied with God's heavenly realities, whether in the wilderness or in the promised land.

PERSONAL REFLECTION

_____

_____

_____

_____

_____

_____

_____

Day 161

THE DAY OF HIS APPEARING

But who can endure the day of His coming? And
who can stand when He appears? For He is
like a refiner's fire and like fullers' soap.
—MALACHI 3:2

ISRAEL WAS GIVEN multiple opportunities to pursue and encounter the manifest presence of God. Their entire life was built around the tabernacle, which was set in the middle of the camp of Israel. God manifested Himself to them according to their surroundings—at night there was the pillar of fire, and in the day there was a cloud. God also spoke to them face to face. But they did not recognize the day of His appearing:

> So watch yourselves carefully, since *you did not see any form* on the day the LORD spoke to you at Horeb from the midst of the fire, *so that you do not act corruptly and make a graven image for yourselves in the form of any figure.*
>
> —DEUTERONOMY 4:15–16, EMPHASIS ADDED

> The LORD spoke to you *face to face* at the mountain from the midst of the fire.
>
> —DEUTERONOMY 5:4, EMPHASIS ADDED

Do you recognize God's presence in your life?

POINT TO PONDER

I will take full advantage of every opportunity God gives
me to pursue and encounter His manifest presence.

PERSONAL REFLECTION

_____

_____

Day 162

SETTLE FOR NOTHING LESS

*These words the Lord spoke to all your assembly at
the mountain from the midst of the fire, of the cloud
and of the thick gloom, with a great voice.*
—DEUTERONOMY 5:22, EMPHASIS ADDED

GOD SPOKE TO the Israelites face to face from the cloud. In other words, there was a revelation of His face in the cloud. But His unwillingness to allow them to see any form of His likeness was because they were prone to idolatry and would most likely create an image to represent His form. Today we fall into the same trap when we create formulas to represent kingdom revelations. People are often tempted to look for shortcuts to kingdom benefits, resulting in Ishmaels instead of Isaacs—counterfeits instead of the real thing. Are you in any way prone to the same kind of idolatry that afflicted the Israelites—willing to settle for a counterfeit instead of God?

POINT TO PONDER

I will not look for shortcuts to kingdom benefits. I want the real God, not a counterfeit.

PERSONAL REFLECTION

_____

_____

_____

_____

_____

_____

LIVING IN THE LIGHT

Search me, O God, and know my heart; try me and know
my anxious thoughts; and see if there be any hurtful
way in me, and lead me in the everlasting way.
—Psalm 139:23–24

GOD ALLOWED MOSES to see His form. God could trust Moses with this level of revelation because his heart had been tested. In His mercy God gives us the level of revelation that our character is prepared to handle. At the same time, He continues to reveal Himself to expose our character and invite us to know Him more. We see this in the following fascinating encounter in John:

> "Now My soul is troubled. What shall I say? 'Father, save Me from this hour'? Instead, for this reason I came to this hour. Father, glorify Your name." Then a voice came from heaven, saying, "I have glorified it, and will glorify it again." The crowd that stood by...said, "An angel has spoken to Him." Jesus answered, "This voice came not for My sake, but for your sakes."
> **—John 12:27–30, MEV**

Will you allow God to test your heart so He can trust you with greater levels of revelation?

POINT TO PONDER

I want to live in the light of His countenance with every corner of my heart exposed to His perfect love.

PERSONAL REFLECTION

_____

_____

_____

Day 164

LET YOUR HEART BE QUICKENED

Call to Me and I will answer you, and I will tell you
great and mighty things, which you do not know.
—JEREMIAH 33:3

THE ENCOUNTER FROM John 12:27 reveals the primary responses that people have to the manifest presence and voice of God. Some who heard the voice thought it had thundered. In other words, they classed the experience as a natural phenomenon. Others believed that an angel had spoken to Jesus. These people recognized that something spiritual or supernatural was going on, but they believed it wasn't for them. Jesus, on the other hand, heard the voice clearly and knew that it *was* for them. He had the heart of His Father, which made Him capable of perceiving not only His Father's voice but also the purpose behind it—to communicate His heart to His people. The Father spoke to make something known to all who could hear. But in doing so, He exposed the level of perception that all those standing by actually possessed. How well are you able to perceive when your loving heavenly Father's speaks? How does Jesus model ways in which you can hear God's voice?

POINT TO PONDER

My heart quickens at the sound of God's voice.

PERSONAL REFLECTION

_____

_____

_____

_____

Day 165
ALL CAN PERCEIVE

Set your mind on the things above, not
on the things that are on earth.
—COLOSSIANS 3:2

THROUGH CHRIST, GOD has made it possible for every person to see the kingdom. Our conversion experience gives us access to that realm, as Jesus explained to Nicodemus, "Truly, truly I say to you, unless a man is born again, he cannot see the kingdom of God" (John 3:3, MEV). However, it is our responsibility to develop this capacity, to train our senses to perceive God through renewing our minds and feeding the affections of our hearts on the truth. Otherwise, we will have no internal paradigm to keep us in tune with the truth amid the prevailing cultural attitudes that surround us. Is your love of earthly things weakening your desire for the things of God? How can you set your mind on the things above?

POINT TO PONDER

My affections are set on the things of God, not the things of this world.

PERSONAL REFLECTION

_____

_____

_____

_____

_____

_____

_____

_____

THE FOOLISHNESS OF THE CROSS

*For the word of the cross is foolishness to those who are
perishing, but to us who are being saved it is the power of God.*
—1 CORINTHIANS 1:18

IN THE WESTERN world setting our minds on the things above
is a challenge because we live in a culture that has embraced an
almost entirely materialistic worldview. This worldview rules out
spiritual reality and makes the physical, material realm the definition of reality. When a materialistic person encounters spiritual things, he has no box in which to put them. He either has
to ignore them completely or explain them by natural means, like
the bystanders who said God's voice was simply thunder. Unfortunately this paradigm influences many believers, leaving them
crippled in their ability to perceive and understand the truth of
Scripture and the spiritual dimensions of their own lives, let alone
supernatural encounters with God. Are you willing to remain
steadfast to the saving grace of the cross even if it means forgoing
success and popularity?

POINT TO PONDER

*I stand on the solid ground of the cross—the heart of
the gospel and the power of God unto salvation.*

PERSONAL REFLECTION

_____

_____

_____

_____

_____

SEEK WISDOM

But if any of you lacks wisdom, let him ask of God, who gives to all generously and without reproach, and it will be given to him.
—JAMES 1:5

THE CONFLICT BETWEEN a materialistic worldview and a biblical one is apparent in the inability or refusal of some Western doctors to acknowledge their patients have been healed by a miracle of God. Many people have gone to their doctors after being healed to have tests to show that they are no longer in the same condition. Though these doctors were the ones who best know the condition that the person was in and they have personally administered these tests, we often hear that many of them insist the problem is in remission or hiding rather than acknowledging that the person has been healed. In their field that's what it looks like to be realistic. But that realism ignores a superior reality—that of the kingdom of God. There are people who have had no evidence of a particular disease for many years whose medical records still declare that they have it, simply because the doctor will not, or is unable to, acknowledge that the person has been miraculously healed. Thankfully a growing number of doctors not only acknowledge miracles but also personally pray for their patients to experience a much-needed miracle. Who is the source of your wisdom—God or man?

POINT TO PONDER

The kingdom of God is a superior reality.

PERSONAL REFLECTION

_____

_____

A DIVINE WORD OF COMMAND

A man in their synagogue who was possessed
by an impure spirit cried out, "What do you want with
us, Jesus of Nazareth? Have you come to destroy us?..."

"Be quiet!" said Jesus sternly. "Come out of him!" The
impure spirit shook the man violently and
came out of him with a shriek.
—MARK 1:23–26, NIV

A DOCTOR FROM BETHEL Church was working with another doctor and several nurses on a patient in a medical crisis. When the patient began to manifest a demon, the others didn't know what to do. Our doctor leaned over that person and quietly bound the devil and commanded it to leave. It did, and the patient was filled with peace. The others in the room were stunned at the manifestation of a demon and the ease at which the name of Jesus solved such a problem. They now know there is a spirit world and another influence in people's lives besides the physical body and the soul.

Every time we are exposed to the miraculous, we are responsible to respond. And our responses, either of faith or unbelief, shape who we are. Unbelief hardens us to God, while faith makes us more alive to Him, more capable of knowing and perceiving Him. Do you live life daily embracing the reality that Jesus has all authority?

POINT TO PONDER

I will respond in faith when I am exposed to the miraculous.

PERSONAL REFLECTION

Day 169

POSITIONING FOR ENCOUNTER

"Look, I am with you, and I will watch over you wherever you go, and I will bring you back to this land. For I will not leave you until I have done what I have promised you." When Jacob woke up, he thought, "Surely the LORD is in this place, and I was unaware of it." And he was afraid and said, "How awesome is this place! This is none other than the house of God; this is the gate of heaven!"
—GENESIS 28:15–17, BSB

JACOB'S CONCLUSION TO his first encounter with God is remarkable. After wakening from the dream in which he saw a ladder standing between earth and heaven with angels ascending and descending upon it, he said, "Surely the LORD is in this place, and I did not know it" (Genesis 28:16).

It's possible to be right next to God and not know it! I often see this truth played out in life. It never ceases to amaze me that in the same meeting one person can be experiencing a powerful touch from the Lord, and at the same moment the person next to him is wondering when the meeting will be over so he can go to lunch. How many times do you think you have been right next to God and were not aware of His presence? How can you sharpen your spiritual senses in this regard?

POINT TO PONDER

God is always present, even when I am unaware of Him.

PERSONAL REFLECTION

_____

_____

HONOR THE POINT

*We have come to know and have believed the love which
God has for us. God is love, and the one who abides
in love abides in God, and God abides in him.*
—1 John 4:16

IT IS POSSIBLE to position ourselves to encounter God by learning to recognize the signs of His presence, not only as we experience them but also as others experience them. My hunting dog is trained to "honor the point" of the other dogs he is hunting with. That means he "points," even when he has not yet picked up a scent of his prey. He assumes the same posture to give me a signal that he has found something. He takes the same posture that the other dogs have. As a result, he eventually picks up the same scent that they have picked up. Likewise, when we recognize that others around us are connecting with the presence of God, even when we are not yet aware of Him ourselves, we set ourselves up to become aware of Him by acknowledging His presence on the basis of others' experience. Who around you connects with the love of God to such an extent that you want to get close and experience God's love also?

POINT TO PONDER

*When I am able to acknowledge the presence of God
in others, I set myself up to receive it too.*

PERSONAL REFLECTION

Day 171

THE FULLNESS OF GOD'S TRUTH

*But when He, the Spirit of truth, comes, He will
guide you into all the truth; for He will not speak on
His own initiative, but whatever He hears, He will
speak; and He will disclose to you what is to come.*
—John 16:13

THE DISCIPLES LEARNED a challenging lesson in Mark 16:14. Jesus
rebuked them because "they had not believed those who had
seen Him after He had risen." Learning to believe God through
another person's experience is one of the most difficult, yet important, lessons in life. Because the Holy Spirit lives within us, we
are required to recognize when someone is telling us the truth
even when we don't understand. Are you inviting the Holy Spirit's
wisdom in those times in life when you feel spiritually blind or do
you tend to rely on your own understanding?

POINT TO PONDER

*The wisdom of the Holy Spirit restores my
sight when I am spiritually blind.*

PERSONAL REFLECTION

_____

_____

_____

_____

_____

_____

_____

_____

FELLOW WORKMEN

*For we are God's fellow workers; you
are God's field, God's building.*
—1 Corinthians 3:9, bsb

WHEN GOD LIFTS the veil of our senses to perceive what is going on in the spiritual realm, we are not spectators who have stumbled upon something that has nothing to do with us. God is communicating with us and allowing us to see what He sees in order to invite us to know Him and partner with what He is doing. The natural realm is such familiar territory that it's easy to get a glimpse of the spiritual realm and keep thinking in the natural. Yet, these glimpses into His realm are given to us by God so that we can better partner with Him in the work of the kingdom. To work alongside God as stewards of creation has been our assignment since the garden. What are you doing with God's glorious invitation to work alongside Him? Do you see it as a great privilege or something you must do in your own strength that is beyond your abilities?

Point to Ponder

*My heart's desire is to walk hand in hand with God,
serving Him faithfully in the power of His Spirit.*

Personal Reflection

_____

_____

_____

_____

_____

Day 173
GREATER REVELATION

The LORD came and stood there, calling... "Samuel! Samuel!"
Then Samuel said, "Speak, for your servant is listening." And the
LORD said to Samuel: "See, I am about to do something in Israel
that will make the ears of everyone who hears about it tingle."
—1 SAMUEL 3:8–11, NIV

IT IS A mistake to think that only certain people with unique gifts can hear and see God. If I think that it's only for others, then I will disqualify myself because I know I'm nothing special. In doing so I remove myself from active faith. One of the essential gestures of faith is to live with the expectation that the God who said that His sheep hear His voice and who gave His life to restore relationship with each of us would like to communicate with us. This faith leads us to lean into His voice—to learn as the prophet Samuel did to say, "Speak, Lord, for your servant is listening." Significantly, it was as soon as he learned to take this posture that he gained access to the greater revelation that God had been inviting him into. What posture are you taking to gain access to the greater revelations that God is inviting you into?

POINT TO PONDER

I will posture myself to recognize God's voice in every situation.

PERSONAL REFLECTION

_____

_____

_____

_____

_____

HE IS LOOKING FOR THOSE HE CAN TRUST

And when they had prayed, the place where they had gathered together was shaken, and they were all filled with the Holy Spirit and began to speak the word of God with boldness.
—Acts 4:31

GOD HAS COMBINED the ultimate quest with the promised outpouring of the Spirit because the ones He intends to clothe with the same anointing that rested upon His Son are those who have the same heart for the face of God that Jesus possessed. Only those with His heart can be trusted to use His power for its intended purpose—to represent Him in all His glory and goodness. This is our challenge—and our destiny. How do you see yourself rising to the challenge to embrace your destiny to represent God as He deserves to be represented?

POINT TO PONDER

I will be found among those whom God can trust to represent Him with all the glory due His great name.

PERSONAL REFLECTION

_____

_____

_____

_____

_____

_____

_____

_____

Day 175

JESUS: THE FACE OF GOD

Look, I am sending My messenger before Your
face, who will prepare Your way before You. The
voice of one crying in the wilderness: "Prepare the
way of the Lord, make His paths straight."
—MARK 1:2–3, MEV

WHAT WAS DIFFERENT about John's life and prophetic ministry? As you read the verses above, consider that Mark's Gospel specifically describes John's ministry as the fulfillment of Isaiah's prophecy. Jesus said of John the Baptist, "Truly I say to you, among those born of women *there has not arisen anyone greater than John the Baptist!*" (Matthew 11:11, emphasis added). Others in Scripture had more dramatic experiences with God. Others did greater exploits against disease, storms, and death itself. Some called down fire or brought an end to famines, and at least one spoke to dry bones that were in a moment's time turned into a living army. And still others installed and deposed kings, directed their armies, and even made declarations that changed the course of history. But John caught heaven's attention as no other prophet had done. He became known as the greatest born of a woman. Are you aware that, like John the Baptist, God has a unique destiny for your life?

POINT TO PONDER

I know that God has a unique destiny for me and He
will reveal it to me from His great heart of love.

PERSONAL REFLECTION

_____

_____

SET APART FOR HIS PURPOSES

Before I formed you in the womb I knew you, before you were
born I set you apart; I appointed you as a prophet to the nations.
—JEREMIAH 1:5, NIV

JOHN LIVED BEFORE the face of God—the ultimate place of favor and responsibility. He had an unusual grace for recognizing the presence of God, even before he was born. When Mary was pregnant with Jesus, she walked into a room to visit Elizabeth, who was pregnant with John. When Mary's greeting reached Elizabeth's ears, John leaped for joy while still in her womb. Amazing—John was still what our culture calls a fetus (in order to ease their conscience about abortion). And that unborn child was able to recognize God's presence. Even more significant was John's ability to recognize the connection that the presence of Christ had to his assignment and eternal destiny. That reality brought great celebration to him, although he was not yet even born. Great joy is always available to anyone who connects with his or her eternal purpose. Have you heard God speak your destiny over you like He did with Jeremiah? If not, are you pressing in, or are you just going through life waiting?

POINT TO PONDER

I have a unique destiny from God that lines up perfectly with His heart.

PERSONAL REFLECTION

_____

_____

_____

_____

Day 177

THE POWER OF THE TONGUE

Set a guard, O Lord, over my mouth; keep
watch over the door of my lips!
—Psalm 141:3, esv

Luke's Gospel records the early years of John's life for several reasons. Not only does it show us that John was in tune with the presence of God from the womb, indicating the potential for what would fully mature in his ministry, but it also makes a point that this capacity was something that had to be protected. Zacharias did not believe the words of the angel sent to him from God with the message of John's birth. Because of this, God made him mute for the entire pregnancy. His tongue loosened only after he responded in obedience to the command of the Lord in naming his child *John*. This is very important, for "Death and life are in the power of the tongue" (Proverbs 18:21). Left unto himself while still in his state of unbelief, Zacharias could have killed with his words the very purpose of God in the promise given to them. Can you think of any words you may have spoken that killed the purpose of God in your life? It is never too late to repent and speak again out of obedience to God.

Point to Ponder

I come into agreement with God regarding His plans
and purposes. I repent of any words I have spoken that
have hindered the purposes of God in my life.

Personal Reflection

_____

_____

_____

BY YOUR WORDS YOU SHALL BE JUSTIFIED

But I tell you that every careless word that people speak, they shall give an accounting for it in the day of judgment. "For by your words you will be justified, and by your words you will be condemned."
—MATTHEW 12:36–37

Z ACHARIAS' WORDS SPOKEN in agreement with the will of God were the key to releasing John's destiny. John was also protected by Elizabeth, who concealed her pregnancy for five months after conception. In other words, only when her pregnancy was becoming inarguably evident did she go public. The implication is that John's exposure to the careless speech of others could have affected what God wanted to do. It takes discipline to tame the tongue. How often do careless words slip from your lips without a thought to their consequences, both for yourself and for those you speak about?

POINT TO PONDER

I will guard my tongue so that the words of my mouth speak blessings, not curses.

PERSONAL REFLECTION

_____

_____

_____

_____

_____

_____

Day 179
LEARNING TO BE FAITHFUL

This, then, is how you ought to regard us: as servants
of Christ and as those entrusted with the mysteries
God has revealed. Now it is required that those who
have been given a trust must prove faithful.
—1 CORINTHIANS 4:1–2, NIV

MANY WOULD ARGUE that God's purposes will be accomplished regardless of the speech of others. Perhaps. But why then does He want us to know the effect of our words if they have no effect at all? The five months in seclusion were probably sufficient for Elizabeth to become strong enough in her own faith to withstand the *well-meaning curses* that people would probably make—things such as, "Oh, aren't you a little old to be having a child? Isn't there a good chance that this child will be born with deformities or retardation?" Being hidden away gave her time to settle into her call and learn how to be unaffected by the careless concern of others. Only with faith and confidence regarding her own call could she become strong enough to correctly steward the anointing on her unborn child. Do you think you have the patience and wisdom of Elizabeth to learn how to steward well what God gives you, or do you find that you tend to struggle to know how to go forward when God is doing something in your life?

POINT TO PONDER

I will stop and wait on God, trusting Him to
show me everything I need to know.

PERSONAL REFLECTION

_____

_____

Day 180
SPEAK LIFE

When Elizabeth heard Mary's greeting, the baby leaped in
her womb; and Elizabeth was filled with the Holy Spirit.
And she cried out with a loud voice and said, "Blessed
are you among women, and blessed is the fruit of your
womb!... For behold, when the sound of your greeting
reached my ears, the baby leaped in my womb for joy."
—Luke 1:41–42, 44

In our Western culture it sounds strange to hear someone talk of the effect of our words on an unborn child. Yet, I remind you, it was the *greeting* from Mary, the mother of Jesus, that caused John to rejoice. Words brought joy to an unborn child. Did he understand them? No, I doubt that very much. But a child has amazing discernment that, unless he or she has parents who understand the way the spirit world works and have learned how to steward their child's anointing and gift, tends to get trampled on through life until that child can no longer discern. When the essence of Mary's words reached his undefiled heart, he rejoiced! Elizabeth was then filled with the Holy Spirit, enabling her to become a good steward of the gift that God had given her son until the time that he was able to watch over it himself. How does it make you feel to think that your words can have such extraordinary impact?

POINT TO PONDER

I am growing in my understanding of the power of my tongue.

PERSONAL REFLECTION

_____

_____

Day 181

JOHN'S ASSIGNMENT

And he asked for a tablet and wrote as follows, "His name is John."
And they were all astonished. And at once his mouth was opened
and his tongue loosed, and he began to speak in praise of God.
Fear came on all those living around them; and all these matters
were being talked about in all the hill country of Judea. All who
heard them kept them in mind, saying, "What then will this child
turn out to be?" For the hand of the Lord was certainly with him.
—LUKE 1:63–66

IN THE STORY of John's birth we see a powerful illustration of partnering with the Lord in speech and action in order to steward the call of God on his life. No prophet ever bore the responsibility that was given to John the Baptist. His assignment was not only to walk before the face of God; he was also *to prepare the way for the face of God to be revealed* for all to see. This was the moment that all the other prophets had longed to see. Now everything would change. How much of a stretch is it for you to think that an assignment God has on your life could have significant impact? Think of Ananias. God instructed him to lay hands on Saul and declare healing in the name of Jesus. That simple act had eternal significance. Have you had an Ananias moment?

POINT TO PONDER

I will trust God and be obedient, not shrinking
back from my Ananias moment.

PERSONAL REFLECTION

_____

_____

_____

THE KING OF ALL KINGS

*The next day he saw Jesus coming to him and said, "Behold,
the Lamb of God who takes away the sin of the world!"*
—JOHN 1:29

PICTURE A COMMON scene of the old world: an army marching
through a town, followed by their king being carried on the
shoulders of his servants. Now picture the same scene, except this
time it's an army of one, dressed in camel's hair, making crooked
places straight with his prophetic declarations. He too is followed
by a King, but this is the King of all kings. John would usher in
the King's face of divine favor. His assignment was to not only
prepare the way for the clearest *revelation* of God but also to prepare the way for an actual *manifestation* of the face of God—Jesus
Christ. In Christ that which had existed in types and shadows
for centuries would be brought into the open. Are you hungry to
be able, like John, to perceive God's special signs and receive His
divine inspiration regarding the things of His kingdom?

POINT TO PONDER

*I am hungry to receive more from God, and I trust His
process as He prepares me for greater revelation.*

PERSONAL REFLECTION

_____

_____

_____

_____

_____

_____

Day 183

THE PRECIOUS HOLY SPIRIT

Do your best to present yourself to God as one
approved, a worker who does not need to be ashamed
and who correctly handles the word of truth.
—2 TIMOTHY 2:15, NIV

WHILE JOHN THE Baptist had the most important assignment ever given to a man, his assignment was not only to make declarations. More needed to be done.

> John testified saying, "... I did not recognize Him, but He who sent me to baptize in water said to me, 'He upon whom you see the Spirit descending and remaining upon Him, this is the One who baptizes in the Holy Spirit.' I myself have seen, and have testified that this is the Son of God."
>
> —JOHN 1:32–34

John made an amazing statement: "I did not recognize Him." Jesus didn't stand out as the Son of God—until the Holy Spirit came upon Him and remained. The Holy Spirit has been positioned to manifest the face of God—first upon Jesus, then through Jesus to the world. How qualified do you feel to testify that Jesus is the Son of God? What would make you feel more qualified?

POINT TO PONDER

I won't be satisfied with my current understanding of God's
Word. I commit to a greater depth and breadth of study,
inviting the Holy Spirit to illuminate the Scriptures to me.

PERSONAL REFLECTION

_____

_____

Day 184

PASSIONATE TO HOST
THE PRESENCE

*Then John gave this testimony: "I saw the Spirit come
down from heaven as a dove and remain on him."*
—JOHN 1:32, NIV

A KEY THOUGHT FOR me in this whole story is found in the phrase,
"He remained upon Him." This punchy prophetic declaration
describes how Jesus did life: He walked through life in such a way
that the dove of the Spirit would not be startled and leave. In Him
we see a lifestyle that was crafted around the passion to host the
presence of the Spirit of God. Being a person on whom the Holy
Spirit can remain has a cost. (Cost in this context has nothing to
do with works. It is passion for Him and a reverence for His presence where every move we make has Him in mind.) Can you say
that you are passionate to host the presence of God, or is it something you've not thought about?

POINT TO PONDER

*I will cultivate passion to host God's presence, walking
every day with a keen awareness of the Holy Spirit.*

PERSONAL REFLECTION

_____

_____

_____

_____

_____

_____

Day 185

OBEDIENCE BRINGS MIRACLES

But He said, "On the contrary, blessed are those
who hear the word of God and observe it."
—LUKE 11:28

MATTHEW'S GOSPEL RECORDS the details of Jesus' baptism by John. At first John resisted Jesus for all the obvious reasons. He was not worthy to untie Jesus' shoes, let alone baptize Him. On top of that, Jesus was not a sinner and had no need of public repentance. Yet John obeyed—and witnessed one of the most amazing moments in history.

> Then Jesus arrived from Galilee at the Jordan coming to John, to be baptized by him. But John tried to prevent Him, saying, "I have need to be baptized by You, and do You come to me?" But Jesus answering said to him, "Permit it at this time; for in this way it is fitting for us to fulfill all righteousness."...After being baptized, Jesus came up immediately from the water;...he saw the Spirit of God descending as a dove and lighting on Him, and behold, a voice out of the heavens said, "This is My beloved Son, in whom I am well-pleased."
>
> —MATTHEW 3:13–17

Do you struggle to obey the Word of God because what you see in the natural seems contrary to what He is saying to you?

POINT TO PONDER

I will grow in radical obedience that brings the miraculous.

PERSONAL REFLECTION

_____

_____

Day 186

THE BAPTISM OF THE SPIRIT

*I baptize you with water for repentance, but he who is coming
after me is mightier than I, whose sandals I am not worthy
to carry. He will baptize you with the Holy Spirit and fire.*
—MATTHEW 3:11, ESV

PREVIOUS TO THEIR encounter at the Jordan, John had announced that Jesus would come with a different baptism than his, the baptism of the Holy Spirit and fire. John was speaking of this baptism when he made the startling statement, "I have need to be baptized by You" (Matthew 3:14). When Jesus came to be baptized by John, it violated everything that John had thought about their different assignments. He knew that his role was to identify the Son of God and prepare people with a baptism of repentance from sin so that they could receive the revelation of the face of God in the Son. He also knew that the Son's role was to reveal this face through His baptism, the baptism of the Spirit. In his statement we see that John's regard was not for his title or his role, but it was entirely for the One he served. John, the one who is called the greatest of those born of women, revealed his biggest need. He needed the baptism that Jesus offered—the baptism in the Holy Spirit and fire. John needed the baptism in the Holy Spirit and so do we. Yet many of us don't realize our great need in this regard. Do you?

POINT TO PONDER

*Baptism in the Holy Spirit is a gift from Jesus that every
believer needs for the power to witness to His great name.*

PERSONAL REFLECTION

_____

_____

Day 187
TRANSFORMED BY LOVE

Now hope does not disappoint, because the love of God has been poured out in our hearts by the Holy Spirit who was given to us.
—ROMANS 5:5, NKJV

JESUS MADE THE statement that the least in the kingdom is greater than John—greater than the greatest born of women. If the people Jesus was referring to are those who are already in paradise, it's a moot point. Jesus didn't waste words. Rather He was giving a significant revelation about the kind of person that would be walking the earth not many days later—people born of the Spirit and baptized in the Spirit. It is in this context that John's confession, "I have need to be baptized by You," makes sense. The one thing he, the greatest prophet of all, lacked is now available to every born-again believer. The baptism in the Spirit, a profound encounter with the face of God, adds the power of heaven to bring transformation to planet Earth. This baptism qualifies *the least in the kingdom to be greater than John*. It is a promise that is in effect now, to the degree we live in and manifest the King's domain. Can you think of at least one instance from Scripture where the baptism of the Spirit poured the love of God into someone's heart in a way that brought transformation to the earth?

POINT TO PONDER

I am thankful for the gift of the Holy Spirit poured out in my heart.

PERSONAL REFLECTION

_____

_____

_____

GOD IS GOOD—ALWAYS

And Jesus said to him, "Why do you call Me
good? No one is good except God alone."
*—*MARK 10:18

WHAT WAS THE nature of God that Christ revealed? This topic would take many volumes of books to address properly. But if I had to pick one word to describe the nature of God revealed in Christ, it is that He is *good*.

I never realized how controversial the subject of the nature of God could be until I began teaching week after week that God is good, *always*. While most believers hold the belief as a theological value, especially because it is so stated in Nahum 1:7 and elsewhere, they struggle in light of the difficulties all around us. Many have abandoned the idea altogether, thinking it doesn't have any practical application. The hardest part is saying He's *always* good. Some say He is *mysteriously good*, which is about the same as saying He's good, but not as we think of goodness. This response doesn't help to clear up confusion over the nature of God. Are you confused by the troubles of this world that seem to contradict the nature of God? If Scripture says He is a stronghold in times of trouble, doesn't that indicate He is not the source of the trouble?

POINT TO PONDER

I declare that God is always good even when things
around me seem to contradict that belief.

PERSONAL REFLECTION

_____

_____

RELATIONSHIP WITH GOD

"The people living in darkness have seen a great light; on those living in the land of the shadow of death a light has dawned." From that time on Jesus began to preach, "Repent, for the kingdom of heaven has come near."
—MATTHEW 4:16–17, NIV

WHEN WE TURN to the Scriptures, we encounter similar apparent contradictions between the statement that God is always good and actual events in which He does not seem to be expressing goodness. While the Old Testament certainly contains revelations of God's compassion and love for people, it is also riddled with many incidents that seem to imply otherwise. To those who do not have a personal relationship with God, this especially appears to be the case. The Old Testament is filled with accounts of all kinds of tragedies and conflicts that God seemed to bring upon people because of their sin and rebellion. The Old Testament seems to portray God as being quite different from the God we see through Jesus Christ in the New Testament. What is the main difference between relationship with God in the Old Testament versus relationship with Him in the New Testament?

POINT TO PONDER

The light of Christ has come into my heart.

PERSONAL REFLECTION

_____

_____

_____

_____

Day 190

CONFUSION IS NOT FROM GOD

Jesus said to Him, "Have I been so long with you, and yet you have not come to know Me, Philip? He who has seen Me has seen the Father; how can you say, 'Show us the Father'?"
—JOHN 14:9

IN THE NEW Testament Jesus works against the tragedies that are devouring people's lives and tries to bring restoration and healing. How many sick and diseased people came to Him and left afflicted and disappointed? How many times did Jesus actually say that the problem a person had was because God the Father was trying to teach a lesson that would ultimately make him more like Him? To how many diseased people did He try to explain that it just wasn't God's timing for them to be well? How many tormented people did He leave in that condition, saying, "This is the result of their choices. I would set them free if they really wanted to be free"? How many storms did Jesus bless? He not only lived differently from their common understanding of God; He lived in complete *contradiction* to their common understanding of God. If Jesus is an exact representation of the Father, why are we confused about the nature of God?

POINT TO PONDER

The more I get to know Jesus, the more I understand God.

PERSONAL REFLECTION

_____

_____

_____

_____

Day 191

THE ULTIMATE CONTRADICTION

*Some of them said, "He casts out demons by Beelzebul, the
ruler of the demons."...He knew what they were thinking
and said to them, "Every kingdom divided against itself
becomes a desert, and house falls on house. If Satan
also is divided against himself, how will his kingdom
stand?...But if it is by the finger of God that I cast out
the demons, then the kingdom of God has come to you."*
—LUKE 11:15, 17–18, 20, NRSV

THE STRIKING DISTINCTION that Jesus lived in complete contradiction to our modern understanding of God has eluded many.
It has become common for believers to think God brings or allows
sickness so that we will become more like Jesus. Leaders teach that
God brings calamity because it will draw us nearer to Him. If that
line of thought were true, then mental hospitals and cancer wards
would be glowing with God's presence as their patients would
have drawn near to God and been transformed into the likeness of
Jesus. Two thousand years ago all sickness was from the devil and
healing was from God; today people teach that sickness is from
God and those who pursue a healing ministry are from the devil
(or out of balance, at best). How far we have fallen! How do you
feel about the ministry of healing in the church today?

POINT TO PONDER

*Jesus has commissioned me to minister healing to the
sick, the broken, and the tormented just as He did.*

PERSONAL REFLECTION

_____

_____

THERE IS MORE!

Truly, truly, I say to you, he who believes in Me, the works that I do, he will do also; and greater works than these he will do; because I go to the Father. Whatever you ask in My name, that will I do, so that the Father may be glorified in the Son.
—JOHN 14:12–13

WHILE IT'S TRUE that believers can respond to disease and calamity with sacrificial acts of love and kindness, ministry should never be reduced to merely that. We are to be Christlike in loving service. But we have defined the responsibility of being like Jesus through this lens alone instead of by the way He dealt with such issues. Jesus stopped storms; He wasn't interested in just helping with the cleanup afterward. He resurrected the dead instead of conducting funerals. He healed the blind instead of training seeing-eye dogs. What do you think of Jesus' statement that you can do greater things than He did? Does that seem impossible? Why is it not impossible?

POINT TO PONDER

I will not let my experience limit my understanding of God.

PERSONAL REFLECTION

_____

_____

_____

_____

_____

_____

Day 193

GOD IS LOVE REVEALED IN JESUS

*He made Him who knew no sin to be sin on our behalf, so
that we might become the righteousness of God in Him.*
—2 CORINTHIANS 5:21

SOME HAVE GONE so far as to say that, like a good-cop-bad-cop
scenario, the Father is the angry One and Jesus is the merciful
One. Nothing could be further from the truth. Confusion over the
nature of the persons of the Trinity has made us welcome deception in our ranks. Most of those who embrace the idea that God
is an angry Father do so in equal proportion to their inability to
demonstrate His power. Powerlessness demands an explanation or
a solution. Blaming God seems to be easier than taking responsibility and pursuing an encounter with Him that changes our capa-
bilities in ministry. Do you see in yourself a tendency to blame
God when you feel powerless? Don't fall into that trap. He is a
good Father.

POINT TO PONDER

The love of God is a foundational attribute of His character.

PERSONAL REFLECTION

_____

_____

_____

_____

_____

_____

_____

_____

Day 194

JESUS—THE EXACT REPRESENTATION OF GOD'S NATURE

And He is the radiance of His glory and the exact representation of His nature, and upholds all things by the word of His power. When He had made purification of sins, He sat down at the right hand of the Majesty on high, having become as much better than the angels, as He has inherited a more excellent name than they.
—HEBREWS 1:3–4, EMPHASIS ADDED

ONE OF THE most important features of the gospel message is that the nature of the Father is perfectly seen in Jesus Christ. Jesus was a manifestation of the Father's nature. Whatever is thought to be in conflict between the Father in the Old Testament and the Son in the New Testament is in fact wrong. All inconsistencies in the revelation of the nature of God between the Old and New Testaments are cleared up in Jesus Christ. Jesus demonstrated the Father in everything He did. In short, Jesus is perfect theology. Are you struggling with what you think are inconsistencies in the revelation of the nature of God? If so, how is that impacting your relationship with Him?

POINT TO PONDER

I need to stop struggling with what seem to be inconsistencies in Scripture concerning God's nature and simply look to Jesus, who is an exact representation of the Father.

PERSONAL REFLECTION

_____

_____

_____

Day 195

DISCIPLESHIP AS DEFINED
BY SCRIPTURE

*Now after John was arrested, Jesus came to Galilee,
proclaiming the good news of God, and saying, "The
time is fulfilled, and the kingdom of God has come
near; repent, and believe in the good news."*
—MARK 1:14–15, NRSV

WHEN REFLECTING ON what seem to be inconsistencies in Scripture regarding the nature of God, some may ask, "What about Job?" I would respond, "I'm not a disciple of Job. I'm a disciple of Jesus. Job was the question, and Jesus is the answer." The entire Old Testament painted a picture of the problem so that it would be easy to recognize the answer when He came. If my study of Job does not take me to Jesus Christ as the answer, then I never understood Job. The Book of Job, along with all other questions about God's nature, are not meant to provide a revelation of God that would preempt the clear revelation of God through Jesus Christ. Who are you a disciple of?

POINT TO PONDER

I am a disciple of Jesus Christ who believes in the good news.

PERSONAL REFLECTION

_____

_____

_____

_____

_____

_____

EXTRAORDINARY COMPASSION FROM A GLORIOUS GOD

So Jesus said to them again, "Peace be with you; as
the Father has sent Me, I also send you."
—John 20:21

For the believer, it is theologically immoral to allow an Old Testament revelation of God to cancel or contradict the perfect and clear manifestation of God in Jesus. I'm not denying that God displays anger and judgment in the Old Testament, as did Jesus to some degree, but by and large Jesus came with a display of extraordinary compassion. This is the revelation of God that believers are responsible to teach and model. This was made clear in Jesus' statement, "As the Father has sent Me, I also send you" (John 20:21). Jesus ministered out of compassion, which is a revelation of the heart of God. How do you see yourself manifesting the compassion of God?

Point to Ponder

I will minister from a heart of compassion just as Jesus did.

Personal Reflection

_____

_____

_____

_____

_____

_____

_____

_____

Day 197

TAKING HOLD OF THE KINGDOM

*From the days of John the Baptist until now the kingdom of
heaven suffers violence, and violent men take it by force.*
—MATTHEW 11:12

THE ONLY JUSTIFIABLE model we have is Jesus Christ. The job
description is fairly simple: heal the sick, raise the dead, cast out
demons, and cleanse lepers. If you say you are not gifted in such
things, then I say, "Find out why." Most of what we need in life
will be brought to us, but most of what we want we'll have to go
and get. God has made these realities available. We must pursue
them. These gifts are the overflow of the *face of God* encounter. It's
not always fashionable to be zealous for God, yet that is what He
desires. How much zeal do you have to pursue His face?

POINT TO PONDER

My desire to zealously pursue God is growing daily.

PERSONAL REFLECTION

_____

_____

_____

_____

_____

_____

_____

_____

_____

_____

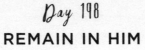

REMAIN IN HIM

Whoever claims to live in him must live as Jesus did.
—1 John 2:6

I DON'T HAVE ANSWERS to all the questions about the differences in the portrait of God throughout Scripture. There are mysteries of the faith that I must learn to be content to live with. But I have found a wonderful key for life: it's best to live from what you know to be true in spite of the mysteries that you can't explain. I cannot afford to stumble over my questions when what I *do* understand demands a response and commitment. The portrait of God the Father, as seen in Jesus Christ, is wonderfully clear. He deserves the rest of my life as I learn how to imitate Him. Most days the rest of my life seems far too short to do Him justice. How are you living from what you know to be true about God as revealed in Jesus?

POINT TO PONDER

I stand on 1 John 4:17, "By this, love is perfected with [me],
so that [I] may have confidence in the day of judgment;
because as He is, so also [am I] in this world."

PERSONAL REFLECTION

Day 199

DRAW AWAY AND DRAW NEAR

*One of those days Jesus went out to a mountainside
to pray, and spent the night praying to God.*
—LUKE 6:12, NIV

JESUS SET ASIDE His divinity, choosing instead to live as a man completely dependent on God. In doing so, He not only modeled a supernatural lifestyle, but He also illustrated that the ultimate quest is for the face of God. His lifestyle of both fasting and praying on the mountain throughout the night—a lifestyle He no doubt had established long before the Spirit descended upon Him—demonstrated His unquestionable priority to seek God's face. How can you take what Jesus modeled in this passage from Luke—to draw away from everything and everyone to be alone with the Father to whom He submits His cares and burdens—and apply it to your own life?

POINT TO PONDER

*With Jesus as my model, I will set apart time to be alone with
the Father, to share my heart, my burdens, and my love.*

PERSONAL REFLECTION

_____

_____

_____

_____

_____

_____

_____

_____

Day 200

THE POWER OF RELATIONSHIP

*Then Jesus was led up by the Spirit into the wilderness
to be tempted by the devil. And after He had fasted
forty days and forty nights, He then became hungry.*
—MATTHEW 4:1–2

To SAY THAT Jesus came both to manifest the face of God and illustrate the quest for His face may sound a little confusing, but both are true. Remember, Jesus modeled for us what it looked like to grow in favor with God as well as with man. The heavenly Father responded to His Son by giving an open heaven, which was followed by words of affirmation, saying, "This is My beloved Son with whom I am well-pleased" (2 Peter 1:17). It was in this encounter that the Father released the Holy Spirit upon His Son, enabling Him to manifest His face to the world. Notice the progression of events from the end of Matthew 3 into Matthew 4—Jesus is baptized by the Spirit, affirmed by the Father, and made manifest to the world. Then, He is immediately tempted by the devil. Jesus, the living Word, responds to evil with the living Word. Are you ready to live out this model in your own life?

POINT TO PONDER

I'm learning to live as Jesus lived, in the power of relationship.

PERSONAL REFLECTION

_____

_____

_____

_____

_____

THE CONFESSION OF CHRIST

Simon Peter answered, "You are the
Christ, the Son of the living God."
—MATTHEW 16:16

THE FATHER, BY the Holy Spirit, directed all that Jesus said and did. It was the intimacy that Jesus had with His heavenly Father that became the foundation for all the signs, wonders, and miracles performed in His three and a half years of earthly ministry.

Ezekiel made the prophetic declaration, "I will not hide My face from them any longer, for I will have poured out my Spirit on [them]" (Ezekiel 39:29). The face of God is revealed in the outpouring of the Holy Spirit. The outpouring of the Spirit also needed to happen to Jesus for Him to be fully qualified. This was His quest. Receiving this anointing qualified Him to be called the *Christ*, which means "anointed one." Without the experience there could be no title. Much of the world would rather we not confess Jesus. How ready are you to make a confession of Christ?

POINT TO PONDER

I confess that Jesus is the Christ, the Son of the living God.

PERSONAL REFLECTION

_____

_____

_____

_____

_____

_____

_____

FULFILLING YOUR ASSIGNMENT

For I have come down from heaven, not to do My
own will, but the will of Him who sent Me.
—John 6:38

IN JOHN 17 we read Jesus' prayer about how He has fulfilled His assignment in ministry, saying, "I have glorified You....I have finished the work....I have manifested Your name....I have given them Your word....As You sent Me into the world, I also have sent them....The glory which You gave Me I have given them....I have declared to them Your name" (vv. 4, 6, 14, 18, 22, 26, NKJV). Clearly, Jesus' assignment was to put His Father's name, work, glory, and Word on display, particularly to this select group of disciples. It's hard to do someone's will if you don't know the person. The intimacy Jesus enjoyed with the Father enabled Jesus to reveal aspects of God's nature that God wants us to know. What aspects of His nature has God revealed to you?

POINT TO PONDER

As I draw near to the Father, He will draw near to me.

PERSONAL REFLECTION

_____

_____

_____

_____

_____

_____

_____

HE IS WITH US ALWAYS

I came forth from the Father and have come into the world;
I am leaving the world again and going to the Father.
—JOHN 16:28

JESUS SHOCKED HIS disciples when He told them He had to leave. Picture this—the face of God had come, and they had encountered Him and beheld His glory. Now they were hearing that this experience, which had become the ultimate encounter with God imaginable, was to be taken away from them. To top it off, Jesus said it would actually be better if He left them. "It is to your advantage that I go away; for if I do not go away, the Helper will not come to you; but if I go, I will send Him to you" (John 16:7). It's not hard to imagine the disciples' confusion. They didn't yet have a full revelation of the cross. We do. With that in mind, how do you respond when God seems confusing?

POINT TO PONDER

I remember God's promises when I find myself in troubled waters.

PERSONAL REFLECTION

_____

_____

_____

_____

_____

_____

_____

_____

_____

Day 204
FROM GLORY TO GLORY

Therefore if anyone is in Christ, he is a new creature; the
old things passed away; behold, new things have come.
—2 Corinthians 5:17

JESUS MANIFESTED THE face of God to mankind. But it was only when He was taken away that He could release His experience to become their experience. And so He sent the Holy Spirit to come upon them. This meant that they could have their own encounter with God's face in a way that was not available through Jesus Himself. In other words, Jesus' experience was to become the normal experience of all who follow. This encounter brings us into the ultimate transformation, that we might become the ultimate transformers. Are you willing to give yourself over to the glorious process of being made more like Jesus? What you give up will pale in comparison to what you gain.

POINT TO PONDER

I want to be changed from glory to glory.

PERSONAL REFLECTION

_____

_____

_____

_____

_____

_____

_____

_____

_____

THE PRACTICAL SIDE OF GLORY

But because of his great love for us, God, who is rich in mercy, made us alive with Christ even when we were dead in transgressions—it is by grace you have been saved.
—EPHESIANS 2:4–5, NIV

WHEN MOSES ASKED to see God's glory, God revealed His goodness. The goodness of God is revolutionary in nature. His goodness is not a token act of kindness but is instead a picture of God's overwhelming pursuit of humanity that He might show us His extreme love and mercy. People get stuck on God's ability to judge and forget that He is the One who looks for the opportunity to show mercy. Many of His own children live in ignorance regarding His goodness and therefore continually misrepresent Him. In fact, no matter how horrible a person's sin or life was, from the woman caught in adultery to the tormented Gadarene man, Jesus revealed the face of God by showing mercy. These actions were never meant to be momentary displays of kindness so that in the twenty-first century God could finally punish people. His heart to forgive and show mercy is clear in the person of Jesus Christ. Jesus is the clearest manifestation of the face of God that mankind has ever seen. How does it make you feel to think that God is in pursuit of you so that He can show you His love and mercy and great goodness?

POINT TO PONDER

I am thankful that I have been saved by grace.

PERSONAL REFLECTION

_____

_____

Day 206

BEHOLDING GOD'S FACE
IN RIGHTEOUSNESS

Blessed are the pure in heart, for they shall see God.
—MATTHEW 5:8

MANY WILL REMIND us that while God is good, He is still the judge of all. And that is true. But in Jesus' time that judgment was only directed at the people who claimed to know God but didn't know Him at all: the religious leaders. Jesus was a continual threat to their empire of selfishness built on religious service. They were good at rejection, punishment, and restriction, but they were clueless about the heart of God—the very thing they claimed to know. They knew little about the boundless love of God and His passion for the freedom of all humanity. Is it possible to be pure in your heart but not in your head?

POINT TO PONDER

I see the glory of God with greater clarity when my heart is pure.

PERSONAL REFLECTION

Day 207

WALKING AS HIS PEOPLE

You yourselves like living stones are being built up as a spiritual house, to be a holy priesthood, to offer spiritual sacrifices acceptable to God through Jesus Christ.
—1 Peter 2:5, esv

AT ONE TIME Jesus said to the Pharisees, "It is not those who are healthy who need a physician, but those who are sick; I did not come to call the righteous, but sinners" (Mark 2:17). The most spiritually diseased people on the planet were the religious leaders. Yet His statement did not make an impact on them because they lacked awareness of their personal need. They were lacking in the genuine righteousness that comes from a relationship with God. Harlots and tax collectors had a step up on the Pharisees simply because they were aware of their need. "Blessed are the *poor in spirit*, for theirs is the kingdom of heaven" (Matthew 5:3, emphasis added). But the Pharisees' lack of awareness of spiritual need disqualified them for the call of God to salvation. Are you living daily with a genuine awareness of your need for Jesus?

POINT TO PONDER

My righteousness is like filthy rags without Jesus.

PERSONAL REFLECTION

_____

_____

_____

_____

_____

_____

Day 208
BLESSED JESUS!

*And so it was with me, brothers and sisters. When I came to you,
I did not come with eloquence or human wisdom as I proclaimed
to you the testimony about God. For I resolved to know nothing
while I was with you except Jesus Christ and him crucified.
I came to you in weakness with great fear and trembling.*
—1 Corinthians 2:1–3, niv

Ironically the greatest sinners were the ones who recognized who Jesus was when He came. The prostitutes, stargazers, tax collectors, and harlots all recognized Jesus as the Messiah. The ones most trained in Scripture were the ones who didn't recognize Him for who He was. It is this single factor of being aware of personal need that enables someone to recognize that which God is doing in the earth. Each one of us has personal need for God although many are not aware of the depth of his or her need. Is your life characterized by a sense of your own weakness and need for God? In what ways do you need Him? Does the depth of your need match the depth of your desire?

Point to Ponder

I resolve to live in Christ's strength instead of my own weakness.

Personal Reflection

_____

_____

_____

_____

_____

_____

Day 209

LIVING IN THE FAITH REALM

For You, Lord, are good, and ready to forgive, and
abundant in lovingkindness to all who call upon You.
—Psalm 86:5

THE AWARENESS OF deep personal need is also the setting where extraordinary faith grows. King David knew extraordinary need, which he expressed beautifully in the psalms. It's there in the psalms that we can also see David's extraordinary response to God in the midst of his needs. When there is no awareness of need, the opportunity to respond to God remains out of reach. For this reason the Pharisees had no access to the realm that pleases God the most—faith. And faith moves God unlike any other thing. David didn't hesitate to call upon God because he had faith in Him. What does your faith level look like in times of need? Do you cry out to God believing that He will answer?

POINT TO PONDER

I will live and walk in the realm of faith, always
mindful of my need for the mercy of God.

PERSONAL REFLECTION

_____

_____

_____

_____

_____

_____

_____

_____

Day 210

SETTING UP AN AMBUSH

Jesus said to them, "I am the bread of life; whoever comes to me shall not hunger, and whoever believes in me shall never thirst."
—JOHN 6:35, ESV

HUNGER FOR GOD is one of the greatest signs of life a person can have. It reveals an inner awareness of the existence of greater destiny and personal fulfillment. Some people have a theological concept about God's presence being with them, but they are stuck with no true interaction or experience. God is eager for us to experience Him. He created us for relationship with Him. Just as He walked with Adam in the evening in the cool of the garden, He wants to walk with you. We must press past intellectual awareness and on to hunger for heartfelt encounters that change and transform. Where do you go, and who do you go to when you are spiritually hungry?

POINT TO PONDER

All of me desires the true bread that is Jesus Christ. Nothing else will satisfy me.

PERSONAL REFLECTION

_____

_____

_____

_____

_____

_____

_____

_____

Day 211

CREATED FOR HIM

My soul longs, yes, faints for the courts of the LORD;
my heart and flesh sing for joy to the living God.
—PSALM 84:2, ESV

THE DESIRE TO seek God itself is testimony that there is more, and the fact that we possess this desire to seek God should encourage us to pursue these encounters. It is nearly impossible to hunger for something that does not exist. I crave sweets only because sweet things exist. In the same way, my heart cries out for God because I was created to find complete fulfillment in Him alone. And the more I come to know Him, the more I become sure that He will be faithful to satisfy the desire He put in me. The desire for God is built into the human heart. When our hearts become corrupt, we begin to desire things in place of God. Some people spend a lifetime trying to satisfy a hungry heart without ever turning to God. Are there any corrupt areas in your heart that you need to deal with?

POINT TO PONDER

God created me to find complete fulfillment in Him alone.

PERSONAL REFLECTION

_____

_____

_____

_____

_____

_____

_____

Day 212
HIS CONSTANT PRESENCE

The LORD is the one who goes ahead of you; He will be with you.
He will not fail you or forsake you. Do not fear or be dismayed.
—DEUTERONOMY 31:8

ONE OF JESUS' most important promises was given to His disciples just prior to His death. "He who loves Me...*I will* love him and *manifest Myself to him*" (John 14:21, NKJV, emphasis added). He promised that they would see Him again. This is clearly not merely a promise that they would see Him in heaven, because that was a given. It was also not a promise for these disciples only, but rather for all who love Him. (Otherwise we might think that this promise only referred to the appearance Jesus made to His disciples before He ascended.) How confident are you that Jesus is always with you? What gives you that confidence?

POINT TO PONDER

I receive every promise of Jesus with confidence in His unfailing love.

PERSONAL REFLECTION

_____

_____

_____

_____

_____

_____

_____

_____

_____

_____

Day 213
BE OF GOOD COURAGE

Then you will call upon me and come and pray to me, and I will hear you. You will seek me and find me, when you seek me with all your heart. I will be found by you, declares the LORD.
—JEREMIAH 29:12–14, ESV

THE PROMISE OF John 14:21—that we would see Jesus again—is for every generation of believers, and it can mean nothing less than that He would make Himself conspicuous to us and that we would surely see Him again and again. We are not only to receive the Holy Spirit in power; we are also to see Jesus over and over again. That has to be the best of both worlds. God has given us these promises explicitly that we might seek Him with abandon, confident that He will be found by those who love Him and seek Him with all their hearts. In what ways are you seeking God with all your heart?

POINT TO PONDER

My greatest joy is to seek God with everything in me.

PERSONAL REFLECTION

_____

_____

_____

_____

_____

_____

_____

_____

Day 214

GOD LOOKS AT THE HEART

After removing Saul, he made David their king. God testified concerning him: "I have found David son of Jesse, a man after my own heart; he will do everything I want him to do."
—Acts 13:22, niv

GOD REVEALS HIMSELF to those who love Him. What kind of people are those who love Him? If we made a list of people in Scripture who illustrate what it looks like to love God, David would probably be at the top of the list. It's amazing to see what this love for God led him into. What characteristics of David revealed in the psalms do you think made God declare that he was a man after His heart? Do you see any of those characteristics in yourself? Take time to think about others in Scripture who illustrate what it looks like to love God. What aspects of their walk with the Lord do you see reflected in your life?

POINT TO PONDER

God searches me and knows my heart, even my anxious thoughts.

PERSONAL REFLECTION

THE TRIAL OF FAITH

*So that the proof of your faith, being more precious
than gold which is perishable, even though tested
by fire, may be found to result in praise and glory
and honor at the revelation of Jesus Christ.*
—1 PETER 1:7

WHEN GOD SENT the prophet Samuel to anoint the man He
had chosen to replace King Saul, He explained to him that He
didn't look on the outward appearance but instead looked on the
heart. It was from that perspective that David was chosen over his
brothers, who were all better suited for greatness in the natural.
Yet David's heart of passion for God attracted God to David. As
a result, he was chosen to be king. While God is very capable of
multitasking—of giving His undivided attention to each person
on the planet all at the same time—He is drawn the most strongly
to the ones whose hearts have been refined in their pursuit of Him.
In what ways has your heart been refined in your pursuit of God?
What brought about the refinement?

POINT TO PONDER

I am guarded by the power of God in the midst of my trials.

PERSONAL REFLECTION

_____

_____

_____

_____

_____

_____

TRUE REPENTANCE

*The sacrifices of God are a broken spirit; a broken
and a contrite heart, O God, You will not despise.*
—PSALM 51:17

DAVID'S PASSION FOR God was first seen on the backside of a mountain while tending his father's sheep. In the quiet part of our day, when no one is looking, the true desires of our hearts can be seen. So it was with David. David was a skilled musician who wrote songs of worship to God. He did this long before this was a normal expression of worship. Up to this point in history Israel had been instructed to offer the blood sacrifice to God as their basic worship expression. But there had been very little instruction about the sacrifice of thanksgiving and praise that could be given from the heart. David discovered that this was important to God as he pursued God. He learned that what really pleased God was the offering of a broken and contrite heart. And David was eager to give it. His zeal for God became evident as he gave himself to the privilege of worship and ministered directly to the Lord. What does this kind of true repentant worship mean to you? How willing are you to get to a deep level of brokenness before God?

POINT TO PONDER

*God will show me every place in my heart
where I am in need of repentance.*

PERSONAL REFLECTION

_____

_____

_____

HIS FACE OF FAVOR

Humble yourselves, therefore, under God's mighty
hand, that he may lift you up in due time.
—1 PETER 5:6, NIV

DAVID EMBRACED RESPONSIBILITY to watch over his father's sheep with equal zeal. (Many have passion for their life's goals and ambitions, but David was rightly directed.) When a lion and a bear attacked his father's sheep, he put his own life at risk to save them. Remember, he did this when no one was looking; it was not done so others would recognize him as a brave young man. It came out of his identity with God. He killed them both, and such courage and integrity set him up for the moment God allowed him to kill Goliath when everyone was looking. A private victory leads to a public victory and a corporate blessing, because God turns His face of favor toward those who will demonstrate character when no one is looking. What private victories have occurred in your life? What flowed from those victories?

POINT TO PONDER

I love the secret place with God, where He
alone sees the things in my heart.

PERSONAL REFLECTION

_____

_____

_____

_____

_____

_____

UNTO THE LORD

Whatever you do, work heartily, as for
the Lord and not for men.
—COLOSSIANS 3:23, ESV

MANY YEARS AFTER David's rule there arose another king. The prophet Elisha gave him instruction to strike the ground with arrows. The king followed his command and did so three times. The prophet became angry at his casual approach to the assignment and announced that if he would have struck the ground five or six times, he would have annihilated their enemies. But instead he would enjoy only three temporary victories. All of Israel would suffer the consequences of his passionless act. The sobering fact is this—leaders who lack passion cost everyone who follows. Not so with David. He endeared himself to God as a man of great passion—for God and for life. How much passion do you really have for God, and how is this passion impacting those around you?

POINT TO PONDER

Passion for God characterizes my life.

PERSONAL REFLECTION

_____

_____

_____

_____

_____

_____

_____

_____

Day 219

THE STRIVING IS OVER

This is what the LORD says: "Stand at the crossroads and look; ask for the ancient paths, ask where the good way is, and walk in it, and you will find rest for your souls."
—JEREMIAH 6:16, NIV

DAVID'S GREAT LOVE for God led him to discover the truth that God will be found by those who seek Him. A great command found in the psalms reveals one of King David's secrets in life. "Rest in the LORD and wait patiently for Him" (Psalm 37:7). The word *rest* used in this verse means one of two things, depending on the context. One is "to be still." That would be consistent with our use of the word in the English language. The other definition is rather fascinating, though. It means "to take a leisure walk." I think automatically of God and Adam walking in the Garden of Eden together in the cool of the day. This illustrates that true rest is found in a right relationship with God. Do you find rest for your soul when you are walking with Jesus?

POINT TO PONDER

I set my feet on the good path that is Jesus Christ.

PERSONAL REFLECTION

_____

_____

_____

_____

_____

_____

_____

Day 220
TRUE FREEDOM

So if the Son sets you free, you will be free indeed.
—John 8:36, niv

We know that all that was stolen because of Adam's sin is restored in the last Adam, Jesus Christ. So, to *rest in the Lord* means basically that the obstacle to the relationship is removed and the striving is over. I don't need to fight to gain God's attention. I already have His favor and will walk favorably with Him in the adventure of a developing personal relationship. All this is provided for in the gift of salvation. It is amazing to realize that David discovered this power of waiting on God while under the old covenant. What are you discovering under the new covenant?

Point to Ponder

Jesus gives me the power to walk free indeed.

Personal Reflection

_____

_____

_____

_____

_____

_____

_____

_____

_____

_____

_____

_____

Day 221

THE UPSIDE-DOWN KINGDOM

But God showed his great love for us by sending
Christ to die for us while we were still sinners.
—ROMANS 5:8, NLT

MANY PEOPLE WORK for God's attention and favor instead of learning to work with God because of His favor. They become so exhausted working *for* Him that there's little strength left to work *with* Him when He opens the doors for significant service. At the root of this problem is ignorance about Christ's acceptance of each of us, and it has cost us dearly. We work so hard to gain favor from God that we might be accepted, when all the while that's the opposite of how life works in the kingdom. Do you find it challenging to wrap your mind around the great love of God for us in Jesus? What about His love challenges you?

POINT TO PONDER

I receive the mercy of God in Jesus as the first
step to upside-down kingdom living.

PERSONAL REFLECTION

_____

_____

_____

_____

_____

_____

_____

_____

THE PERFECT ONE

*For from him and through him and for him are all
things. To him be the glory forever! Amen.*
—ROMANS 11:36, NIV

BECAUSE JESUS IS my righteousness I am already accepted. From that acceptance comes favor, and that favor gives birth to authentic Christlike works of service. I serve *from* Him, not merely *for* Him. This simple progression really is the key to ministry. This was the model that Jesus gave us. He only did what He saw His Father do and said what He heard His Father say. So many are busy serving Him with little knowledge of their identity as beloved sons and daughters of their loving heavenly Father. They live as outsiders, constantly striving to win the Father's affection when they already have it through no effort of their own. Are you living as one of God's beloved? How would you describe the ways in which you serve God?

POINT TO PONDER

Jesus is my righteousness.

PERSONAL REFLECTION

_____

_____

_____

_____

_____

_____

_____

CHOOSE THE GOOD PART

But the Lord answered and said to her, "Martha, Martha, you are worried and bothered about so many things; but only one thing is necessary, for Mary has chosen the good part, which shall not be taken away from her."
—LUKE 10:41–42

THE STORY OF Mary and Martha illustrates the difference between how we often respond in the presence of Jesus and how He desires we respond. Mary chose to sit at Jesus' feet while Martha chose to work in the kitchen. Mary sought to please Him by being with Him while Martha tried to please Him through service. When Martha became jealous, she asked Jesus to tell Mary to help her in the kitchen. Most servants want to degrade the role of the friend to feel justified in their works-oriented approach to God. Jesus' response is important to remember: "Mary has chosen the good part." Martha was making a meal that Jesus never ordered. Doing more for God is the method servants use to get God's attention that they might increase in favor. A friend has a different focus entirely: they enjoy the favor they have and use it to spend time with their master. Do you use the favor God has given you to spend time with Him, or do you tend to stay busy serving rather than sitting?

POINT TO PONDER

I am a friend of God, and I want to spend as much time with Him as I can.

PERSONAL REFLECTION

_____

_____

_____

JOY UNSPEAKABLE

You will make known to me the path of life; in Your presence is fullness of joy; in Your right hand there are pleasures forever.
—PSALM 16:11

To say we need both Marys and Marthas is to miss the point entirely. And it simply isn't true. Perhaps you've heard it said that nothing would ever get done if we didn't have any Marthas. That too is a lie. That teaching comes mostly from Marthas who are intimidated by the lifestyle of Marys. Mary wasn't a nonworker. Rather she was beginning to be like her Master, who only did what He saw the Father do. Jesus was talking, so Mary set aside other distractions and sat down to listen. She didn't get caught up in making the sandwiches that Jesus didn't order. She was learning that working from His presence is much more effective than working for His presence. Have you experienced joy unspeakable in God's presence? Is it something you long for? How is Jesus suggesting you receive such joy?

POINT TO PONDER

I want to look more like Jesus every day—to be a Mary, not a Martha.

PERSONAL REFLECTION

_____

_____

_____

_____

_____

_____

Day 225

ANOTHER LOOK AT WAITING

For this purpose also I labor, striving according to
His power, which mightily works within me.
—Colossians 1:29

ONE OF THE problems that we have in our study of Scripture is that we tend to interpret things through our own experience and culture. *Waiting patiently for God* is a great example. For most of us this statement brings a passive image to mind. Many have found this to be a way to blame God for their spiritual laziness: "Oh, we're just waiting on God." And they've done so for years, wasting valuable time, hoping that God will invade their lives with some sense of significance. Do you put things off under the guise of "waiting for God" when in fact it is *you* that you are waiting on?

POINT TO PONDER

God has already invaded my life with more significance
than I can handle—He has given me Jesus.

PERSONAL REFLECTION

_____

_____

_____

_____

_____

_____

_____

_____

_____

_____

ACTIVELY WAITING

*So then, my beloved, just as you have always obeyed, not
as in my presence only, but now much more in my absence,
work out your salvation with fear and trembling.*
—PHILIPPIANS 2:12

HOWEVER, WAITING ON God is not a passive, lean-back-in-the-recliner attitude that says, "When God wants to touch me, He knows my address." There are still people who sit back and say, "Boy, I hear God is doing great things all over the world. I just wish He would move in my life or my church. I wish He'd do something great in my city." This kind of *waiting on God* attitude is not the one we see in the Scriptures. There are those who wait and those who go. Which one are you? Can you lay aside your own agenda, or lack thereof, and embrace His good direction even when it means actively waiting?

POINT TO PONDER

*I will wait on God, not out of avoidance, but because
I know He will show me a better way.*

PERSONAL REFLECTION

_____

_____

_____

_____

_____

_____

_____

LET PASSION LEAD THE WAY

For where your treasure is, there your heart will be also.
—MATTHEW 6:21, NIV

THIS HEBREW WORD *patiently* is in the Bible fifty-three times. Four times it is defined as "waiting patiently," "to wait," "waiting," or "waited." Forty-nine times it is defined as "writhing in pain, as in childbirth" or "whirling in the air in dance." The characteristics involved in childbirth and the dance give us the needed insight on how to practice waiting patiently on God. We could never watch someone involved in giving birth to a child or dancing skillfully to music and think that they were passive about what they were doing. Passion is the nature of both expressions. And passion leads the way in waiting patiently on God. What is leading your wait on God?

POINT TO PONDER

When passion leads my heart, God's blessings abound.

PERSONAL REFLECTION

_____

_____

_____

_____

_____

_____

_____

_____

_____

BRING GOD YOUR BEST

My heart is confident in you, O God; my heart is
confident. No wonder I can sing your praises!
—PSALM 57:7, NLT

IN OUR CULTURE *patience* connotes the attitude expressed by words such as these: "I'm just going to put up with this annoyance for another day because I'm patient." That's not the biblical patience David was talking about. If *waiting patiently* is seen in the activity of leaping and whirling about in a dance, then the person who is waiting will have to be incredibly focused. Their love for the dance takes them into a discipline that brings out creative excellence. Dancers must be intensely focused on their bodies, the music, and where they're going to land. At minimum, without that much-needed discipline and focus, injuries would be certain. In what areas of your life does your love for God bring out excellence? What areas need more work (more love)?

POINT TO PONDER

When I bring God my best, He makes it even better.

PERSONAL REFLECTION

_____

_____

_____

_____

_____

_____

_____

_____

Day 229
OUR HIGH PRIEST

*Therefore, holy brothers and sisters, who share in the
heavenly calling, fix your thoughts on Jesus, whom
we acknowledge as our apostle and high priest.*
—HEBREWS 3:1, NIV

I HAD THE PRIVILEGE of being present for the birth of each of my children. When my wife was giving birth to our third child, Leah, I made the mistake of turning my head toward someone else in the room during a contraction. I quickly discovered that it was definitely the wrong time to have done so. When I turned my attention elsewhere, it affected her ability to keep her focus, which was essential in keeping her writhing in pain at a minimum. I made this mistake when my wife needed my help the most. Her death grip on my arm helped me to return to my senses and realize that there was really only one person who should have all my attention at that moment. How often do you make God the absolute center of your attention to the exclusion of everything else?

POINT TO PONDER

*I fix my eyes on Jesus who gives me wisdom, fresh
motivation to love, and confidence to face every day.*

PERSONAL REFLECTION

_____

_____

_____

_____

_____

Day 230

RADICAL LIVING

*As the time approached for him to be taken up to
heaven, Jesus resolutely set out for Jerusalem.*
—LUKE 9:51, NIV

THERE'S SOMETHING ABOUT both the dance and giving birth
that requires incredible resolve to reach an intended end. This is
waiting patiently for God. It has intense focus, disciplined resolve,
and a conviction that *nothing else will satisfy*. God is attracted to
people who have that kind of tenacity and who are not satisfied
with inferior things. Too often we are tenacious about things that
are not of God because we have set our hearts elsewhere. He wants
us to center our hearts on His heart. Is there something in your
life right now that demands tenacious resolve? How do you think
God would have you respond?

POINT TO PONDER

I live radically when my heart is centered on God's heart.

PERSONAL REFLECTION

_____

_____

_____

_____

_____

_____

_____

_____

_____

Day 231
EAGER PURSUIT

Lead me in Your truth and teach me, for You are the
God of my salvation; for You I wait all the day.
—PSALM 25:5

DAVID USES ANOTHER word to expand his portrait of our waiting on God. "But those who *wait* for the LORD, they will inherit the land" (Psalm 37:9, emphasis added). Here the word *wait* means "to lie in wait," as in setting up an ambush. That is about as far away from the passive definition as can be imagined. It is almost militant, still carrying the discipline of the intense focus mentioned earlier, but along with an eager pursuit. Isaiah expressed the same idea: "And I will wait for the LORD who is hiding His face from the house of Jacob; I will even look eagerly for Him" (Isaiah 8:17). How do you wait for God? Eagerly? Impatiently? With faith?

POINT TO PONDER

When I set an ambush for God, I will always find
Him because He has already found me.

PERSONAL REFLECTION

_____

_____

_____

_____

_____

_____

_____

_____

Day 232

STOP AT NOTHING

And when they could not get near him because of the crowd,
they removed the roof above him, and when they had made
an opening, they let down the bed on which the paralytic lay.
—Mark 2:4, esv

I F I WANT to hunt deer, I won't set up an ambush on Wall Street
in New York City or in the middle of the Pacific Ocean. To set
up an ambush with any hope of success, I must do so in areas that
deer frequent. But many do not realize that the same is true of
waiting on God. There are many who need a miracle, but they
won't go across town to a church where miracles are common. We
play a mental game of pride when we refuse to humble ourselves
and go to lie in wait in the places that God frequents. Are you
willing to set up an ambush just to encounter Jesus? If not, what is
getting in the way?

Point to Ponder

I will look for every opportunity to be positioned to receive from Jesus.

Personal Reflection

_____

_____

_____

_____

_____

_____

_____

_____

Day 233

I SURRENDER ALL

You will seek Me and find Me when you
search for Me with all your heart.
—JEREMIAH 29:13

PLEASE DON'T STUMBLE over the concept of ambushing God as though it violates His sovereignty—He is the One who has promised to be found by us if we seek Him with all of our hearts. And He is the One who said He would make Himself conspicuous as we pursue Him. This is His idea. It is our test to see if we believe Him enough to *look eagerly* for Him. God is looking for someone who will get out of his or her routine and set up an ambush. If you were to get out of your routine to look for God, would it be an inconvenience or a joy?

POINT TO PONDER

I will let go of everything in my heart that is
getting in the way of my pursuit of God.

PERSONAL REFLECTION

_____

_____

_____

_____

_____

_____

_____

_____

A GREATER REALITY

Then know this, you and all the people of Israel: It is by the name of Jesus Christ of Nazareth, whom you crucified but whom God raised from the dead, that this man stands before you healed.
—Acts 4:10, niv

SOME PEOPLE GET really upset when they see believers traveling all over the world because those believers have heard that God is doing something significant in a particular place. Their reasoning: "God is everywhere. Seek Him where you are, and He will come to you." Similarly, preachers with little breakthrough anointing will say, "You're not supposed to follow signs. They are supposed to follow you!" That looks good on paper and carries a measure of truth. But if signs are not following you, you had better follow them until they follow you. Remember, signs point to a greater reality. We are not to follow them for their own sake but because they lead us to the One who created them. Getting in touch with Him is how we become those whom signs follow. When you hear of a miracle of God, how do you respond? Does it make you hungry for the things of God that are beyond what you know in the natural, or do you try and minimize it because you haven't experienced much of the miraculous yourself?

Point to Ponder

I embrace faith to believe for the supernatural of God to break into my natural.

Personal Reflection

_____

_____

_____

Day 235

DRAW NEAR

*And a woman who had a hemorrhage for twelve years, and could
not be healed by anyone, came up behind Him and touched the
fringe of His cloak, and immediately her hemorrhage stopped.*
—LUKE 8:43–44

WHILE THEY MAY not realize it, many who travel anywhere at
any cost just because of their hunger for God are doing exactly
what David taught about waiting on God. They go to where He is
working and lie in wait, anticipating His every move, looking for
the chance to reach out and touch God. Matthew described such
an extraordinary act in the story of a woman who had been hem-
orrhaging for twelve years. She positioned herself in such a way
that she was able to touch the hem of Jesus' garment as He was
making His way down the road. It was no easy feat. There were
large crowds of people pressing in upon Him. Yet she was the only
one who saw the dimension of heaven that He was carrying and
touched Him in a way that put a demand on the anointing of the
Holy Spirit that was resident in Him. That is the kind of faith that
pleases God. It is the classic example of how God welcomes being
ambushed. Are you willing to ambush God with great faith?

POINT TO PONDER

When Jesus draws near, I will reach out to Him.

PERSONAL REFLECTION

_____

_____

_____

_____

FOLLOWING IN JACOB'S FOOTSTEPS

I will not let you go unless you bless me.
—GENESIS 32:26

JACOB, DESPITE HIS deep personal issues with deception and manipulation, had an intense desire for the blessing of the Lord. He would not be well liked today by those who criticize the ones who are constantly looking for God's blessing. He simply wanted God to be real in his life. His pursuit culminated when he had to face what he believed would be the most dangerous situation of his life—meeting his brother, Esau, for the first time after obtaining Esau's birthright and stealing his blessing. The circumstances were desperate— he believed that his brother wanted vengeance. Not everyone turns to God in desperate circumstances. Some might throw a last-ditch prayer up, but few take the step of grabbing on to God as their only hope and holding on for dear life until His answer comes. Jacob did this, and it was this focused passion and faith that attracted the Lord to him. In response God sent an angel to wrestle with him.

Jacob put his fears before God and ended up in a wrestling match. Have you ever wrestled with God this way? If so, what was the outcome? If not, what is holding you back?

POINT TO PONDER

God's grace alone brings me victory. His joy comes in the morning.

PERSONAL REFLECTION

_____

_____

_____

_____

HOLDING ON TO GOD

So he said to him, "What is your name?" And he said, "Jacob."
He said, "Your name shall no longer be Jacob, but Israel; for you
have striven with God and with men and have prevailed." Then
Jacob asked him and said, "Please tell me your name?" But he said,
"Why is it that you ask my name?" And he blessed him there. So
Jacob named the place Peniel, for he said, "I have seen God face to
face, yet my life has been preserved." Now the sun rose upon him
just as he crossed over Penuel, and he was limping on his thigh.
—GENESIS 32:27–31, EMPHASIS ADDED

IN RESPONSE TO his persistence Jacob received a name change. This name change reflected the character change that had occurred with him in his pursuit of the blessing. His name was changed from *Jacob* ("deceiver") to *Israel* ("God strives"). He was injured in this encounter with God, and he limped for the rest of his life— that was the cost for his persistence. Such resolve always has a cost. Look around and you will find people who are willing to pay a price for things that are not of God, while ignoring what He has to offer. This is the condition of many believers. How persistent are you in your pursuit of God, and what price are you willing to pay?

POINT TO PONDER

The fire burning down in my soul can't be quenched
by anything but His magnificent presence.

PERSONAL REFLECTION

_____

_____

_____

THE GENEROSITY OF GOD

*Don't you see how wonderfully kind, tolerant, and patient
God is with you? Does this mean nothing to you? Can't you
see that his kindness is intended to turn you from your sin?*
—ROMANS 2:4, NLT

I GUESS THAT WHEN you realize you survived looking at the face of God, surviving an angry brother seems easy. Significantly, when Jacob later met Esau and found favor with him, he said, "No, I pray you, if I have now found favor in your sight, then receive my gift from my hand. For I have seen your face, and it is as though I have seen the face of God, with you having received me favorably" (Genesis 33:10, MEV). This episode clearly reveals the power of the blessing and favor that came upon Jacob's life after his encounter and name change—his brother treated him like a completely different person. Are there instances in your life when God has brought ungodly hidden motives or actions to light and then blessed you? Would you consider those instances to be His generosity or a rebuke?

POINT TO PONDER

The loving-kindness of God leads me to repentance.

PERSONAL REFLECTION

_____

_____

_____

_____

_____

THE QUEST THAT PERFECTS

For if, while we were God's enemies, we were reconciled to
him through the death of his Son, how much more, having
been reconciled, shall we be saved through his life!
—ROMANS 5:10, NIV

THE QUEST FOR God's face started a change in Jacob. His life is
a great reminder that one does not need to be perfect to begin
this journey. In fact, it is this quest that perfects. The ultimate
encounter in life was given to Jacob. His conclusion was, "I have
seen God face to face, yet my life has been preserved." It saddens
me to see the great number of people who feel they have to clean
up their lives before they meet the only One who cleanses. It's an
impossible task that creates pressure and striving for a relationship with God. Just being able to follow, without distraction, our
hearts' desire to know God—that's what causes more transformation than any list of rules found in religion. Do you struggle to
relate to God because you think your life is too messy—that you
need to clean things up before you can pursue Him?

POINT TO PONDER

When God bids me to come and be reconciled to Him, I
will go with all my brokenness and receive His love.

PERSONAL REFLECTION

_____

_____

_____

_____

_____

FOLLOWING IN ELISHA'S FOOTSTEPS

*When the LORD was about to take up Elijah by a whirl-
wind to heaven,...Elijah went with Elisha from Gilgal.
Elijah said to Elisha, "Stay here please, for the LORD has
sent me as far as Bethel." But Elisha said, "As the LORD
lives and as you yourself live, I will not leave you."*
—2 KINGS 2:1–2

ELISHA ILLUSTRATES THAT our capacity to wait determines
whether we will experience spiritual breakthroughs that release
a new measure of power and authority in our lives.

Elisha spent years in training as Elijah's assistant, and eventually the time came for the Lord to take Elijah home. Strangely, on
this day it seemed that Elijah tried to ditch his spiritual son at every
turn. But Elisha followed Elijah and wouldn't let him out of his sight.
When Elijah asked him what he could do for him before he was
taken, Elisha shot for the moon. He said, "Please, let a double portion of your spirit be upon me" (2 Kings 2:9). What Elisha asked for
was very difficult because of the price involved. The Lord showed
Elijah how Elisha would be tested to see if he had what it would take
to carry a double portion of Elijah's anointing. How is God testing
you in order to prepare you to carry greater anointing?

POINT TO PONDER

*I will wait patiently, enduring God's testing so
that I can receive His greater anointing.*

PERSONAL REFLECTION

_____

_____

_____

Day 241
THROUGH THE SPIRIT

But we who live by the Spirit eagerly wait to receive
by faith the righteousness God has promised to us.
—GALATIANS 5:5, NLT

GIFTS OF THE Spirit rest best on the fruit of the Spirit. That's why the Bible says that faith actually works through love. The word for *works* or *working* in Galatians 5:6 is *energeo*, from which we get our word *energy*. In other words, *faith is energized through love*. Gifts are energized by character. And without the energy of character flowing through our lives, we won't be able to exercise the gifts consistently and with excellence. The anointing of the Spirit from which these gifts flow is given to bless and release the reality of heaven to earth. But it is weighty. In what ways is God working on your character, and to what degree are you cooperating with Him?

POINT TO PONDER

My faith is energized by the love of God. My gifts are
energized by His character formed in me through His love.

PERSONAL REFLECTION

_____

_____

_____

_____

_____

_____

_____

Day 242

TIMES OF TESTING

As they were going along and talking, behold, there appeared
a chariot of fire and horses of fire which separated the two
of them. And Elijah went up by a whirlwind to heaven.
—2 Kings 2:11

ONLY INTEGRITY JOINED with passion could enable Elisha to carry a double measure of Elijah's anointing. The test was simple but not easy. Elijah said, "You have asked a hard thing. Nevertheless, if you see me when I am taken from you, it shall be so for you; but if not, it shall not be so" (2 Kings 2:10). Then God created an incredible distraction that would have caused most people to take their eyes off Elijah. It is interesting to note that the Lord chose to test Elisha in the very thing he was already doing—keeping his eyes on his master. Elisha was probably already dogging Elijah's steps to the point where Elijah couldn't go to the bathroom without Elisha being present. God simply arranged the circumstances in order to see whether what he was doing out of instinct had enough force of character behind it to be sustained in spite of the kind of distractions he would face, should he be entrusted with a double portion. What distractions have caused you to take your eyes off God? How did you get back on track?

POINT TO PONDER

I will keep my eyes fixed on the One who is worthy of
it all no matter what is going on around me.

PERSONAL REFLECTION

_____

_____

_____

CARRYING THE ANOINTING

Elisha saw it and cried out, "My father, my father, the chariots of Israel and its horsemen!" And he saw Elijah no more. Then he took hold of his own clothes and tore them in two pieces.
—2 KINGS 2:12

As ELISHA KEPT his assignment to watch Elijah, the unexpected happened. A chariot of fire came down out of heaven. The chariot didn't take Elijah to heaven, as some have surmised. The Scriptures tell us that Elijah was actually taken up in a whirlwind. So what was the chariot of fire for? It was the test. If Elisha were to carry a double portion of Elijah's anointing, it would mean that there would be many unusual signs and wonders surrounding his life. Could Elisha keep his eyes on his assignment (Elijah in this case), even when the activities of heaven invaded the atmosphere? Could he anchor his heart to the will of God and not be pulled away by the wonder of his gift? Most of us would have failed this test. After all, how could we go wrong by putting our attention on God's activities? But Elisha's quest for the double portion anointing was fulfilled in this encounter, for Elisha wouldn't be distracted by his own gift and anointing. How do you anchor your heart to the will of God and not get distracted by the gifts and anointing He has placed on you?

POINT TO PONDER

I am very thankful for the gifts God has given me, but I am most thankful for Him.

PERSONAL REFLECTION

Day 244

THE CALL TO ENDURANCE

Therefore, since we have so great a cloud of witnesses
surrounding us, let us also lay aside every encumbrance
and the sin which so easily entangles us, and let us
run with endurance the race that is set before us.
—Hebrews 12:1

GOD DESIRES TO release gifts to us more than we desire to receive them. He is just too merciful to release gifts upon us that He would have to judge us for later because we failed to carry them with integrity. However, we must also realize that even when we pass a particular character test and are entrusted with a greater measure of anointing, we have not *arrived*. We all know those who have begun well in the race of faith and have been entrusted with a wonderful anointing to bless the body of Christ, only to fall later in life. This is a lifelong race that we are running, and God works in every part of it to groom us to carry what He wants to give us, both for this life and the next. Are there times when you are tempted to feel as if you've arrived? How do you counterbalance those feelings in order to stay focused for the long haul?

POINT TO PONDER

I will continue to run the race set before me, going
from glory to glory, strength to strength.

PERSONAL REFLECTION

FOLLOWING IN JESUS' FOOTSTEPS

*For we do not have a high priest who is unable to empathize
with our weaknesses, but we have one who has been
tempted in every way, just as we are—yet he did not sin.*
—Hebrews 4:15, niv

OUR KEY TO running a successful race is the same as Elisha's. As
Hebrews tells us, the key is to fix our eyes on our Master. We
are successful when we fix our eyes on Jesus precisely because He
is the One who has run the race ahead of us. He had to undergo
the same tests of character that Elisha faced and that we must face.
He modeled success for us by keeping *His* eyes fixed on the Father
at all times. Like Elisha's ultimate test, Jesus' test required Him to
keep His focus in the face of separation from His Father. How do
you keep your focus when you feel distant from God?

Point to Ponder

I will keep my eyes fixed on the Father at all times.

Personal Reflection

_____

_____

_____

_____

_____

_____

_____

_____

_____

Day 246

TO THE CROSS

Just at that time some Pharisees approached, saying to
Him, "Go away, leave here, for Herod wants to kill You."
And He said to them, "Go and tell that fox, 'Behold, I cast
out demons and perform cures today and tomorrow, and
the third day I reach My goal.' Nevertheless I must journey
on today and tomorrow and the next day; for it cannot
be that a prophet would perish outside of Jerusalem."
—LUKE 13:31–33

IN HIS JOURNEY to the cross Jesus demonstrated the ultimate example of the kind of passionate focus that we've been considering. He set His face toward Jerusalem, knowing He was about to die. Even some of His beloved disciples tried to dissuade Him from going because they didn't yet have knowledge of the ultimate outcome of the cross. What obstacles have been thrown in your path to take your focus off where God is leading you? How did you deal with these obstacles?

POINT TO PONDER

Following Jesus' example, I will be steadfast
toward whatever God puts in front of me.

PERSONAL REFLECTION

_____

_____

_____

_____

_____

Day 247

GOD'S PERFECT TIMING

Peter took Him aside and began to rebuke Him, saying,
"God forbid it, Lord! This shall never happen to You."
—MATTHEW 16:22

IT'S IMPORTANT TO realize that Jesus pursued this focus without any support from those closest to Him. He carefully took the time to prepare His disciples for His death. But no matter how much He talked with them, they didn't understand. Not only did they not comprehend the issue of the cross, they opposed the little they did understand. At one point Peter actually rebuked Jesus for His repeated references to His personal death. God's timing was perfect in not giving the disciples revelation of the cross before the resurrection even though the lack of revelation made it difficult for both Jesus and His followers. Will you trust in God's perfect timing even when it is hard to maintain your focus?

POINT TO PONDER

God's timing is always perfect. Therefore, I will learn to walk with perseverance and faith in spite of what I know or don't know.

PERSONAL REFLECTION

_____

_____

_____

_____

_____

_____

_____

PERFECT LOVE

About three in the afternoon Jesus cried out in a loud voice, "Eli, Eli, lema sabachthani?" (which means "My God, my God, why have you forsaken me?").
—MATTHEW 27:46, NIV

H IS DEATH WAS to be unlike any other in all of history. Jesus Christ was without sin, yet He would bear the sins of all mankind from all time. The weight of such a burden is beyond comprehension. In His death the Son of God was separated from His Father for the first and only time. This separation is another unimaginably difficult experience that Jesus embraced for our sakes. How amazing is the mercy of the cross—to know and understand that Father, Son, and Holy Spirit were willing to allow a time of separation in their perfect union so that you and I could become partakers of that union. Are you undone in the light of such great sacrifice?

POINT TO PONDER

I am doing my best to receive the perfect love of God in Jesus.

PERSONAL REFLECTION

_____

_____

_____

_____

_____

_____

_____

Day 249

COUNT IT ALL JOY

Consider it pure joy, my brothers and sisters,
whenever you face trials of many kinds.
—James 1:2, niv

W E READ IN Scripture that Jesus did what He did "for the joy set before Him" (Hebrews 12:2). His eyes were fixed on something beyond the cross—the reconciliation of many sons to His Father. Likewise, in the race of each of our lives, God has set a joy before us, and it is the joy of sharing in this reconciliation that Christ has purchased for us. But as we become people who can drink of that joy in its fullness, we may pass through testing and sacrifice when it feels like God has turned His face from us.

It is a precious and vital secret to discover that, for those who seek the face of God, these moments are actually God's invitations into greater power and intimacy. Have you experienced moments of joy with the Lord in the middle of trials? How wonderful that God invites us into such intimacy with Him.

POINT TO PONDER

I trust God to direct me to His joy even in the midst of trials.

PERSONAL REFLECTION

_____

_____

_____

_____

_____

_____

ANOTHER PARADOX

*Beloved, now we are children of God, and it has not appeared
as yet what we will be. We know that when He appears, we
will be like Him, because we will see Him just as He is.*
—1 John 3:2

WE LIVE IN an hour when the face of God is being revealed in
a wonderful outpouring of the Holy Spirit. *There's no limit to
what is possible for one person, church, city, or nation to experience.*
The Bible points to what has been made available, but how, when,
or how much of it can be accessed has never been defined for us.
Boundaries have never been set. While the glory of God in its fullness would kill us, there are measures of His presence that have
been enjoyed by people in the past that far surpass what we now
experience. It is my personal conviction that God has made available to us whatever measure of His glory our bodies can handle.
How do you think you would handle an extraordinary measure of
God's glory? What person from Scripture models this well for you?

POINT TO PONDER

*God knows me well enough not to give me more than
I can handle. His grace is sufficient for me.*

PERSONAL REFLECTION

_____

_____

_____

_____

_____

_____

Day 251

HOLY BALANCE

For we are God's handiwork, created in Christ Jesus to do
good works, which God prepared in advance for us to do.
—EPHESIANS 2:10, NIV

IT MAY SEEM like a strange thing to encourage people to go after something in God with reckless abandon and in the same breath to exhort them to rest. But somehow it's the unique combination of those two things that defines our challenge in this hour. This is the "rest that pursues." What God has done for me is so far beyond my wildest dreams. In one sense I could live in this place with God forever because He is so completely satisfying, yet being with Him stirs up dreams and passions that won't allow me to be stationary. There is so much at stake. I am alive for more! In what ways are you navigating the paradox of being satisfied with the richness of God in your life while at the same time feeling a hunger to engage even more with Him because of this richness?

POINT TO PONDER

I am aiming for a holy balance between that place of
resting in Him while hungering for more of Him.

PERSONAL REFLECTION

_____

_____

_____

_____

_____

_____

BE STILL AND EXPERIENCE GOD

It is like the precious oil upon the head, coming down upon the beard, even Aaron's beard, coming down upon the edge of his robes.
—PSALM 133:2

I LOVE THE PRIVILEGE of spending time with God—the more the better. Being still before Him is an often-underrated activity by those of us who like to accomplish and achieve things in prayer for the King and His kingdom.

This is how it looks for me. Sometimes I'll take just a few minutes in the middle of a workday for His pleasure. I get before the Lord and say something to this effect, "God, I'm here, but I'm not going to ask for anything or perform in any way for You. I'm just going to sit here simply as an object of Your love and let You love me." This is a big deal for me because my usual prayer time is about 75 percent worship and 25 percent petition. Not doing stuff is sometimes hard. Sometimes when I enter that place of rest I get a picture of Him pouring a honey-colored oil all over me as a symbol of His love. It's an overwhelming picture of drowning in His love. Something wonderful begins to happen as He awakens every part of my life to His presence. Have you experienced the oil of His blessings?

POINT TO PONDER

I want the ointment of God's love poured over my life, every day, in generous measure.

PERSONAL REFLECTION

_____

_____

_____

LIVING IN THE GLORY OF GOD

And David was dancing before the LORD with all his might, and David was wearing a linen ephod. So David and all the house of Israel were bringing up the ark of the LORD with shouting and the sound of the trumpet.
—2 SAMUEL 6:14–15

DAVID SAID, "My soul thirsts for You, my flesh yearns for You" (Psalm 63:1). Think about this—before it was possible to be born again through the blood of Jesus, David said that his body actually hungered for God. It is possible to be so drenched in the glory of God through a lifestyle of worship that our bodies discover one of the great purposes for which they were created. We were born to live in the glory of God. Whether it is five minutes or five hours, taking the time with God outside of the need for Christian performance is one of the most important decisions we can make. How do you feel about abandoning yourself in worship simply because He is so worthy?

POINT TO PONDER

I am pressing in for the freedom of abandoned worship.

PERSONAL REFLECTION

_____

_____

_____

_____

_____

_____

_____

Day 254

THE CREATIVE MOMENT

Through him all things were made; without him
nothing was made that has been made.
—JOHN 1:3, NIV

WHEN I SIT before the Lord in times of inactivity, I often remember things that must be done or ideas that will be good for my life or ministry. In my younger years I thought this was always the devil trying to distract me from my time with God. But as I get older, I realize that God is merely showing me that He is concerned about whatever concerns me. Time with Him releases a creativity that is paramount to fulfilling our assignments in life. How often do you tune your ears to the creative whisperings of God in your quiet time with Him? What happens when you do?

POINT TO PONDER

I will listen for God's whisperings and count it all as bless-
ings that He shares His creativity with me.

PERSONAL REFLECTION

_____

_____

_____

_____

_____

_____

_____

_____

_____

Day 255

REVELATION THAT
SATISFIES THE HEART

Delight yourself in the LORD; and He will
give you the desires of your heart.
—PSALM 37:4

I NOW BRING A pen and paper with me into my quiet times with God. As ideas come, I give thanks to God and write them down. By doing so I don't have to try to remember what God has said, but I can return my attention to Him. Not having the pressure to remember details releases me into a creative process. In this kind of prayer time I don't go before Him to get answers and directions. I am there simply to experience His love. But I have found that in that place of communion and love it is His pleasure to give revelation that satisfies our hearts. I just don't want anything to become the chariot that pulls me away from my opportunity to delight myself in the Lord. So I receive what He's giving me and then turn my attention back to the giver Himself. What is the focus of your quiet times? Do you find yourself longing to receive something from God or simply to be in His presence? Or both?

POINT TO PONDER

I long for the place of communion and love
that the Father delights to give me.

PERSONAL REFLECTION

_____

_____

_____

_____

THE NECESSARY FRUIT

*Therefore do not be foolish, but understand
what the Lord's will is.*
—EPHESIANS 5:17, NIV

W E NEED TO develop the capacity to sustain great passion and focus if we are going to become those who set up ambushes for God. There's a word in Scripture that describes this capacity: it is the word *self-control*. Self-control is first and foremost a fruit of the Spirit, which means that you can only get it through intimacy with Him. The fruit of our lives is not something that we work to produce; it is merely the evidence of whatever we spiritually commune with. Self-control in our lives is the evidence of the Holy Spirit's control and influence over us. This particular fruit of the Spirit produces its own fruit. To what degree do you allow the Holy Spirit to control and influence your life, and what are the fruits that flow when He is in control?

POINT TO PONDER

I agree to surrender every aspect of my life to the control and influence of the Holy Spirit.

PERSONAL REFLECTION

———————————————————
———————————————————
———————————————————
———————————————————
———————————————————
———————————————————
———————————————————

Day 257
THE FRUIT OF LOVE

For our proud confidence is this: the testimony of our conscience, that in holiness and godly sincerity, not in fleshly wisdom but in the grace of God, we have conducted ourselves in the world, and especially toward you.
—2 CORINTHIANS 1:12

THERE ARE MANY people in the world who appear to be very self-controlled because they have very disciplined lives in certain areas. Religion offers plenty of ways to control our behavior, as do popular psychology, prescription drugs, and diets. But the practice of these disciplines fails to bring people to the place where the qualities of righteousness, peace, and joy in the Holy Spirit are continually present in their lives. God's love shed abroad in our hearts brings freedom from religion and empty pursuits. This love bears the fruit of self-control that enlivens the lives of believers. What kind of fruit is His love bearing in your heart and your life?

POINT TO PONDER

I will forgo the control of religion for the freedom of the Spirit, bearing much fruit for His kingdom.

PERSONAL REFLECTION

_____

_____

_____

_____

_____

_____

Day 258

IMITATING CHRIST

Therefore be imitators of God, as beloved children.
—Ephesians 5:1

THOSE WHO ARE the most fruitful in the Spirit are not necessarily those who make a first impression of being very controlled and disciplined. If you get to know them, you will find that they are indeed disciplined, but that *discipline* is in fact an inadequate factor for measuring their success in life. It's like coming into the home of a proverbial loving couple and describing the husband as disciplined for going to work and the wife as disciplined for keeping the house clean and cooking dinner. They would probably reply that discipline has nothing to do with it—if they are disciplined, it is simply the fruit of their love and commitment to each other. What does your love and commitment look like?

POINT TO PONDER

I want love to be the overriding fruit of God's Spirit in my life.

PERSONAL REFLECTION

_____

_____

_____

_____

_____

_____

_____

_____

_____

Day 259

GUARD YOUR HEART

Watch over your heart with all diligence, for
from it flow the springs of life.
—PROVERBS 4:23

THE CENTER OF the Christian life is passion for God, and it is this passion that defines the boundaries of our lives. Self-control is the by-product of living in covenant with God. To demonstrate the character trait of true self-control, one must be able to illustrate what it looks like to live in perfect harmony with the values of the Spirit of God. We also show self-control in the way we protect our connection with God from other influences that could distract and dissuade us. When we fail to protect our heart, ungodly influences can flow in. What comes in determines what goes out. Are you mindful to guard your heart? How do you do that?

POINT TO PONDER

Protecting my heart for God is a priority for me.

PERSONAL REFLECTION

_____

_____

_____

_____

_____

_____

_____

_____

_____

Day 260

SET YOUR FACE

For in Him all the fullness of deity dwells in bodily form.
—Colossians 2:9

SELF-CONTROL IS NOT only the ability to say no to all the options and voices that are contrary to the values of the kingdom of God. It is also the ability to say yes to something so completely that all other voices and values are silenced. Jesus demonstrated this best of all. He set His face to go to Jerusalem and die. Nothing could distract Him from His purpose.

The same challenge is yours: set your face toward His purposes, and you will experience the greatest privilege known to humanity. Set your face, and you'll see His face. Jesus is calling you to say yes so completely that all else in your life pales in comparison. Are you willing to do that? Don't wait! Say yes today.

POINT TO PONDER

Today I say yes to Jesus completely.

PERSONAL REFLECTION

Day 261
HOLY INNOVATION

For the creation waits in eager expectation
for the children of God to be revealed.
—ROMANS 8:19, NIV

THROUGHOUT HISTORY THERE have been great numbers of people who refused to settle for whatever had become the norm. We applaud political leaders for being this way, and the same is true for innovators in education and entertainment. The leaders of business and especially technology and medicine attract great accolades from society for breaking out of the confines of past achievements. No doubt this is due in large part to the fact that their breakthroughs bring such benefit to the masses. God is the author of creativity, and He will unleash His creativity through you if you make yourself available. He will put His Spirit upon you and give you great freedom to be a holy innovator. How is He leading you to be innovative in your sphere of influence?

POINT TO PONDER

God is calling me to be a holy innovator who
releases the creativity of heaven on earth.

PERSONAL REFLECTION

_____

_____

_____

_____

_____

_____

SOUND WISDOM—A TREASURE FOR THE RIGHTEOUS

He stores up sound wisdom for the upright; he
is a shield to those who walk in integrity.
—PROVERBS 2:7, ESV

NEW IDEAS CAN be threatening; we tend to want to keep a distance from those who push the edge. The ideas that end up lasting the longest have usually been rejected first. Then they were tolerated, and eventually they are accepted. Jesus is the most radical example of this. When He brought the kingdom of God to earth, many kept their distance because what He did threatened their way of thinking. Even His disciples struggled to understand what He was doing. When you see someone who appears to be pushing the edge spiritually, how do you go about sorting out what you see going on? Do you judge, or do you go to the Lord for His wisdom?

POINT TO PONDER

I will seek the Lord's wisdom and wait on it,
especially when I am confused by what I see.

PERSONAL REFLECTION

Day 263

PASSIONATE HUNGER

It is the glory of God to conceal things, but the
glory of kings is to search things out.
—**PROVERBS 25:2**, ESV

SPIRITUAL LEADERS WHO live on the edge as pioneers tend to suffer conflict. They are also the ones most likely to be rejected at first. Opponents will often do most anything to silence the voice of one who says there is more. Feeling good about ourselves has become such an idol that many have become blind to the prophetic edge of the Scriptures. But some won't settle for what presently exists because they see how much more is available, as illustrated in the life of Jesus. Instead of being blind to the prophetic edges of the Scriptures, they seek them out and embrace them because they know God will burn away the dross. They understand that their place of sonship demands nothing less than their best. How willing are you to let God refine you in the fire of His Word?

POINT TO PONDER

Scripture contains all I need for godly living.

PERSONAL REFLECTION

_____

_____

_____

_____

_____

_____

_____

_____

GOING HIGHER

Ask of Me, and I will surely give the nations as Your inheritance, and the very ends of the earth as Your possession.
—PSALM 2:8

JESUS' LIFE DEMONSTRATES that there is more. And to pull us into our destiny, He said, "Greater works than these he will do; because I go to the Father" (John 14:12). It's hard to imagine, but Jesus declared that there would be a generation that would rise *above* His high watermark. That boggles the mind of many believers because they haven't yet learned what it means to live as beloved sons and daughters in the Father's house. When you live in the Father's house, you get His inheritance. And He wants you to do something with that inheritance. He makes it available so that you can do the greater works that Jesus spoke of. Remember— Jesus only said what He heard the Father say. I don't know about you, but I'm claiming my full inheritance. I'm going for the *more*. How about you? Is anything holding you back?

POINT TO PONDER

I am ready for Jesus to pull me into my destiny.

PERSONAL REFLECTION

_____

_____

_____

_____

_____

_____

_____

Day 265

BUILDING ON FIRM FOUNDATIONS

*Brothers and sisters, I do not consider myself yet to
have taken hold of it. But one thing I do: Forgetting
what is behind and straining toward what is ahead, I
press on toward the goal to win the prize for which
God has called me heavenward in Christ Jesus.*
—PHILIPPIANS 3:13–14, NIV

WE ARE IN the throes of change; a reformation will impact
society on all fronts. This is happening largely because today
there is a new breed of believer. They may look quite different
from each other, but they are known by their love and faith. They
just won't settle for what has been. While there is great admira-
tion for those who have gone before, this group won't stop long
enough to build them a monument or memorial. In fact, this generation knows that the best way to honor past accomplishments is
by building on top of their breakthroughs. Whose breakthroughs
are you building upon?

POINT TO PONDER

I am hungry for the more of God who is always in front of me.

PERSONAL REFLECTION

_____

_____

_____

_____

_____

_____

THE VOICES OF HISTORY

We will not hide these truths from our children; we will
tell the next generation about the glorious deeds of the
Lord, about his power and his mighty wonders.
—Psalm 78:4, nlt

SOME OF OUR most notable heroes of the faith had moments in which God invaded their lives in ways that were often unique, sometimes hard to believe. Their lives were changed dramatically, often in equal proportion to the strangeness of their encounter. Yet all of them were able to manifest an aspect of heaven throughout the remainder of their lives and to blaze a trail for future believers. I encourage you to read the stories of some who made their mark on history—Evan Roberts, John G. Lake, Smith Wigglesworth, Charles Finney, T. L. Osborn, and others. These revivalists are my personal heroes. They helped to shape the course of history. Yet their experiences are but a drop in the bucket compared to what is being released now around the world. Read these stories of divine encounters and their fruit. Hunger in the same way they did. And watch how God chooses to manifest Himself in your life. Who from your generation is blazing a trail for those to come as a result of a dramatic encounter with God?

POINT TO PONDER

I stand ready to receive and run with what God is
currently releasing in the earth to His beloved.

PERSONAL REFLECTION

NOW WHAT?

*But if I say, "I will not remember Him or speak
anymore in His name," then in my heart it becomes
like a burning fire shut up in my bones; and I am
weary of holding it in, and I cannot endure it.*
—JEREMIAH 20:9

I**T IS IMPOSSIBLE** for me to read the stories of these men and
women of God and remain the same. As a result, the fire burning
in my soul gets hotter and brighter for more of God. Through their
testimonies I know that such possibilities exist and the pursuit of
them is worth any price. They inspire me to take risks for God and
pursue Him even more. But most of all I learn to be grateful but
not satisfied. When you think of heroes of the faith, who inspires
you to a place of grateful dissatisfaction?

POINT TO PONDER

*I am grateful but not satisfied, doing my best to
tend God's holy fire down in my soul.*

PERSONAL REFLECTION

_____

_____

_____

_____

_____

_____

_____

_____

_____

HE IS WORTH THE RISK

Then the Spirit of the LORD will come upon you mightily,
and you shall…be changed into another man.
—1 SAMUEL 10:6

I REMEMBER WHEN I was a child and my parents would have guests come over to our house to visit. It was always exciting to be a part of the food and the fun. But it was painful to have to go to bed while they were still there, sitting in our living room, talking and having fun. The laughter that echoed back into my room was just torture. It was impossible for me to sleep in that atmosphere. Sometimes, when I couldn't take it any longer, I would sneak quietly into the hallway, just to listen. I didn't want to miss anything. If my parents caught me, they usually sent me back to bed. But there were a few times when they thought my curiosity was humorous enough to let me come out to be with them just a little longer. The risk was worth it!

I'm in the hallway again. And the thought of missing something that could have been the experience of my generation is pure torture. I can't possibly sleep in this atmosphere, because if I do, I know I'll miss the reason for which I was born. Are you content to sleep through this mighty move of God, or will He find you in the hallway?

POINT TO PONDER

I will not miss even a minute of what God is doing.

PERSONAL REFLECTION

_____

_____

_____

JOY: THE REWARD

A person's wisdom yields patience; it is to
one's glory to overlook an offense.
—PROVERBS 19:11, NIV

THE BIRTH OF Christ was proclaimed with this declaration: "I bring you good news of great joy" (Luke 2:10). Apparently there is *normal* joy and then there is *great* joy. The coming of the Son of God to earth was joyful news that would bring all who received Him into joy itself.

For reasons unknown to me, one of the greatest offenses in this present move of God is the manifestation of joy. Every season that brings new outpourings of the Holy Spirit (revival) interjects a new experience and manifestation that causes offense. It is necessary. Only when we are able to get past the fear of the criticism of others that such an experience brings are we poised to receive all that God has for us. How do you respond when you see someone overcome with the joy of the Lord?

POINT TO PONDER

When I put down the spirit of offense, my
hands are free to receive from God.

PERSONAL REFLECTION

_____

_____

_____

_____

_____

Day 270
MOVING VIOLATION

And I say to you, My friends, do not be afraid of those who kill the body, and after that have no more that they can do.
—LUKE 12:4, NKJV

THE FEAR OF man is the heart and soul of religion—form without power. And most of us are prone to try and bottle up what God is doing so we can analyze and control it to keep us comfortable. It is the way of death. And it must be defeated in us. People seem to be good with the idea of joy as a theological value, but they disdain it as actual experience, especially as a corporate expression. It appears to be out of order. And it is. But whose order does joy actually violate? Have you had an experience of utter joy in the Lord that lifted you up to a place where you cared not what others thought of you? If so, how did it change you? If not, are you hungry for it?

POINT TO PONDER

Nothing else matters when God's joy comes over me.

PERSONAL REFLECTION

_____

_____

_____

_____

_____

_____

_____

_____

_____

DISORDERLY ORDER

Each one of them was hearing them speak in his own language.
They were amazed and astonished, saying, "Why, are not all
these who are speaking Galileans? And how is it that we each
hear them in our own language to which we were born?...But
others were mocking and saying, "They are full of sweet wine."
—ACTS 2:6–8, 13

I WAS PRESENT AT the birth of all three of my children. It was wonderful, amazing—and very offensive. Even though there was laughter and celebration, there was also a big mess with pain and tears. Those in charge didn't seem to be bothered by any of it. But to the uninitiated, it appeared chaotic. The nurses' and doctors' lack of panic helped to calm any misgivings I may have had.

I wonder how often God has purposed to do something wonderful for His people, and then we get nervous and take over because we don't feel comfortable with the situation. I've come to realize that He is not all that concerned about us feeling comfortable. That's why He gave us the Comforter—He planned to make us uncomfortable first. The first outpouring of the Holy Spirit made a lot of people uncomfortable because it was outside their understanding. Many tend to respond the same way today. How do you respond when the presence of God makes you uncomfortable?

POINT TO PONDER

I will trust the Holy Spirit, the Comforter, to help me be comfortable when God does things that are outside my understanding.

PERSONAL REFLECTION

Day 272

JOY MADE FULL

These things I have spoken to you so that My joy may
be in you, and that your joy may be made full.
—John 15:11

THE BIGGEST OFFENSE in joy is laughter. The question comes
often: Where is that in the Bible? It's not that complicated.
Laughter is to salvation what tears are to repentance. We are not
commanded to cry at an altar when we come to Christ. But it happens often, as it should. Our twisted set of values has distorted the
nature of life with Christ. "In Your presence is fullness of joy; in
Your right hand there are pleasures forever" (Psalm 16:11). Is not
laughter at least a part of joy? Does not "fullness" mean that all the
parts are joined together in the whole, whether it include laughter,
smiling, inner happiness, or whatever else? While laughter should
not be our only response to His presence, it is an acceptable and
normal expression of being with God. The fullness of God's joy
is optional for believers—we can take it or leave it. What do you
choose to do?

POINT TO PONDER

I will not settle for less than the fullness of joy that Jesus
offers even if it means looking foolish to others.

PERSONAL REFLECTION

_____

_____

_____

_____

_____

Day 273

REJOICE IN GOD'S GREAT LOVE

*He led me to a place of safety; he rescued
me because he delights in me.*
—Psalm 18:19, nlt

I HAVE FOUND THAT it usually takes greater faith to rejoice in His presence than it does to weep. To rejoice I have to believe that I am acceptable to God. I used to weep a lot with a sense of unworthiness. Hiding behind that was my inability to see that I was acceptable to God. But when people discover that not only are they acceptable to God, but also that He actually delights in them, it's time to rejoice! Paul in his letter to the Philippians said, "Rejoice in the Lord always; again I will say, rejoice!" (Philippians 4:4). It's pretty simple—if you want joy, rejoice. God loves you with an everlasting love. Nothing can quench it. Do you have enough faith in who God is to rejoice in His presence when your heart wants to weep?

POINT TO PONDER

God delights in me and I delight in Him.

PERSONAL REFLECTION

_____

_____

_____

_____

_____

_____

_____

THE EASE OF DIS-EASE

And He did not do many miracles there because of their unbelief.
—MATTHEW 13:58

MUCH OF THE present Christian culture has unintentionally fostered ways of life and thought patterns that allow for people to be heavily burdened and discouraged as the norm. That habit often takes us into the stronghold of unbelief. In this mode we are much better at applauding tears over laughter, poverty over wealth, and the endurance of affliction over receiving quick answers and getting breakthroughs. We are quicker to believe in the supremacy of disease than to believe that God heals, to believe that God's love has limits. God so loved the world that He gave His best. What more does He need to do to show His love? Are you living in a way that unintentionally fosters thoughts and behaviors that bring discouragement and doubt about the goodness of God? What will it take to break you out of that mind-set?

POINT TO PONDER

I will not let unbelief get in the way of what Jesus makes available.

PERSONAL REFLECTION

_____

_____

_____

_____

_____

_____

_____

THE KING HAS COME

Jesus went through all the towns and villages, teaching in their synagogues, proclaiming the good news of the kingdom and healing every disease and sickness.
—MATTHEW 9:35, NIV

OUR PERSPECTIVE IS in need of change. An incorrect view of suffering has allowed the Trojan horse of disease to come in through the gates of the community of the redeemed. Misunderstanding this simple subject has invited the thief to come through the front door, often escorted by the teaching from our greatest pulpits. When we wrestle with the agony of defeat, it is easier to view suffering as the will of God than to accept that we don't fully understand everything about Him. We want an explanation for the unexplainable. Jesus is our explanation and yet we tend to see Him and still not see the Father. Jesus brought the kingdom of God with Him (Mark 1:15). The King has come! Have you accepted what Jesus brought or are you still struggling to receive the great gift of God's Son?

POINT TO PONDER

The kingdom of God has come in my heart in the person of Jesus Christ.

PERSONAL REFLECTION

_____

_____

_____

_____

_____

_____

Day 276

THE LAMB OF GOD

But he was pierced for our transgressions, he was crushed for our iniquities; the punishment that brought us peace was on him, and by his wounds we are healed.
—Isaiah 53:5, NIV

THE SUFFERINGS OF Jesus were realized in the persecution He endured and in the burden He carried for people. He did not suffer with disease. That must be removed from our idea of Christian suffering. It is vain to carry something under the guise of the will of God when it is something that He purchased that He might destroy its power over us. An additional concept to remember is that He suffered that we *might not* have to suffer. For example, He bore stripes on His body applied by a Roman soldier so that they could become His payment for our healing. Take time today to reflect on the great love that Jesus has for you. What is His great love making available and possible for you?

POINT TO PONDER

I can love because He first loved me.

PERSONAL REFLECTION

_____

_____

_____

_____

_____

_____

_____

Day 277

OUR RULE OF LIFE

*Finally, brothers and sisters, whatever is true, whatever
is noble, whatever is right, whatever is pure, whatever is
lovely, whatever is admirable—if anything is excellent or
praiseworthy—think about such things. Whatever you have
learned or received or heard from me, or seen in me —put
it into practice. And the God of peace will be with you.*
—Philippians 4:8–9, niv

If this suffering of His was insufficient, then what did it
accomplish? This error, if carried through, brings the whole issue
of conversion and forgiveness of sins into question. It's true that
the sufferings of Jesus are not yet complete, but they have to do
with our call to righteous living in an unrighteous world. This
brings pressures upon our lives that range from the realm of persecution for living for Christ to the burdens we bear as interces-
sors before our heavenly Father where we plead the case of the lost.
What intentional plan of spiritual disciplines have you set up in
your life to help keep you on the path to growth in holiness?

Point to Ponder

*I am called to righteous living in an unrighteous
world, continually growing in maturity in Christ.*

Personal Reflection

_____

_____

_____

_____

_____

Day 278

UNASHAMED OF THE GOSPEL

My people are destroyed for lack of knowledge.
—Hosea 4:6

IGNORANCE THAT EXALTS itself with a false sense of accomplishment for meeting religious requirements is one of our greatest enemies. For ignorance creates tolerance. And what we tolerate dominates. It dishonors the Lord to disregard His work in order to justify our difficulty to believe for the impossible. It is time to own up to the nature of the gospel and preach it for what it is. It is the answer for every dilemma, conflict, and affliction on the planet. Declare it with boldness and watch Him invade earth once again. Forget about looking foolish. Scripture says that the message of the cross is foolishness to those who have not received it (1 Corinthians 1:18) and the power of God for salvation to everyone who believes (Romans 1:16). Jesus is the One who draws all men to Himself. Preach His gospel with boldness and let Him do the rest. Is anything holding you back?

POINT TO PONDER

*I am not ashamed of the gospel—it is the power of God
for salvation to everyone who believes (Romans 1:16).*

PERSONAL REFLECTION

_____

_____

_____

_____

_____

IT IS FINISHED

*But he endured the suffering that should have been ours,
the pain that we should have borne. All the while we
thought that his suffering was punishment sent by God.*
—Isaiah 53:4, gnt

WHEN WE ALLOW sickness, torment, and poverty to be thought of as the God-ordained tools He uses to make us more like Jesus, we have participated in a very shameful act. There is no doubt He can use them, as He is also known to be able to use the devil himself for His purposes. (He can win with a pair of twos.) But to think these things are released into our lives through His *design*, or that He approved such things, is to undermine the work at Calvary. To do so one must completely disregard the life of Christ and the purpose of the cross. None of us would say that He died for my sins but still intends that I should be bound by sin habits. Neither did He pay for my healing and deliverance so I could continue in torment and disease. His provision for such things is not figurative: it is actual. Is it difficult for you to understand that God is not the author of suffering? Why? Do your reasons line up with God as revealed in Jesus?

POINT TO PONDER

I believe in the full and finished work of the cross.

PERSONAL REFLECTION

FEED ON HIS FAITHFULNESS

*And the work of righteousness shall be peace; and the
effect of righteousness quietness and assurance for ever.*
—Isaiah 32:17, kjv

A FALSE APPROACH TO the Christian life also tends to inflate the power of the devil in the minds of believers. In the wrong atmosphere, complaining and criticism masquerades as information needed for our prayer lives. This mind-set leads us away from the kingdom where there is righteousness, peace, and joy and takes us to a realm of heaviness that emphasizes the devil's strategies and accomplishments. We were not commanded to keep a record of the devil's accomplishments. We were commanded to keep the testimony of God's wonderful work on the earth, making His works our delight and the object of our fascination and study. We are commanded to "feed on His faithfulness" (Psalm 37:3, nkjv). The atmosphere established around us is determined by what treasure we keep (the treasure revealed in our conversations). What treasure, revealed to you at your conversion, do you keep close to your heart?

Point to Ponder

All the treasure I need is found in Jesus.

Personal Reflection

_____

_____

_____

_____

_____

STAND IN AWE OF GOD

You are from God, little children, and have overcome them;
because greater is He who is in you than he who is in the world.
—1 JOHN 4:4

IT IS NOT healthy to have a big devil and a small (impractical) God. It's not that the devil has no power or should be ignored. The apostle Paul taught us against such ignorance. We just can't afford to be impressed by the one who is restricted in power when we serve an all-powerful God. I try to live in such a way that nothing ever gets bigger than my awareness of God's presence. When I lose that perspective, I find that I need to repent, change my focus, and come into the awe of God again. One sure way to be aware of the devil's attempts to gain power in my life is the presence of fear. When I start to become fearful about something, I'm in danger of being more impressed by the devil than by God. The only fear that has any place in the life of the believer is the healthy fear of God. Every other kind of fear should be kicked to the curb immediately. Has the devil been able to dupe you into thinking he has the upper hand? Don't believe him!

POINT TO PONDER

I declare that all things are under the feet of Jesus.

PERSONAL REFLECTION

_____

_____

_____

_____

_____

SHOUT FOR JOY!

At that same time Jesus was filled with the joy of the Holy Spirit, and he said, "O Father, Lord of heaven and earth, thank you for hiding these things from those who think themselves wise and clever, and for revealing them to the childlike. Yes, Father, it pleased you to do it this way."
—Luke 10:21, nlt

Allowing the facts of the devil's work to masquerade as truth undermines joy, the obvious trait of those who are in the kingdom of God. Truth becomes evident only in the mind of Christ, and the mind of Christ is given to joy. "At that very time He rejoiced greatly in the Holy Spirit" (Luke 10:21). Here the word *rejoiced* suggests *shouting and leaping*—not quite the picture of Jesus given to us in movies or sermons. Do you find it hard to imagine Jesus shouting and leaping for joy over who God is? How does that image change the way you think about Jesus and the way you respond to God?

Point to Ponder

I will follow Jesus' example of unashamed adoration of the Father.

Personal Reflection

_____

_____

_____

_____

_____

_____

_____

_____

THE MOTIVATION OF JESUS

Fixing our eyes on Jesus, the pioneer and perfecter of faith.
For the joy set before him he endured the cross, scorning its
shame, and sat down at the right hand of the throne of God.
—HEBREWS 12:2, NIV

JESUS LIVED IN perfect obedience, both in motive and in action.
Everything that Jesus did He did as a man dependent on God.
We also know that Jesus took delight in doing His Father's will.
But it was the Father who brought another element into the equation: "Jesus, the author and perfecter of faith, who for the joy set before Him endured the cross" (Hebrews 12:2). The Father added a reward that was so significant that it would bring the Son of Man through the greatest suffering ever known to a human being. And this One, who was to pay the ultimate price, would receive the ultimate reward—joy. Joy is the reward. Is His joy your ultimate reward?

POINT TO PONDER

Because joy is Jesus' ultimate reward, it will be mine also.

PERSONAL REFLECTION

_____

_____

_____

_____

_____

_____

_____

_____

THE REWARD OF PERSEVERANCE

Therefore, do not throw away your confidence, which has a great reward. For you have need of endurance, so that when you have done the will of God, you may receive what was promised.
—Hebrews 10:35–36

THERE IS A price to pay for following Christ. And there is also a reward for following Christ. Emphasizing the price without the reward is morbid. Going through the pain of discipline for any reason must have an outcome that is worthy of the pain. When the Father wanted to give the best reward to His own Son, He chose to give Him joy. What will people who do not like joy do when they get to heaven? We each have the choice to live in the overflow of His joy or not. Perhaps so many choose the *not* because they haven't tasted real joy that flows from the heart of the Father. He makes it available to each of us. It's our reward. Will you take it?

POINT TO PONDER

I want to taste the real joy that flows from the heart of the Father, no matter the price.

PERSONAL REFLECTION

_____

_____

_____

_____

_____

_____

_____

Day 285
PRAISE HIM!

For you will go out with joy and be led forth with peace; the
mountains and the hills will break forth into shouts of joy
before you, and all the trees of the field will clap their hands.
—Isaiah 55:12

JESUS KNEW THAT the reward of joy was well worth the price.
This is difficult to comprehend. But joy is such a priceless commodity in heaven that it also became the reward for the believer.
"Well done, good and faithful slave....*Enter into the joy of your*
master" (Matthew 25:21, emphasis added). The implication is not
only that joy is the reward but also that we are to enter into our
Father's personal joy. "He who sits in the heavens laughs" (Psalm
2:4). It is the very nature of God that we get to enjoy and celebrate
for eternity. And part of that nature is seen in joy. Think of it as
a mansion you have inherited. Your great privilege is to *enter* each
room of that place with wonder and delight. While it's an honor
just to be there, the shocking reality is that it is your inheritance.
How amazing is this picture from Isaiah, of all of creation—even
the mountains and the hills and the trees—joining together in
great joy and peace to praise God? Does it make you want to shout
His praises?

POINT TO PONDER

I will exalt my God and make His praise glorious!

PERSONAL REFLECTION

_____

_____

_____

THE REALM OF THE FATHER'S JOY

*But grow in the grace and knowledge of our Lord
and Savior Jesus Christ. To him be the glory
both now and to the day of eternity. Amen.*
—2 PETER 3:18, ESV

THE WHOLE UNENDING realm of the Father's joy is your personal possession, and it's yours to explore for eternity. And for you, eternity started the moment you were born again. There are some who think it is carnal to do things to get a reward. Jesus' example should dispel such a notion. Rewards are a part of heaven's economy and are legitimate motivators. In fact, those who lose sight of their reward have not kept a healthy view of eternity. And we don't do well without eternity in mind. Heaven's economy isn't anemic. The shelves of the storehouses in heaven are never in danger of going bare. They are overflowing now and forever. Realms of the Father's joy aren't reserved for some later date. He has made them available in His Son Jesus for your inheritance now. How do you feel about that? Can you receive what Jesus died to give you in this life and the next?

POINT TO PONDER

*I receive everything Jesus makes available
to me now and for all eternity.*

PERSONAL REFLECTION

_____

_____

_____

_____

Day 287

THE JOY OF HIS FACE

*Rejoice in the Lord always; again I will
say, rejoice!... The Lord is near.*
—PHILIPPIANS 4:4–5

JOY IS AN important part of the Father's nature. We experience His joy, and now we inherit His joy as our own. "Righteousness and justice are the foundation of Your throne; lovingkindness and truth go before You. How blessed are the people who *know the joyful sound*! O LORD, *they walk in the light of Your countenance. In Your name they rejoice all the day, and by Your righteousness they are exalted*" (Psalm 89:14–16, emphasis added). How marvelous is this! "See what great love the Father has lavished on us, that we should be called children of God! And that is what we are! The reason the world does not know us is that it did not know him" (1 John 3:1, NIV). When you think of God, do you see Him as joyful, or as one who is too majestic to engage in joy?

POINT TO PONDER

My heavenly Father is a joyful Father. His joy is my inheritance.

PERSONAL REFLECTION

_____

_____

_____

_____

_____

_____

_____

HEAVENLY INVASION

The kingdom of God has come near to you.
—Luke 10:9

OUR JOY IS a direct result of being before the face of God. A countenance filled with joy is the reflection of the Father's delight in us. Those who live before the face of God know the sound of joy, for the sound of joy is the actual sound of heaven. There is no darkness in heaven, not even a shadow, because the light of His face is everywhere. In the same way, there is no discouragement or depression in heaven, because the sound of joy radiates from the face of God. Praying for the kingdom of God to come now "on earth as it is in heaven" (Matthew 6:10) is in essence a prayer for the atmosphere of heaven to permeate the earth and that includes the joy of heaven. How do you see God's kingdom coming on the earth today? Joyfully or otherwise?

POINT TO PONDER

I am thankful that God's kingdom is here now and I can be a part of it.

PERSONAL REFLECTION

_____

_____

_____

_____

_____

_____

_____

_____

TRAINING FOR JOY

*My heart says of you, "Seek his face!" Your
face, Lord, I will seek.*
—Psalm 27:8, niv

IT IS SAID that the mind of a child is trained in joy at an early age. It's as though boundaries are established much like a surveyor would go out onto a piece of property and drive stakes into the ground to mark the property lines. So children's capacity for joy and wholeness is set by their relationship with loving adults who are delighted in them. There is a part of the brain that some call the joy center. This area is activated through the joyful countenance of the parents as they look into the child's eyes. This affirming experience is their actual training for joy. Throughout life we allow ourselves to be trained in many things and take great pride in our accomplishments. Yet, most of us never consider allowing God to train us for joy. Why is that? Are you allowing God to train you for joy?

POINT TO PONDER

I will live joyfully, gazing into His eyes and partaking of His joy.

PERSONAL REFLECTION

_____

_____

_____

_____

_____

_____

_____

TRUST AND SECURITY IN GOD

*The boundary lines have fallen for me in pleasant
places; surely I have a delightful inheritance.*
—Psalm 16:6, NIV

So MANY STRUGGLE with joy. Most people in the church have so little joy in their personal lives. They've not seen the favor and approval from their heavenly Father. The church is crippled in most of its Christian life because people view God as the One who longs to punish instead of save, the One who reminds them of sin instead of forgiving. The church has come to consider lack of joy as pious, as if God created us to drag through life with weighty seriousness. That kind of thinking illustrates our lack of understanding about the nature of God. How do you see God—as stern judge or loving heavenly Father? Based on the example of Jesus, how do you think God wants you to see Him?

Point to Ponder

*I trust God. He is a loving Father, and I am His treasure. He takes
great delight in me even when I fall short of who He intends me to be.*

Personal Reflection

_____

_____

_____

_____

_____

_____

_____

HIS JOYFUL KINGDOM

Every good and perfect gift is from above, coming down from the Father of the heavenly lights, who does not change like shifting shadows.
—James 1:17, niv

Jesus taught His disciples to seek the face of His Father. Those who do so get the affirming realization that we are the "sparkle in His eyes." From this place of intimacy with God we find answers and solutions. Concerning this, Jesus said, "Until now you have asked for nothing in My name; ask and you will receive, so *that your joy may be made full*" (John 16:24, emphasis added). Once again we see that joy is the expected result of a right relationship with God. It is normal. Everything below that is not. Some teach of the balanced Christian life as though we needed equal measures of joy and depression. Foolishness! The kingdom is one of joy. And I don't ever have to leave. Are you in the habit of receiving the good gifts that the Father has for you? Is joy on your list?

Point to Ponder

I receive every good gift the Father has for me.

Personal Reflection

_____

_____

_____

_____

_____

_____

JOY BRINGS STRENGTH

*All the people were weeping when they heard the words of
the law. Then he said to them, "Go, eat of the fat, drink
of the sweet, and send portions to him who has nothing
prepared; for this day is holy to our Lord. Do not be
grieved, for the joy of the LORD is your strength."*
—NEHEMIAH 8:9–10

ONE OF THE greatest revelations of joy is found in the Old Testament. God allowed Israel to taste of the coming reality that would be had by all who were covered in the redemptive work of Christ. But it came when the children of Israel had been standing from early morning until the evening listening to the priests read from the book of Law. Many of them were hearing the Law of God for the first time. When the people didn't understand what was read, priests would run out among the people giving explanation. They saw that God's standard of requirement for their lives was extremely high. They also saw that they had miserably failed God in what He required. This was a shocking moment. And they responded in the most natural way imaginable: with tears. However, Nehemiah and Ezra let the people know that joy and not weeping was the proper response. Was there a time when God turned your weeping into joy? Did it bring you strength?

POINT TO PONDER

The joy of the Lord is what gives me strength.

PERSONAL REFLECTION

_____

_____

Day 293

CULTIVATING YOUR HEART

*I will give you a new heart and put a new spirit in you; I will
remove from you your heart of stone and give you a heart of flesh.*
—EZEKIEL 36:26, NIV

GRIEVING AND WEEPING over sin is thought to be very consistent
with the subject of holiness. Tears are almost synonymous with
repentance. Yet not in the context of Nehemiah 8:9–10, as we read
yesterday. In this context it was a violation. It seems quite strange
that there are times when God's holiness is actually violated by tears.
But it's true. They were mourning and weeping because they saw
they had not even come close to God's purposes for their lives. That
could only come about with an overwhelming conviction of the Holy
Spirit that would give them the chance to see their hearts as He did.
In all honesty, this is the kind of moment many of us preachers look
for—the people are aware of their need for God and His forgiveness.
We look for moments when people are ready to make permanent
changes in their lives. Such brokenness is the climate of the heart
that makes change possible. Yet the Spirit of God has another tool
to bring about His intended transformation. It is the power of celebration—the power of joy. What seasons have you gone through
that brought change? Did they involve repentance or joy?

POINT TO PONDER

*I invite the Holy Spirit to come whenever He will and till the soil
of my heart in preparation for God's seasons of change in my life.*

PERSONAL REFLECTION

_____

_____

SOW IN TEARS, REAP IN JOY

*For His anger is but for a moment, His favor is
for a lifetime; weeping may last for the night, but
a shout of joy comes in the morning.*
—Psalm 30:5

In Nehemiah chapter 8 the priests saw their tears and realized that this was in violation of what God was doing. Their responsibility was now to run out among the people and tell them to stop weeping! They were not only to stop weeping; they were to take it a step further into rejoicing and celebrating. The reason? They *understood* the law. Understanding what God was saying to them was to become the point of their joy, and thus the birth of their joy. When it comes to relationship with God, ignorance is not bliss. God intends that we live as children of the light, understanding who He is and what He has for us. Are you walking as a child of God's light? How does His gift of repentance impact you?

Point to Ponder

*God has called me to know Him and rejoice
in everything He has for me.*

Personal Reflection

ENTER HIS COURTS WITH JOY

How lovely is your dwelling place, O LORD of hosts!
My soul longs, yes, faints for the courts of the LORD;
my heart and flesh sing for joy to the living God.
—PSALM 84:1–2, ESV

I F EVER THERE were a moment in the Old Testament that gave a sneak peak of New Testament life, it is the story from Nehemiah 8, when the people wept before the Lord as they came to understand the Law. It violates all our understanding of the severity of the Law and even violates our understanding of how God moves in revivals. For this reason, many have missed the much-needed revelation of joy through grace that came forth in this present move of God. It is legitimate. It started with joy. How like our loving heavenly Father to revive us with joy. Are you allowing God to joyfully bring restoration to your life?

POINT TO PONDER

I give God permission to revive me with His joy.

PERSONAL REFLECTION

_____

_____

_____

_____

_____

_____

_____

_____

Day 296
SAY YES

Forget the former things; do not dwell on the
past. See, I am doing a new thing! Now it springs
up; do you not perceive it? I am making a way in
the wilderness and streams in the wasteland.
—ISAIAH 43:18–19, NIV

TRUE BELIEVERS ARE being positioned to display the wonders of
the almighty God to the world around us. The Bible actually
calls us a new creation, a new race of people that had never existed
before. Many of the prophecies that Jesus made concerning His
church have never been fulfilled. The "greater works" of John 14:12
are yet to come upon an entire generation. But this is the hour all
the prophets spoke of. Kings and prophets longed to see what we
have seen. It is important that we say yes to all that has been provided for us through the blood of Jesus. It is time for the people of
God to rise as one and display the power and glory of God. Are
you willing to say yes to *all* that has been provided through the
cross?

POINT TO PONDER

I say yes to everything that Jesus made available to me.

PERSONAL REFLECTION

_____

_____

_____

_____

_____

_____

Day 297

THE ULTIMATE TEST

If I do not do the works of My Father, do not believe Me;
but if I do them, though you do not believe Me, believe
the works, so that you may know and understand
that the Father is in Me, and I in the Father.
—John 10:37–38

JESUS ONCE TOLD a crowd of people, "If I do not do the works of My Father, do not believe Me" (John 10:37). Angels, the prophets, nature, and Scripture all testified about who Jesus was. Yet He was willing to hang the credibility of all those witnesses on one thing—the works of the Father. Without question, the works of the Father that Jesus is referring to are the miracles recorded throughout the Gospel of John. If Jesus didn't do miracles, people were not required to believe. I look for the day when the church, His body, makes the same statement to the world around us: if we don't do the works of our Father, do not believe us. Are you willing to make such a statement?

POINT TO PONDER

If I do not do the works of my Father, do not believe me.

PERSONAL REFLECTION

_____

_____

_____

_____

_____

_____

JESUS—PERFECT THEOLOGY

If a house is divided against itself, that
house will not be able to stand.
—Mark 3:25

JESUS CHRIST IS perfect theology. For anyone who wants to know the will of God, look at Jesus. He is the will of God. Some pray, "If it be Thy will," as though God's will is unclear. You would have to ignore the life of Christ to come to such a conclusion.

How many people came to Jesus for healing and left sick? None. How many came to Him for deliverance and left His presence still under torment? None. How many life-threatening storms did Jesus bless? None. How many times did Jesus withhold a miracle because the person who came to Him had too little faith? Never. He often addressed their small faith or unbelief, but He always left them with a miracle as a way to greater faith. Jesus Christ, the Son of God, perfectly illustrates the will of God the Father. To think otherwise is to put the Father and the Son at odds. And a house divided will fall. Is Jesus your perfect theology?

POINT TO PONDER

God's perfect will is revealed in Jesus.

PERSONAL REFLECTION

_____

_____

_____

_____

_____

_____

Day 244

GOD IS IN CHARGE

So then do not be foolish, but understand
what the will of the Lord is.
—EPHESIANS 5:17

WHY DID JESUS raise the dead? Because not everyone dies in God's timing. We cannot have the Father choosing to do one thing and Jesus contradicting it with a miracle. Not everything that happens is God's will. God gets blamed for so much in the name of His sovereignty. We have concealed our irresponsibility regarding the commission that Jesus gave us under the veil of God's sovereignty for long enough. Yes, God can use tragedy for His glory. But God's ability to rule over bad circumstances was never meant to be the evidence that those circumstances were His will. Instead it was to display that no matter what happens, He is in charge and will rework things to our advantage and to His glory. Our theology is not to be built on what God hasn't done. It is defined by what He does and is doing. What do you do when circumstances cause you to question the will of God?

POINT TO PONDER

God is in charge. I will trust what He has
done and what I see Him doing.

PERSONAL REFLECTION

_____

_____

_____

_____

THE WILL OF GOD

*I can of Myself do nothing. As I hear, I judge; and
My judgment is righteous, because I do not seek My
own will but the will of the Father who sent Me.*
—JOHN 5:30, NKJV

THE WILL OF God is perfectly seen in the person of Jesus Christ. No one who ever came to Him was turned away. The Bible celebrates the man healed by the pool of Bethesda. If that were done today, the Christian periodicals would interview the people by the pool who were not healed. Theologians would then use the absence of a miracle for the others as a proof text, saying, "It's not always God's will to heal." In the absence of experience bad theology is formed. God wants you to experience Him and His kingdom so that you can know Him better. Because when you know Him better you can receive Him more fully and represent Him with the honor due His great name. When you know His will, you can do His will. In one sense it's quite simple. How complicated or simple is the will of God to you?

POINT TO PONDER

I won't let my experience define my theology.

PERSONAL REFLECTION

_____

_____

_____

_____

_____

_____

Day 301
THE GREAT JOURNEY

As You sent Me into the world, I also
have sent them into the world.
—John 17:18

EVERYONE WHO CONFESSES to know Jesus Christ in a personal relationship is assigned the privilege of re-presenting Him. "As the Father has sent Me, I also send you" (John 20:21). The mandate is clear and strong, and there are no options. Discovering who He is and what He is like is the great journey for the believer. It is an eternal quest, one that we will delight in forever. But in our discovery is the responsibility to make Him known. Do we do so by preaching the Word? Yes. But He is also to become manifest through our lives. We are to become a portrait of God. This is part of what being the body of Christ means. How are you a portrait of God, manifesting Him to the world around you?

POINT TO PONDER

I am discovering who God is so that I can look like Him in the world.

PERSONAL REFLECTION

_____

_____

_____

_____

_____

_____

_____

_____

SEEING CLEARLY

*Lord, I have heard of your fame; I stand in awe of
your deeds, Lord. Repeat them in our day, in our time
make them known; in wrath remember mercy.*
—HABAKKUK 3:2, NIV

W E BECOME LIKE what we worship. Seeing God changes us. Worship increases our capacity to see. But if we view God through an incomplete Old Testament lens, then we are likely to carry a message of wrath and anger, thinking we are honoring God. It's not that God cannot show anger. The whole point is that He wants to show mercy, and He looks for those who will intercede on behalf of those who have no hope. He is the One who said mercy is victorious over judgment. An incomplete revelation from the old covenant cannot produce fruit of the new. Those who don't see Him through the New Testament revelation in Scripture try to re-create who He is through human reasoning. It is usually a distorted view of an angry God. But sometimes it's the other extreme—a God who ignores sin. Neither is correct, and both are products of the minds of those who cannot see.

He is perfect in *love, power, character,* and *wisdom.* These expressions of His nature must be seen in and through us. How are you an expression of God's perfect nature to others?

POINT TO PONDER

*The perfect expression of God's nature seen in
me and through me is my act of worship.*

PERSONAL REFLECTION

_____

_____

Day 303
SACRIFICIAL LOVE

We love, because He first loved us.
—1 JOHN 4:19

IT IS AN honor to love, for God loved us first. We only give away what we've received. God set the standard for giving love that demands nothing in return. He also set the standard for love that is sacrificial. "For God so loved the world, that He gave..." (John 3:16). It is our privilege to give time, money, attention, friendship, and so on. Sacrificial giving is sacrificial living. While we can give without loving, we can't love without giving. By nature, love does not require anything in return, or it is not love. The real test of love is when we are able to love the unlovely, who are unable to give in return. Our human nature can make this kind of love very challenging. But with God's nature, sacrificial love becomes possible. Is sacrificial love a part of the way you live?

POINT TO PONDER

God sets my standard for love.

PERSONAL REFLECTION

_____

_____

_____

_____

_____

_____

_____

_____

THE "GO" OF THE GOSPEL

Go therefore and make disciples of all the nations.
—MATTHEW 28:19

MANY OF US grew up thinking that the way we reach out to our community is to pray hard that people would attend church meetings in hopes of them being converted. It's hard for us to be effective in demonstrating the love of God if people are required to come to us. It is in *going* that we are most likely to give authentically. The story of the good Samaritan stands out as a good example of love. He adopted the problems of the injured stranger as his own. When he couldn't stick around to help the man firsthand, he hired someone to do what he was unable to do. It is an amazing story of loving a total stranger. How do you "go" for the gospel?

POINT TO PONDER

The gospel comes into the world as I go into the world.

PERSONAL REFLECTION

_____

_____

_____

_____

_____

_____

_____

_____

_____

_____

Day 305

DEMONSTRATE HIS LOVE

*For God so loved the world, that He gave His
only begotten Son, that whoever believes in Him
shall not perish, but have eternal life.*
—JOHN 3:16

I HAVE HEARD TEACHING on the subject of giving to the poor and needy that emphasizes our stewardship instead of compassion. It basically means that you don't want to give to someone who will not use what was given properly. My opinion is that there is too much concern about giving something to someone who might misuse what is given. That didn't stop God. While we do have a responsibility for good management of what God has given us, we are not responsible for what another person does with what we've given them. We are responsible to love, and love requires giving. Even if a person misuses the money or gift I gave him, the message of love has been demonstrated. Giving His love away is the goal.

People who get breakthroughs in the miracle realm face a temptation: it's easy to pursue miracles for miracles' sake. But the greater ambition ought to be that in all we do we display the love of God. What are you doing to display the love of God?

POINT TO PONDER

Giving away God's love is my responsibility and my goal.

PERSONAL REFLECTION

_____

_____

_____

_____

Day 306

IN ALL FAITH, BELIEVE

And walk in love, as Christ loved us and gave himself
up for us, a fragrant offering and sacrifice to God.
—EPHESIANS 5:2, ESV

THE TENDENCY TO embrace the concept of God being an angry Father is done in equal proportion to a person's inability to demonstrate His power. There is a connection between our belief system and what actually flows through us. If we don't see Jesus' life as ultimate illustration of the will of God, we will continually undermine our ability to display it. Jesus Himself said many times that He only did what He saw the Father doing and only said what He heard the Father say. Love is His greatest commandment and His greatest gift. If we live with all faith, believing in Him, what is in Him will flow through us. What is your concept of God, and what is flowing through you as a result? Do you accept the fragrant offering of Jesus as an illustration of the love of the Father?

POINT TO PONDER

The life of Jesus is the ultimate illustration of the will of God.

PERSONAL REFLECTION

ONE IN THE SPIRIT

But the one who joins himself to the Lord is one spirit with Him.
—1 Corinthians 6:17

POWERLESSNESS IS SUCH an aberration that we are either compelled to seek for a fresh baptism in the Spirit until the power that was promised becomes manifested through us, or we create doctrinal reasons to comfort ourselves in powerlessness. I don't want comfort. I want power. It is never OK to live short of the miraculous. I am indebted to Him in this matter: He gave the example, sent the wonderful Holy Spirit, and gave us His Word in our commission. What else must He do? We owe Him miracles as a testimony that He is alive and that His face is turned toward us. The Spirit of the resurrected Christ, that same Spirit that anointed Jesus for ministry, lives within us. The gospel makes sufficient provision for this issue to be settled for anyone who seeks His face with reckless abandon. Christ is in you, the hope of glory! Will you seek His face with reckless abandon today?

POINT TO PONDER

*I will seek with reckless abandon the face
of the One who lives within me.*

PERSONAL REFLECTION

_____

_____

_____

_____

_____

_____

A HOLY COMBINATION

*But I say, walk by the Spirit, and you will
not carry out the desire of the flesh.*
—GALATIANS 5:16

I'VE HEARD PEOPLE say that if they had to choose between purity and power, they'd choose purity. That sounds good, but it's an illegal choice. The two must not be separated. They are two sides of the same coin, and they must remain intact. I have told our church family, "I'm not impressed with anyone's life that does not have character. But I'm not happy with that life until there is power." It's not OK to settle for one or the other. God intends that both be present in the life of the believer. A life of purity opens the door to His power. But His power does not flow when purity is absent. If you are struggling with a lack of purity or power in your life, what needs to be done to remedy your situation?

POINT TO PONDER

*I will walk by the Spirit, in the purity and
power that is available to me.*

PERSONAL REFLECTION

_____

_____

_____

_____

_____

_____

_____

Day 309

ABIDING IN CHRIST

I am the vine, you are the branches; he who
abides in Me and I in him, he bears much fruit,
for apart from Me you can do nothing.
—John 15:5

CHRISTLIKE CHARACTER IS not merely being victorious over sin issues. It is the realized effect of the life of faith, which is righteousness, peace, and joy, which is, as I have already made clear, Paul's definition of the kingdom. These three things demonstrate the character of Christ in the life of a believer. When you live in the realm of God's kingdom by faith, what is His becomes available to you. You take on the character of Christ as you grow more like Him, from glory to glory. You live as a branch attached to the vine, rooted deeply enough in Christ to demonstrate His character and His kingdom. What a marvelous way to live! If this doesn't describe your life, perhaps you have become disconnected from the vine. How can you reconnect to Jesus?

Point to Ponder

I will abide in the vine that is Jesus so that my
life continually reflects His character.

Personal Reflection

_____

_____

_____

_____

_____

_____

THE SON OF RIGHTEOUSNESS

*But for you who fear My name, the sun of righteousness
will rise with healing in its wings; and you will go
forth and skip about like calves from the stall.*
—MALACHI 4:2

LIVING RIGHTEOUSLY MEANS that I live completely for God, with no attachments to ungodly things. Living for God means I reject the inferior things that give temporary satisfaction because only the kingdom of God satisfies. Righteousness has been reduced to morality for some. Morality is essential, but it is the bottom rung of the ladder. It's the first step. But true righteousness is demonstrated in Christlike indignation toward injustice. It seeks to vindicate mistreatment of the poor, the widow, and the unborn. It also stirs our hearts toward those who are bound by disease, for it was the sun of *righteousness* that rose with healing in His wings. Healing is an expression of His righteousness on our behalf. What rung of the ladder are you currently standing on?

POINT TO PONDER

*Let my heart be so stirred by injustice that
righteous living becomes my norm.*

PERSONAL REFLECTION

_____

_____

_____

_____

_____

_____

Day 311

SANCTIFIED BY HIS TRUTH

*I do not ask You to take them out of the world, but to keep them
from the evil one. They are not of the world, even as I am not
of the world. Sanctify them in the truth; Your word is truth.*
—John 17:15–17

IT SADDENS ME to see Christians who will not associate with
unbelievers because they want to be separate from the world,
yet their lifestyles are the same as unbelievers. The early church
associated with unbelievers but didn't live like them. That day is
returning as the issue of character is being addressed once again,
this time rightly partnered with power. Unless we live in relationship with Him, we don't know Him and He will not know us.
"Many will say to Me in that day, 'Lord, Lord, have we not prophesied in Your name, cast out demons in Your name, and done many
wonders in Your name?' And then I will declare to them, 'I never
knew you; depart from Me, you who practice lawlessness!'" (Matthew 7:21–23, NKJV). Do you see your life sanctified by His truth
in such a way that you are fully known to Jesus?

POINT TO PONDER

I will live in the righteousness of Christ, sanctified by His truth.

PERSONAL REFLECTION

———————————————————
———————————————————
———————————————————
———————————————————
———————————————————
———————————————————

REIGNING IN LIFE

For if, because of one man's trespass, death reigned through that one man, much more will those who receive the abundance of grace and the free gift of righteousness reign in life through the one man Jesus Christ.
—ROMANS 5:17, ESV

LIKE PEACE AND joy, righteousness is a gift. "Those who receive the abundance of grace and of the gift of righteousness will reign in life through the One, Jesus Christ" (Romans 5:17). The word *reign* in this verse means "to be king." The imagery is strong. Righteousness enables a person to exercise dominion over their life and not live as a victim. Abraham's nephew, Lot, fell short of this reality when the Scriptures say that he was "oppressed by the sensual conduct of unprincipled men" (2 Peter 2:7). The conduct of others affected and oppressed him. Life in God has been designed in such a way that righteousness in our lives actually affects the people around us, much the same way as a king's reign affects everyone under his influence. This is a central theme in the subject of city transformation. Are you eager to see cities transformed? Is righteous living being expressed in your life to the degree that it affects those around you?

POINT TO PONDER

I can reign in life through Jesus Christ.

PERSONAL REFLECTION

_____

_____

_____

Day 313

ABIDING IN HIS PEACE

Now may the Lord of peace Himself continually grant you
peace in every circumstance. The Lord be with you all!
—2 Thessalonians 3:16

PEACE IS MORE than the absence of noise, conflict, and war. It is the presence of the One who exercises military authority over everything that is in conflict with His dominion. As we enjoy His order and calm, the powers of darkness are destroyed by His overwhelming magnificence. It is a life of *rest* for us but a life of *terror* for the powers of darkness. For this reason the Bible declares, "The God of peace will soon crush Satan under your feet" (Romans 16:20). As His peace comes upon us, our enemies are destroyed. When anxiety and fear approach, we must get back to our place of peace. It is our rightful inheritance in Christ and is the place from which we live. This attribute of heaven is the evidence of a victory that has already been won. It is this characteristic that so frustrates the devil. Our not being terrified by him because of our abiding peace actually terrifies the enemy of our soul. What do you do when anxiety and fear start to creep into your thinking? Where do you turn, and who do you turn to?

POINT TO PONDER

I embrace the peace of God that is always available to me.

PERSONAL REFLECTION

_____

_____

_____

_____

RECEIVING HIS LOVE

I will greatly rejoice in the LORD; my soul shall exult in my God, for he has clothed me with the garments of salvation; he has covered me with the robe of righteousness, as a bridegroom decks himself like a priest with a beautiful headdress, and as a bride adorns herself with her jewels.
—ISAIAH 61:10, ESV

JOY BELONGS TO the believer. Joy is to salvation what tears are to repentance. It is one of the most essential expressions of abiding faith. Being stern and harsh is overrated. Any unbeliever can do that. Jesus was only this way toward those who rejected Him but should have known better. They called Him a drunk and glutton simply because drunks and gluttons experienced His love and acceptance. Faith believes I am accepted by God, and there is no power or authority that can take that away. Are you humbled by the knowledge that nothing can separate you from the love of God?

POINT TO PONDER

I am loved by God, and nothing can take His love from me.

PERSONAL REFLECTION

_____

_____

_____

_____

_____

_____

_____

HE HAS MADE ME GLAD

*For You, O LORD, have made me glad by what You have
done, I will sing for joy at the works of Your hands.*
—PSALM 92:4

IF YOU LACK joy, there is one way you can engage in the process
of gaining ever-increasing joy: learn to rejoice. A choice to rejoice
cannot depend on circumstances, because it operates from the
heart of faith. It lives regardless of what has happened, embracing
the realities of His world that can only be accessed by trust in God
and His Word. Rejoicing releases joy. Isaiah 61:3–4 says that God
will give us "a crown of beauty for ashes, the oil of joy instead of
mourning, and a garment of praise instead of a spirit of despair.
They will be called oaks of righteousness, a planting of the LORD
for the display of his splendor. They will rebuild the ancient ruins
and restore the places long devastated; they will renew the ruined
cities that have been devastated for generations" (NIV). This is an
incredible picture of transformation in the midst of joy. When
we joyfully celebrate who God is and what He has done, joy is
released in a way that changes things. Are you ready to become a
joyful transformer?

POINT TO PONDER

I will allow God to transform me so that I can be a joyful transformer.

PERSONAL REFLECTION

REJOICE IN HIS LOVE

So he brought his people out with joy, his chosen ones with singing. And he gave them the lands of the nations, and they took possession of the fruit of the peoples' toil.
—Psalm 105:43–44, esv

PERHAPS THE GREATEST secret regarding joy is in discovering God's joy over us. The Bible tells us, "The joy of the Lord is your strength" (Nehemiah 8:10). God has joy. And it's His joy over us that makes us strong! That truth sets us free unlike anything else. Rejoice, for He is delighted in you! His Word says He will bring you out with joy and singing from whatever is oppressing you, into a place of plenty. And into your hands He will put the nations and all that they possess. God has blessings for you that are released when you rejoice in Him and receive His joy. He is waiting. Will you set aside time today to receive His love and rejoice that He delights in you?

POINT TO PONDER

God's joy over me sets me free.

PERSONAL REFLECTION

_____

_____

_____

_____

_____

_____

_____

Day 317

WISDOM

But the wisdom that comes from heaven is first of all pure; then peace-loving, considerate, submissive, full of mercy and good fruit, impartial and sincere.
—JAMES 3:17, NIV

JESUS IS CALLED *the Desire of the Nations.* To make us successful in the commission to disciple nations He chose to live inside of us. This gives us the potential of appealing to the world around us. That is far from the present experience of most of us. While sinners loved to be with Jesus, they seldom like to be with us. It is up to us to find out why and fix it. Part of the reason is because we tend to be very impractical, answering questions that few people are asking, bringing direction that no one is looking for. How can you be more like Jesus to those around you who are outside of Christ?

POINT TO PONDER

I want the wisdom of heaven so that I can bring the bread of heaven to the hungry.

PERSONAL REFLECTION

_____

_____

_____

_____

_____

_____

_____

_____

_____

Day 318
LIVING WATER

*Many of the Samaritans from that town believed in him
because of the woman's testimony, "He told me everything
I ever did." So when the Samaritans came to him, they
urged him to stay with them, and he stayed two days. And
because of his words many more became believers.*
—JOHN 4:39–41, NIV

IT IS GOD'S time for His people to become highly esteemed by unbelievers again (we prefer to call them "pre-believers"). Jesus has all the answers to all the world's problems. We have legal access to the mysteries of the kingdom. His world is the answer for this one. No matter the problem, whether it is medical, political, or as simple as a traffic-flow problem in our neighborhood or a conflict on the local school board, Jesus has the answers. Not only that, but He also desires to reveal them to us and through us. His method of choice is to use His children, the descendants of the Creator, to represent Him in such matters. Are you ready and willing to represent Jesus, the living water, to those who are thirsty?

POINT TO PONDER

Christ in me, the hope of glory, is an unending fountain of living water.

PERSONAL REFLECTION

_____

_____

_____

_____

_____

Day 319

OUR GREAT INHERITANCE

Then the King will say to those on his right, "Come, you
who are blessed by my Father, inherit the Kingdom
prepared for you from the creation of the world."
—Matthew 25:34, NLT

IT'S HARD FOR us to bring solutions for this world's dilemmas when our hope (end-time theology) is eagerly anticipating the destruction of the planet. Both Jesus and the apostle Paul said we inherit this world. Our correct stewardship should start now. To ignore this part of the commission because of the conviction that the world cannot be made perfect before Jesus' return is very similar to ignoring the poor because Jesus said they'd always be with us. It is irresponsible stewardship of our commission and anointing. What is your end-time theology and is it helping or hindering your desire to properly steward your kingdom inheritance?

POINT TO PONDER

Jesus will return for a spotless bride, restoring that which
was lost. I receive my inheritance and give Him everything
so that I can participate in this restoration process.

PERSONAL REFLECTION

_____

_____

_____

_____

_____

_____

Day 320

WISDOM CELEBRATES GOD

Oh, the depth of the riches both of the wisdom and
knowledge of God! How unsearchable are His
judgments and unfathomable His ways!
—ROMANS 11:33

SOLOMON'S WISDOM SILENCED the queen of Sheba when he answered her questions about life. But when God chose to list the things that impressed her, He recorded a list that would normally be boring, that is, outside of wisdom. The Scriptures list them this way: "the house that he had built, the food on his table, the seating of his servants, the service of his waiters and their apparel, his cupbearers, and his entryway by which he went up to the house of the LORD" (1 Kings 10:4–5, NKJV). These are all everyday things. Only the creative expression of God could arrest the heart of a queen with the ordinary. She had already seen wealth and treasures. But she was now looking at mundane things that had taken on meaning through the creative expression of God through a man. And it made her speechless.

It's time for the world to become speechless again as they become aware of our approach to the simplicities of life—this time with divine wisdom. Are you eager for the world to become speechless in the presence of God? Are the simple and mundane things around you being transformed by the expression of God through you?

POINT TO PONDER

I want to effect transformation through God's wisdom.

PERSONAL REFLECTION

320

Day 321

THE RENEWED MIND

*You were taught, with regard to your former way of
life, to put off your old self, which is being corrupted
by its deceitful desires; to be made new in the attitude
of your minds; and to put on the new self, created to
be like God in true righteousness and holiness.*
—EPHESIANS 4:22–24, NIV

YOU KNOW YOUR mind is renewed when the impossible looks log-ical. The most consistent way to display the kingdom of God is through the renewed mind. It is much more than thinking right thoughts. It is how we think—from what perspective. Done cor-rectly, we are to "reason" from heaven toward earth.

Four *cornerstones of thought* have changed how we do life. They must become more than doctrines that we agree with. They must become perspectives that change how we approach life—attitudes that define the culture we have chosen to live in. What are some of your attitudes that are defining the spiritual culture in which you currently live?

POINT TO PONDER

I choose to live in the culture of heaven.

PERSONAL REFLECTION

_____

_____

_____

_____

_____

_____

Day 322
GOD IS GOOD

If you then, being evil, know how to give good gifts to
your children, how much more will your Father who is
in heaven give what is good to those who ask Him!
—MATTHEW 7:11

I OFTEN OPEN OUR meetings on Sunday with this announcement: "God is in a good mood." It shocks people. As simple as it is, it is not really believed by very many people. But God is really secure in His sovereignty, and He rejoices in the bride of His Son. God thinks the price paid is worth what they're getting. The ones with the angry messages from our pulpits just need to meet the Father. He is really good all the time. He's better than we think, so let's change the way we think. If you encountered someone who was struggling to believe that God is good, how would you explain His goodness to them?

POINT TO PONDER

The fullness of the goodness of God is found in Jesus Christ.

PERSONAL REFLECTION

NOTHING IS IMPOSSIBLE

For nothing will be impossible with God.
—LUKE 1:37, ESV

NOTHING IS IMPOSSIBLE" has become a slogan that defines our approach to life. As believers we are assigned to invade what has previously been called impossible. Some Christians shy away from the pursuit of miracles because they consider them impossible. The saddest part of their story is that they think the rest of the Christian life is possible. Not so! The whole thing is impossible to the natural mind. Only God can say from experience, "Nothing is impossible." But to give us access to a realm that only He enjoys, He added, "All things are possible for him who believes" (Mark 9:23). Do you live from a place where all things are possible with God? If not, are you getting closer?

POINT TO PONDER

I believe all things are possible with God.

PERSONAL REFLECTION

_____

_____

_____

_____

_____

_____

_____

_____

_____

Day 324

WE FIGHT FROM THE VICTORY OF CHRIST

For our struggle is not against flesh and blood, but against the rulers, against the powers, against the world forces of this darkness, against the spiritual forces of wickedness in the heavenly places. Therefore, take up the full armor of God, so that you will be able to resist in the evil day, and having done everything, to stand firm.
—EPHESIANS 6:12–13

WE DO NOT do warfare in order to win. Rather it is to enforce the victory that Jesus has already won on our behalf. We war from His victory toward a given situation. That changes our perspective, which is half the battle. For the believer, most closed heavens are between the ears. When we believe things are dark and feed our soul on that reality, we have a big battle to fight. Through intimidation the enemy has succeeded in putting us into a defensive posture. It's the wrong position—we are on offense, and we have the ball. We've had it ever since Jesus commanded us to *"go into all the world"* (Mark 16:15, emphasis added). If you *have the ball,* then what does it look like for you to fight from His victory?

POINT TO PONDER

I fight from the victory of Christ toward every situation in life because He has already won the victory.

PERSONAL REFLECTION

_____

_____

_____

Day 325

I AM SIGNIFICANT

*God chose the lowly things of this world and the despised
things—and the things that are not—to nullify the
things that are, so that no one may boast before him.*
—1 CORINTHIANS 1:28–29, NIV

IT IS EASIER to say that *we are* significant, instead of saying *I am
significant.* Yet it is the discovery of this truth that liberates us
into true humility. Anyone who speaks of his or her own significance, but goes into pride, never really got this important revelation. There is a humility that comes from seeing our past. But the
greater measure of humility comes from seeing our future. What
is before us is impossible without God's favor, strength, and guidance. Dependence on Him is the result of the discovery of personal significance. Have you undertaken the discovery of your
significance to God? If not, get started. He wants you to know
who you are!

POINT TO PONDER

*I face the future dependent on God because without Him
nothing is possible and with Him all things are possible.*

PERSONAL REFLECTION

_____

_____

_____

_____

_____

_____

GOD'S ULTIMATE PLAN

Devote yourselves to prayer, being watchful and thankful.
—COLOSSIANS 4:2

GOD HAS TURNED our hearts once again to seek His face. Prayer movements are springing up in most every stream of the body of Christ. What Lou Engle has done with TheCall is literally shaping the course of history as an entire generation is being summoned by God to change a nation through prayer and intercession. In light of this shift in the Spirit, we too must embrace the call to pray. But as we do, let's learn to pray as Jesus did—for God's will to be done on earth as it is in heaven. We must be diligent to have no other agenda. Jesus is our model. He has demonstrated what it looks like to passionately adhere to the will of God in all things. And He has given us His Spirit to help us. If God is stirring your heart to prayer, to partake in the great joy of coming before His throne with confidence, don't delay. If prayer is not one of your strengths, what can you do to increase your prayer time and your confidence to pray?

POINT TO PONDER

I will pray continually and give thanks in all circumstances (1 Thessalonians 5:16–17).

PERSONAL REFLECTION

_____

_____

_____

_____

_____

Day 327

EFFECTIVE PRAYER

And if we know that He hears us in whatever we ask, we know that we already possess what we have asked of Him.
—1 John 5:15, bsb

THERE IS NO record of Jesus asking His Father to heal someone, nor is there record of Him crying for the Father's deliverance in a life-threatening storm. Instead He had gained a place of authority in prayer so that He could simply bring the command and watch the will of His Father being done.

It's time to use a good part of our prayer time to actually seek His face. The result will be clearly seen, for when we speak, things will happen—and when we touch people in ministry, we will bring them into an encounter with God that changes everything. Do you trust God to answer your prayers in His timing, in accordance with His good and perfect will?

Point to Ponder

I have confidence that God hears my prayers and answers them according to His perfect will.

Personal Reflection

_____

_____

_____

_____

_____

_____

_____

Day 328

A PEOPLE OF HIS GLORY

But now in Christ Jesus you who formerly were far off
have been brought near by the blood of Christ.
—Ephesians 2:13

JESUS CHRIST WAS entirely God. He was not a created being. Yet He became a man and lived entirely within man's limitations. His ability to demonstrate power, walk on water, and carry out countless other divine manifestations was completely due to the fact that He was without sin and was totally yielded to the Holy Spirit. He became the model for everyone who would experience the cleansing of sin by the blood of Jesus.

The forgiveness that God gives puts every believer in a place without sin. The only question that remains is how empowered by the Holy Spirit we are willing to be. How will you answer that question?

POINT TO PONDER

I am washed clean by the blood of Jesus to do
good works to the glory of His name.

PERSONAL REFLECTION

_____

_____

_____

_____

_____

_____

_____

_____

EXAMPLES FOR US

Jesus answered, "My Kingdom is not an earthly kingdom. If it were, my followers would fight to keep me from being handed over to the Jewish leaders. But my Kingdom is not of this world."
—John 18:36, NLT

MOST OF THE experiences of Jesus recorded in Scripture were prophetic examples of realms in God available to the believer. The Mount of Transfiguration raised the bar significantly on potential human experience. The goal should never be to talk with Moses and Elijah, and anyone who has that as a focus would concern me. The overwhelming lesson in this story is that Jesus Christ, the *Son of Man*, had the glory of God upon Him. Jesus' face shone with God's glory, similar to Moses' after he came down from the mountain. But Jesus' clothing also radiated the glory of God, as if to say this was a new era as compared to Moses' day. In this era the boundaries had changed—a veil could not be used to cover Jesus' face as it shone with glory, as the veil itself would also soon radiate with the same glory. We impart what God has given us to change the nature of whatever we touch. Remember that touching the edge of Jesus' garment healed a woman. In this kingdom things are different. When you pray, "Your kingdom come," do you think of His kingdom coming on the earth or into your heart, or both?

POINT TO PONDER

I can extend Jesus' supernatural kingdom into the world.

PERSONAL REFLECTION

_____

_____

Day 330

COVENANT POWER

*Do not leave Jerusalem, but wait for the gift my
Father promised, which you have heard me speak
about. For John baptized with water, but in a few
days you will be baptized with the Holy Spirit.*
—ACTS 1:4–5, NIV

ONLY PETER, JAMES, and John were part of the transfiguration. It was so extreme that Jesus warned them not to tell anyone about what they had seen until after His resurrection. Certain things have no place in our hearts until we know of the resurrection through our own conversion experience. Through the Spirit living in us we are designed to carry the same glory that transfigured Jesus' face. But we still must go up the mountain—to the place where we meet with God face to face.

Before this experience Jesus declared, "There are some standing here who will not taste death before they see the kingdom of God come with power" (Mark 9:1, MEV). I do not think He was referring to the Mount of Transfiguration experience, which was only six days later. He was referring to the baptism in the Holy Spirit that would become available after His death and resurrection. That is "the kingdom of God come with power." How well do you understand the baptism in the Holy Spirit and all that it contains for you?

POINT TO PONDER

The baptism of the Spirit empowers me for greater kingdom living.

PERSONAL REFLECTION

_____

_____

Day 331
WHY NOT NOW?

I pray that the eyes of your heart may be enlightened, so that you will know what is the hope of His calling, what are the riches of the glory of His inheritance in the saints.
—EPHESIANS 1:18

IT IS THEOLOGICAL irresponsibility to have the great promises of Scripture and put them off into a period of time for which we have no responsibility. It has become way too easy to place everything that's good into the millennium and keep the trials and dark seasons for this era. My greatest difficulty with that line of thinking is that it requires no faith to achieve it, and that seems to be inconsistent with the rest of God's dealings with humanity. It also places an unhealthy emphasis on future generations to the point where we lose our sense of purpose, call, and destiny. While I live to leave a legacy, each generation has been given enough favor from the Lord to consider themselves capable of being the "final" generation that lives in the glory of God, for the glory of God. Will you put off the responsibility of carrying God's glory to future generations or are you embracing it now?

POINT TO PONDER

I will live my life for the glory of God.

PERSONAL REFLECTION

Day 332

JESUS, THE LIGHT OF THE WORLD

Then Jesus again spoke to them, saying, "I am the
Light of the world; he who follows Me will not walk
in the darkness, but will have the Light of life."
—John 8:12

ONE OF MY favorite declarations in Scripture is found in Isaiah 60:1, "Arise, shine; for your light has come." People stumble over determining the audience to which this command is addressed. Some would put this off into God's future dealings with Israel, which I believe to be a great mistake. While God's great plan is being worked out in His people Israel, the command is brought to *all who have received* His light. What is that light, and to whom has this light come? Jesus Christ is the light of the world. He enlightens every person that comes into this world. How much are you allowing the light of Christ to enliven your life so that you can be one who lights the world?

POINT TO PONDER

Today I will rise again to new life, radiant with the glory of Christ.

PERSONAL REFLECTION

_____

_____

_____

_____

_____

_____

_____

ARISE AND SHINE

You are the light of the world. A city
set on a hill cannot be hidden.
—MATTHEW 5:14

WHEN ISAIAH MADE the declaration to *arise* and *shine*, it was a command reserved for those who received the light that Jesus brought into the world. He is that light. And those who received His light unto salvation are required to *arise*. It is a command. Many wait for something else to happen to them. But He says, "Get up, now! And while you're getting up, shine!"

This amazing declaration began to unfold in Jesus' day, because the second part of the declaration was fulfilled—He, the light, *had* come. But before Jesus left, He told His disciples that they were the light of the world. That statement is often considered figurative language, which is disastrous when God is speaking literally. The church *is* the light of the world. Are you living as a light to the world? If not, what will it take for you to arise and shine?

POINT TO PONDER

Jesus is the light of the world. He lives in me.
Therefore, I too am the light of the world.

PERSONAL REFLECTION

_____

_____

_____

_____

_____

Day 334

A GLORIOUS INHERITANCE

*While you have the Light, believe in the Light, so
that you may become sons of Light.*
—John 12:36

WHEN THE LIGHT of God touches you, you become light. In whatever fashion God touches our lives we become a manifestation of that very reality. It's one of the great mysteries in the gospel, testifying of its ability to completely transform the nature of everything it touches. This issue of *becoming light* is not an isolated illustration, which we will see. It is the power of the gospel that completely transforms the nature of whatever it touches. Through Jesus you have the ability to become a light bearer. It is your inheritance. John 3:34 says, "For He whom God has sent speaks the words of God; for He gives the Spirit without measure." God wants you to allow the power of the gospel to transform your nature so that you can become one who transforms. Are you willing to welcome His process of transformation?

POINT TO PONDER

I welcome God's process of transformation.

PERSONAL REFLECTION

_____

_____

_____

_____

_____

_____

Day 335

MANIFESTATIONS OF HIS GRACE

And now I commend you to God and to the word of
His grace, which is able to build you up and to give you
the inheritance among all those who are sanctified.
—Acts 20:32

JESUS IS OUR righteousness. But when we are touched by His righteousness, we not only became righteous, but we also became *the righteousness of God*. Consider this extreme effect of the gospel. We don't just carry this grace from God. We become a manifestation of that grace. When we think only in figurative and symbolic language we undermine the power of God's intent. With such extraordinary promises we must not be a people restricted by the boundaries set by a prior generation. We must instead build upon their experience and go where they didn't have time to go. Who among believers from the previous generation inspires you to press higher, and what is it about them that inspires you?

POINT TO PONDER

With a grateful heart I will stand on the shoulders of those who came
before me so that I might bring fresh glory to God in this generation.

PERSONAL REFLECTION

Day 336

THE FREE MERCY OF FORGIVENESS

Bear with each other and forgive one another if any of you has a grievance against someone. Forgive as the Lord forgave you.
—Colossians 3:13, NIV

GOD TAKES RIGHTEOUS living to another extreme in the subject of forgiveness. When you are forgiven, you become a forgiver. Jesus pressed way past my comfort zone by saying, "If you forgive the sins of any, their sins have been forgiven them; if you retain the sins of any, they have been retained" (John 20:23). We actually broker God's forgiveness. At minimum God is saying that when we forgive people, He moves upon them with His forgiveness. Again, our nature has been changed by the way in which God touched us. When you think of a time when you or someone you know brokered God's forgiveness, what was the result?

POINT TO PONDER

I want to be a trusted agent of God's forgiveness.

PERSONAL REFLECTION

_____

_____

_____

_____

_____

_____

_____

_____

_____

_____

Day 337

PREPARED FOR THE SAVIOR

Do not think that I have come to abolish the Law or the
Prophets; I have not come to abolish them but to fulfill them.
—MATTHEW 5:17, NIV

UNDER THE OLD Testament, if you touch a leper, you become unclean. The primary message of that covenant was to reveal the power of sin. But the Law of God was not the answer to the problem of sin. It was incapable of being the solution. It was the tutor that was intended to lead people to Christ. As people discovered they could not become righteous on their own, the Law created such a tension in people's lives that it successfully prepared Israel for the Savior. And so, touching the leper made you unclean. God has to train us to reign. What lepers has God had you touch as part of your training for reigning?

POINT TO PONDER

I submit to His training for reigning even when it
means going against what I know in the natural.

PERSONAL REFLECTION

_____

_____

_____

_____

_____

_____

_____

_____

AUTHENTIC LOVE—KINGDOM POWER

Little children, let us not live in word or
talk but in deed and in truth.
—1 John 3:18, esv

In the New Testament we touch the leper and the leper becomes clean. That's because the primary message of this covenant is the power of God's love to make us whole. When we demonstrate authentic love, He backs it up with kingdom power. The one who is cleansed by the blood of Jesus is now able to cleanse; this was in the commission Jesus gave to His disciples: "Cleanse the lepers" (Matthew 10:8). Jesus is giving you the same commission—to cleanse the lepers. However, fulfilling that commission requires a heart of compassion, the same kind of compassion that compelled Jesus to touch the unclean. None of us possess that kind of compassion outside of the love of God. We need His authentic love to move in His kingdom power. It's a lifelong process. Where are you on the journey?

Point to Ponder

I want to cleanse the lepers with the same degree of faith that
drove the leper to Jesus in the first place (Mark 1:40–45).

Personal Reflection

_____

_____

_____

_____

_____

THE WAR OF THE FLESH
AND THE SPIRIT

*Those who live according to the flesh have their minds set on
what the flesh desires; but those who live in accordance with
the Spirit have their minds set on what the Spirit desires.*
—ROMANS 8:5, NIV

By THE HUNDREDS of millions, people recognize the power of
sin. They live under the realization that they cannot change
their nature. And so they spend their lives changing the color of
their hair, taking off pounds, and learning new skills to somehow
quench that internal desire for personal transformation. Some
rebel against that desire and surrender to the inevitable by giving
themselves over to a sin nature they cannot control. The results are
in our newspaper headlines daily. You have been given the gift of
a changed nature through relationship with the living God. How
well are you stewarding that gift?

POINT TO PONDER

*My inward transformation is ongoing. I am
pressing on toward the prize.*

PERSONAL REFLECTION

_____

_____

_____

_____

_____

_____

THE POWER OF AUTHENTIC LOVE

For I am not ashamed of the gospel, for it is
the power of God for salvation to everyone who
believes, to the Jew first and also to the Greek.
—ROMANS 1:16

THE POWER OF sin is old news! The news needed in this day is that the power of the authentic love of God transforms everything it touches. Those changed by His love are true lovers, and those who don't love others have no evidence of ever having experienced God's love. As we face Him, our nature is changed into the nature of the One who touched us, and we release the power of His love to those around us. His authentic love conquers every foe. It has put all things under His feet. Jesus wants you to live full of His authentic love. This begins by experiencing God's love for you and the world. If you haven't fully experienced His love, you are living with a partially full tank. He wants to fill up your tank. In fact, He intends for you to have more than enough for the journey. How full is your tank?

POINT TO PONDER

I will allow myself to be filled up and changed by His love every day.

PERSONAL REFLECTION

Day 341

WE MUST SHINE

*I have given them the glory you gave me, so
they may be one as we are one.*
—John 17:22, NLT

ONE OF THE issues that must be settled in the minds of believers if we are going to obey God's command to arise and shine is the issue of being glorious. For many Christians the idea of being glorious sounds prideful or ridiculous. But there is a glory that exists in humanity simply because we were made in His image. There is a glory in animals, the sun, the stars, and all other created things. He made it this way.

To downplay our role in these last days and to *play small* in life restricts the measure of glory we possess and are able to give to God. Our capacity to give glory ends up being reduced by our unbelief in our significance. What measure of His glory do you see yourself possessing? Are you playing small in life, or are you going big for God?

POINT TO PONDER

I am significant, made in God's image to reflect His glory.

PERSONAL REFLECTION

_____

_____

_____

_____

_____

_____

ABIDE IN HONOR

So that, as it is written, "Let the one
who boasts, boast in the Lord."
—1 Corinthians 1:31, esv

OUR SIGNIFICANCE IS not based on anything in and of us. It is entirely based on the One who calls us to Himself. Solomon seemed to know this, saying, "Let another praise you, and not your own mouth; a stranger, and not your own lips" (Proverbs 27:2). God warns against boasting in ourselves, but He adds that we are to allow others to do it to us. Honor is a kingdom value. If we don't know how to receive it correctly, we will have no crown to throw at His feet. Our war against pride is misguided when it is inconsistent with God's Word. False humility is the most dangerous form of pride as it is often mistaken for a virtue. Do you struggle with false humility? If so, God wants you to learn how to receive the honor that is yours. Are you ready and willing?

Point to Ponder

I will learn true humility so I do not suffer a downfall (Proverbs 18:12).

Personal Reflection

_____

_____

_____

_____

_____

_____

_____

Day 343

HE IS WORTHY

Because He is Lord of lords and King of kings, and those
who are with Him are the called and chosen and faithful.
—REVELATION 17:14

WHEN PEOPLE GIVE me honor, I thank them for their thought-fulness. But I refuse to respond with the nauseating religious jargon, "It wasn't me; it was Jesus." Rather, when I get alone with God, I bring the honor given to me and give it to Him, saying, "Look what someone gave to me. I believe this belongs to You." There's no question in my mind about who really deserves it. I don't want to hold on to something that belongs to God. If my heart isn't overflowing with love for Him that leads me to give Him all honor and glory, then I'm in need of a course correction. I will receive honor for His name's sake and then I'll gather it up in my arms and bring it to Him because He is so worthy. What do you bring to God at the end of the day?

POINT TO PONDER

I was in need of a Savior and found Him—the One worthy of it all.

PERSONAL REFLECTION

_____

_____

_____

_____

_____

_____

_____

LIVING IN THE LIGHT

No one lights a lamp and puts it under a basket. Instead, a lamp is placed on a stand, where it gives light to everyone in the house.
—MATTHEW 5:15, NLT

IT'S JUST FASCINATING to me that God enjoys having us be *in the line of fire* when glory and honor are being released. They affirm our eternal significance and destiny. And if we make the mistake of taking that honor to ourselves, then we have already received our reward in this life. The eternal aspect has been removed. That which is invested into eternity pays eternal dividends. Is it possible that the scriptural standard of going from *glory to glory* also carries with it the principle of going from living in the glory of man to living in the glory of God?

Jesus added to this command, saying, "Let your light shine before men in such a way that they may see your good works, and glorify your Father who is in heaven" (Matthew 5:16). There is a way in which we can shine that causes others to worship God and give Him glory. It was in this context that Jesus taught us that our lights were not to be hidden but put in the open for others to see. Others are attracted to God by our shining. Have you noticed from the Gospels that Jesus' ministry was a very public ministry? He didn't bring the kingdom in secret. How is He calling you to bring the kingdom?

POINT TO PONDER

I will live in the light and be bold to bring the kingdom of God everywhere.

PERSONAL REFLECTION

_____

_____

HOW TO SHINE

*The LORD bless you, and keep you; the LORD make His
face shine on you, and be gracious to you; the LORD lift
up His countenance on you, and give you peace.*
—NUMBERS 6:24–26

To LEARN HOW to shine in response to God's command in Isaiah 60 we must learn how God shines. We represent Him. Just as Aaron and his sons were to release a blessing over the children of Israel, so too are we to release this blessing today over God's children.

When God shows His favor to people, He is giving us a model to follow. He is teaching us how to shine. Showing favor to others is one way to follow His example. Being accepted by God enables us to accept others, once again demonstrating that we become a manifestation of the nature of God's touch in our lives. How good are you at accepting others? Is it sometimes hard for you? What would make it easier?

POINT TO PONDER

I will accept and love others just as I am accepted and loved by God.

PERSONAL REFLECTION

_____

_____

_____

_____

_____

_____

Day 346

RELEASING DIVINE FAVOR

*Let no unwholesome word proceed from your mouth, but only
such a word as is good for edification according to the need
of the moment, so that it will give grace to those who hear.*
—EPHESIANS 4:29

OD'S FACE SHINES on us when He releases His favor and
blessing in our lives. We have been given the power to release
life and death through our speech. In this place of responsibility
we are able to speak words that encourage according to the needs
a person has at the moment. But the part of the verse that amazes
me the most is that we are able to *give grace to those who hear.* Grace
is divine favor. In a sense we broker God's favor. It is as though He
is saying, *"To whomever you show favor, I will show favor."* Every
time you bring encouragement to someone, you release divine
favor. They are marked for God's attention because of your words.
That is shining! To what degree are you able to shine and release
God's divine favor to others? Does it bring you joy when you do?

POINT TO PONDER

*I am ready to be more of an encourager and
release the favor of God to others.*

PERSONAL REFLECTION

_____

_____

_____

_____

_____

_____

Day 347

GIVING AWAY THE FARM

Give, and it will be given to you. A good measure, pressed down,
shaken together and running over, will be poured into your
lap. For with the measure you use, it will be measured to you.
—LUKE 6:38, NIV

IT'S COMMONLY SAID, "You can't out-give God." And it's true. He makes sure that we receive mostly according to what we've given away. But it's not simply because God gives back to us according to what we've given. It's largely because He changes our nature when He touches us, to the point that we actually produce the very thing we gave away. That is not to say any of it originates with us; all good gifts come from God. Period. But what a man sows, that shall he also reap. Some are too insecure to sow honor. It is almost as though they think that they will be lacking if they give it away. Not so. All heavenly commodities increase as they are released. Those who show mercy have mercy returned to them. It's how this kingdom works.

If we have received something from God, we shine as we give it away. It's the act of releasing internal realities and experiences that help to redefine the nature of the world we live in. Internal realities become external realities. That is the act of shining. When you release God's internal realities to the world around you, what happens?

POINT TO PONDER

I am growing in my ability to give away Jesus.

PERSONAL REFLECTION

_____

_____

_____

THE RICHES OF HEAVEN

The kingdom of God is within you.
—LUKE 17:21, MEV

I WON'T WRITE A check if I don't know that I have money in the bank. It is the discovery of the treasure that is in us through encountering the face of God that enables us to write checks that are consistent with His account, not ours. Peter said to the lame man, "Silver and gold have I none; but *such as I have give I thee*" (Acts 3:6, KJV, emphasis added). He then wrote a check that only God could back up. That is the way this kingdom works. God's bank account is always full. There is no lack in heaven. You can't overdraw God. He's always got you covered. Do you tend to write little checks against God's big account? Perhaps it's time to check His balance.

POINT TO PONDER

I will learn to write bigger checks for God because the riches of heaven, which are within me, are without measure.

PERSONAL REFLECTION

_____

_____

_____

_____

_____

_____

_____

_____

THE KINGDOM WITHIN

But to each one of us grace was given according
to the measure of Christ's gift.
—**Ephesians 4:7**

At one point Jesus invited all of humanity to come to Him and drink. "If anyone is thirsty, let him come to Me and drink.... 'From his innermost being will flow rivers of living water'" (John 7:37–38). The picture drawn by Jesus is once again very extreme. If I take a drink of refreshing from Him, a river of refreshing flows from me! A drink becomes a river. There is an exponential increase in everything that God releases into our lives as we release it. It grows through use. The waters of refreshing that pour through us don't diminish as we give it away. The opposite is true. Our heartfelt capacity to give increases in the giving. What is seemingly small on the outside becomes eternally significant once it's on the inside—the kingdom within. Receiving grace from God defines the kind of grace we can distribute. Are you a good steward—continually giving according to the measure given you? If not, perhaps you don't know your measure. Ask God to show you.

Point to Ponder

Christ dwells in me without measure. Therefore, I
can give Him away without measure.

Personal Reflection

_____

_____

_____

_____

Day 350

THE RIVER THAT NEVER RUNS DRY

He who believes in Me, as the Scripture said, "From
his innermost being will flow rivers of living water."
But this He spoke of the Spirit, whom those who
believed in Him were to receive; for the Spirit was
not yet given, because Jesus was not yet glorified.
—JOHN 7:38–39

THE RIVER JESUS is speaking of in John 7:38–39 is actually the
Holy Spirit Himself. He is in us as a river, not a lake. He's not
merely with us to comfort us and abide in us. He is in us to flow
through us to transform the nature of the world around us. This
is what Peter released to the lame man at the gate. He gave what
he had. In his survey of his inheritance in Christ he discovered a
river that can never run dry. It flows from the temple of God, getting deeper as it flows, and works to change the course of world
history—through you and me. What do you have from Jesus that
you release to those around you who are in need? Is it His living
water or something else?

POINT TO PONDER

I have His river of life flowing through me!

PERSONAL REFLECTION

_____

_____

_____

_____

_____

_____

Day 351

GOD'S PERFECT TIMING

*If you then, being evil, know how to give good gifts
to your children, how much more will your heavenly
Father give the Holy Spirit to those who ask Him?*
—LUKE 11:13

AT SOME POINT we have to believe in the significance of God's touch in our lives. Many stand in line for prayers of impartation, week after week, hoping to finally get something powerful. It's noble to have such hunger to travel around the world in order to receive from great men and women of God. I do it and believe in it. But the frequency must not be tied to unbelief that God has not released what I've asked for in previous encounters. To keep us from being impartation junkies, He sometimes places His biggest impartation in something like *a time-release capsule.* It's a strange picture, but it is true. There are times when God touches us so significantly that its effect has to be spread out over time, or it might distract us from His purposes. Our faith cannot depend merely on our *felt* experience. It must be on the promises of God. How much faith do you have to stand on the promises of God and wait believing that His timing is perfect?

POINT TO PONDER

I trust that God will give me what He knows I need when I need it.

PERSONAL REFLECTION

_____

_____

_____

_____

Day 352

RELEASING THE KINGDOM
THROUGH DECLARATION

And the Word became flesh, and dwelt among us,
and we saw His glory, glory as of the only begotten
from the Father, full of grace and truth.
—JOHN 1:14

JESUS IS THE Word of God made flesh. But when He spoke, the Word became Spirit. And that Spirit gave life. This passage reveals one of the ways that the Spirit of God is released into a situation: through declaration. When we follow the example that Jesus gave us and say only what the Father is saying, our words also become Spirit. He is released into the environment as we speak. This concept is consistent with the whole of Scripture. "The kingdom of God is…in the Holy Spirit" (Romans 14:17). When the Holy Spirit is released into a situation, the King's dominion is manifested. The Spirit always works to demonstrate liberty and freedom, which are signs that the King is present. God wants you to live with faith enough to boldly release His kingdom through declarations of His Word. Are you currently living with that kind of bold faith?

POINT TO PONDER

I will release the kingdom by boldly declaring His Word.

PERSONAL REFLECTION

_____

_____

_____

_____

RELEASING THE KINGDOM THROUGH ACTS OF FAITH

Now when Jesus heard this, He marveled and said to those who were following, "Truly I say to you, I have not found such great faith with anyone in Israel."
—MATTHEW 8:10

THERE IS A release of the Spirit through acts of faith. Faith so impressed Jesus that it caused Him to announce that certain stories of faith would be told throughout eternity, wherever His story is told. Realizing that faith brought about extraordinary miracles, and the miracles happened because of the Holy Spirit's work, it's not hard to see how the Holy Spirit is released through acts of faith. An act of faith is an action that is an evidence of the faith a person has. I have witnessed people who did not receive healing until they attempted to do what was impossible for them to do. The miracle was then released in the act. Do you engage in acts of faith and see the impossible released? If not, what is holding you back?

POINT TO PONDER

Great faith produces great fruit. Therefore, I will seek greater measures of His faith.

PERSONAL REFLECTION

_____

_____

_____

_____

_____

Day 354

RELEASING THE KINGDOM THROUGH OUR HANDS

They will lay their hands on the sick, and they will recover.
—Mark 16:18, esv

SOMETIMES THE SPIRIT of God is released through touch—more specifically, the laying on of hands. The power of God dwells within a person. Laying our hands on someone who is sick releases the power of God to destroy the affliction. When it's a proper place to touch, I like to lay my hand on the location of the disease or injury. I have felt tumors disappear under my hands. One woman had a tumor in her abdomen that was so large it was as if she was six months pregnant. I laid my hands on her abdomen and the tumor disappeared. Because Jesus established this way of praying, I will follow it. Are you ready to follow Jesus' example and lay hands on the sick as you pray for healing?

POINT TO PONDER

I believe in the laying on of hands for healing the sick.

PERSONAL REFLECTION

_____

_____

_____

_____

_____

_____

_____

_____

_____

RELEASING THE KINGDOM THROUGH PROPHETIC ACTS

Then the man of God said, "Where did it fall?" And
when he showed him the place, he cut off a stick
and threw it in there, and made the iron float.
—2 KINGS 6:6

PERHAPS THE MOST unusual way to release the Spirit of God is through a prophetic act. This is where an action is taken in the natural that has nothing to do with the needed miracle. The prophet threw a stick in the water because a borrowed ax head fell to the bottom of the river. The ax head floated to the surface and was recovered. There isn't a natural law that says that sticks in the water make iron float. Yet when it is an act that is directed by God, it will always release the Spirit of God to accomplish His purposes. This particular manifestation is especially important for those who only like to do what they understand. God loves to address this weakness in us. How comfortable are you to operate in the divine wisdom of a prophetic act or any other act that you do not fully understand? What would give you more confidence to release the kingdom in this way?

POINT TO PONDER

I am pressing in for greater faith to operate in prophetic acts.

PERSONAL REFLECTION

_____
_____
_____
_____

GIVING WHAT YOU HAVE

And the peace of God, which surpasses all comprehension,
will guard your hearts and your minds in Christ Jesus.
—Philippians 4:7

J**esus slept in** a boat during a life-threatening storm. Some said it was because He was exhausted. I don't think so. The world He was dwelling in has no storms. Paul would later find language for Jesus' example saying that we live in "heavenly places in Christ" (Ephesians 1:3). Jesus lived from heaven toward earth. That is the nature of faith. When it came time to stop the storm, He did so by releasing peace. He had it to give. Because His peace was authentic and was truly dwelling in Him, He could release it over the storm. And the storm was no match. Like Jesus, we have authority over any storm we can sleep in.

Through declaration His internal reality became His external reality. The peace that was ruling in Him soon became that which was released to rule around Him. That is the nature of the Christian life. We give away what we have, and as we do, the world around us conforms. His is a superior kingdom in which much has been given to us. What are you giving away?

Point to Ponder

When I receive peace from the One who is peace, it
becomes available for me to give away.

Personal Reflection

———————————————————————————————
———————————————————————————————
———————————————————————————————

Day 357

THE GLORY OF GOD
BECOMES MANIFEST

*For behold, darkness will cover the earth and deep
darkness the peoples; but the LORD will rise upon you
and His glory will appear upon you. Nations will come
to your light, and kings to the brightness of your rising.*
—ISAIAH 60:2–3

THE WONDERFUL PART of shining for God is that He backs it up.
He literally shines through us when our glory is used for Him
and our efforts are surrendered to His purposes. This is the role of
co-laboring with Christ. In your Bible reading today take a look at
Isaiah 60:1–5. Notice that God's glory is released as His crowning
mark upon a people who shine as He assigned for them to do.

Herein lies the challenge—we are commanded to arise and shine
in the midst of deep, depressing darkness that covers those around
us. God responds to our obedience by releasing His glory. Our
shining attracts His glory! And it's His glory released that brings
about the greatest transformation in lives, cities, and nations. We
are not to merely glow for God. We are called to shine brightly. Are
you hiding your light under a bushel, or are you shining brightly
enough to attract His glory?

POINT TO PONDER

I will shine with the brilliance of the One who lives within me.

PERSONAL REFLECTION

_____

_____

_____

Day 358
THE ONE THING

His glory will appear upon you.
—Isaiah 60:2

THROUGH THIS PROPHETIC promise in Isaiah, God provides specific instruction about our approach to life and what kind of results He is looking for through that approach. We are to live intentionally, knowing the kind of impact we are to have even before we see it for ourselves. The ramifications of this prophetic word go far beyond most of our hopes, dreams, and visions. Isaiah declared entire nations and their leaders would be transformed. We'd then see the wealth of the nations released to the church for kingdom purposes. But all the fruit and breakthrough provided in these promises are connected to one thing—the manifest presence of God upon His people. It's the manifestation of His glory. God intends for you to live intentionally, fully aware of the impact His glory through you can have on the world. To that end, how purposeful is your life in light of His great glory?

POINT TO PONDER

I will live with an intentional awareness of the manifest presence of God's glory upon me.

PERSONAL REFLECTION

_____

_____

_____

_____

_____

_____

Day 359

FOR SUCH A TIME AS THIS

However, the Most High does not live in houses made by human hands. As the prophet says: "Heaven is my throne, and the earth is my footstool. What kind of house will you build for me? says the Lord. Or where will my resting place be?"
—ACTS 7:48–49, NIV

THE HANDS OF man built every house of God in the Bible. God always gave the instructions on how it was to be built. But God Himself is building the church as His eternal dwelling place. If He filled the houses He didn't build with His glory, how much more will He fill the one He is building? It's not right to put that event off into the future after Jesus returns. It has to be now. How do we know this is for now? Because in Scripture it occurs when deep darkness is on people. It describes a time like now. Furthermore, the release of His glory is promised to the people who have the capacity to arise and shine with divine purpose. This can only happen to people to whom the light of God has come. We are that people, and Jesus Christ, our light, has come. It can be intimidating to think we are to stand as light in the darkness until we remember it isn't something we do in our flesh. Jesus came so we might become more than conquerors through Him. Can He count you as one who will arise and shine with His divine purpose in a dark world?

POINT TO PONDER

I am a house in which the Lord Himself lives.

PERSONAL REFLECTION

_____

_____

Day 360

A SUPERIOR COVENANT

*But now Jesus, our High Priest, has been given a
ministry that is far superior to the old priesthood,
for he is the one who mediates for us a far better
covenant with God, based on better promises.*
—HEBREWS 8:6, NLT

IF YOU'VE SPENT time in the Old Testament, you're probably
familiar with how dramatically God displayed His presence in
the houses built for Him by men. Studying these events should
help put God's promise to fill His church into an even better context for you. We must remember that inferior covenants cannot
provide superior blessings. For example, because it is in Scripture,
we often take for granted the things that were released to Israel in
the wilderness on their way to the land of promises, not only the
miracles of provision and victories in battle but also the abiding
presence of God in the cloud and the fire. They weren't born again,
they were living in rebellion, and yet God was seen among them.
That all happened under an inferior covenant. We need to look at
these things and ask, "If He did that for them, how much more will
He do for us?" Which covenant are you living under, a covenant of
works or the covenant of grace given to you by Jesus?

POINT TO PONDER

I am living under the superior covenant given to me by Jesus Christ.

PERSONAL REFLECTION

_____

_____

_____

LOOKING IN A MIRROR

Now the Lord is the Spirit. And where the Spirit of the Lord is, there is liberty. But we all, seeing the glory of the Lord with unveiled faces, as in a mirror, are being transformed into the same image from glory to glory by the Spirit of the Lord.
—2 CORINTHIANS 3:17–18, MEV

THE GLORY OF God ought to be seen upon His people. It makes little difference to me whether it is a physical manifestation that is seen by the natural eye or it is something that people perceive through the eyes of their hearts.

There is an unusual lesson found in the third chapter of 2 Corinthians. The apostle Paul is discussing Moses' experience with the glory of God and how Israel insisted that he put a veil over his face because the glory frightened them. Paul then says, "The veil is taken away in Christ" (2 Corinthians 3:14, NKJV). That means that whatever was hidden under the veil is now available for all to see. The fear element that Israel struggled with has been removed because the Spirit of Christ has come to make us free. Which spirit do you walk with—a spirit of fear or the Spirit of freedom?

POINT TO PONDER

I walk in God's Spirit of freedom with His glory resting upon me.

PERSONAL REFLECTION

_____

_____

_____

_____

Day 362
HIS SPOTLESS BRIDE

*That He might present to Himself the church in all
her glory, having no spot or wrinkle or any such
thing; but that she would be holy and blameless.*
—EPHESIANS 5:27

THE FREEDOM THAT the Holy Spirit brings releases us to behold the glory! And strangely, that glory is seen as though we were looking in a mirror. In other words, that is what we look like. That is what the Holy Spirit's job has been—to make us glorious. Jesus is returning for a bride whose body is in equal proportion to her head. The command to *arise and shine* is the process through which we are able to step into the reality of who God says we already are. You were created to arise and shine. In Jesus the old has gone, the new has come. Where are you in the process of stepping into the reality of who God says you already are?

POINT TO PONDER

I am being transformed from glory to glory, called to arise and shine.

PERSONAL REFLECTION

_____

_____

_____

_____

_____

_____

_____

_____

Day 363

REDISCOVERING OUR MESSAGE

And just as we have borne the image of the earthly man, so shall we bear the image of the heavenly man.
—1 Corinthians 15:49, NIV

I CAN THREATEN PEOPLE with hell and have a measure of breakthrough in getting converts. Hell is real and must not be ignored. But that is not plan A. It is plan B. Plan A is, "The kindness of God leads you to repentance" (Romans 2:4). This truth must affect our attitude. When this concept affects our approach to humanity we are much more likely to use our favor to serve them effectively, which better represents life in the kingdom.

We are entering a period of time where we will see more and more people coming to Christ because of His face shining upon the people of God. Sometimes it will be His raw power that manifests through us, and other times it will be His selfless love with works of kindness. But His face will be seen, as it must. Who do you want others to see when they look at you?

POINT TO PONDER

When others look at me, I want them to see Jesus.

PERSONAL REFLECTION

_____

_____

_____

_____

_____

_____

_____

Day 364

UNDONE IN HIS PRESENCE

Let your light shine before men in such a way that they may see
your good works, and glorify your Father who is in heaven.
—MATTHEW 5:16

THE FACE OF God will be encountered over and over again. It is shining on the church right now. It is time to see and be enlarged, for it changes our capacity to represent Him in this world as it changes the nature of who we are. We tend to manifest His likeness in equal measure to how deep our encounters have been.

A fear of God is about to come upon the church. We've experienced it at times because of trial and discipline. But there is something that is about to overtake the people of God that comes from a revelation of His kindness. This kind of blessing does not promote arrogance. On the contrary: there's such an overwhelming sense of His goodness that we are undone. We will become a trembling group of people because we consciously live so far beyond what we deserve. God wants you to be undone in His presence, to fully understand His goodness and His kindness because your light will shine brightest when you are totally overwhelmed in the brilliance of His presence. Are you hungry for such a magnificent encounter? He is hungry for you.

POINT TO PONDER

It is the Father's good pleasure to give us the
kingdom (Luke 12:32). I receive it!

PERSONAL REFLECTION

_____

_____

_____

A CHURCH WITH AUTHORITY

For no man can lay a foundation other than the
one which is laid, which is Jesus Christ.
—1 CORINTHIANS 3:11

A REVELATION OF GOD'S kindness does not mean that there will be an end to our present problems and conflict will be gone. It just means that for the first time in history those problems will consistently yield to a church with authority. It is the contrast that is spoken of in Isaiah 60—darkness covers the earth, but His glory is upon His people. That realization will provoke us to fear God in a new way that ultimately stirs up the nations around us to come to Christ. We become the "city set on a hill" (Matthew 5:14). There is a realm of the blessing in God that has not yet been experienced. And it is the Lord's intent to release this upon His people before the end comes. This blessing enables us to function more like brokers of His world rather than beggars for His invasion. Are you ready to receive what the Lord is going to release upon the church? Are you ready to walk the path of the righteous, shining brighter and brighter until midday, to become the visible representation of Christ on the earth? The Spirit and the bride say come!

POINT TO PONDER

I am a city set on a hill, ready to receive God's blessing
and live with the authority of heaven on earth.

PERSONAL REFLECTION

_____

_____

_____

_____

CONCLUSION

PSALM 67 CAPTURES this prophetic picture of God's heart for His people as the method He would like to use to reach the nations. We can be groomed by His Spirit through divine encounters to be qualified to carry such a responsibility. The face of His favor is available for those who are desperate. He longs for us to be able to carry His likeness into any setting. His blessing upon us will bring the fear of God back to the nations. Let's become candidates for this mandate by embracing the quest for face-to-face encounters with God. The time is now.

> May God be gracious to us, and bless us,
> and cause His face to shine on us; Selah
> that Your way may be known on earth,
> Your salvation among all nations.
> Let the peoples praise You, O God;
> let all the peoples praise You.
> Oh, let the nations be glad and sing for joy;
> for You will judge the people uprightly,
> and lead the nations on earth. Selah
> Let the peoples praise You, O God;
> let all the peoples praise You.
> Then will the earth yield its produce,
> and God, our God, will bless us.
> God will bless us,
> and all the ends of the earth will fear Him.
> —PSALM 67:1–7, MEV

NOTES

NOTES

NOTES

NOTES

NOTES

NOTES